Gender and Theory

Gender and Theory

Dialogues on Feminist Criticism

Edited by

Linda Kauffman

Basil Blackwell

First published 1989

Basil Blackwell Ltd
108 Cowley Road, Oxford OX4 1JF, UK

Basil Blackwell Inc.
432 Park Avenue South, Suite 1503
New York, NY 10016, USA

British Library Cataloguing in Publication Data

Kauffman, Linda S., *1949-*
  Gender and theory: dialogues on feminist
  criticism.
  1. Literature. Feminist criticism
  I. Title
  801′.95

  ISBN 0-631-16355-7
  ISBN 0-631-16356-5 Pbk

Library of Congress Cataloging in Publication Data
Gender and theory: dialogues in feminist criticism / [edited by]
Linda Kauffman.
    p. cm.
  Bibliography: p.
  Includes index.
  ISBN 0-631-16355-7. ISBN 0-631-16356-5 (pbk.)
  1. Feminist literary criticism. I. Kauffman, Linda S., 1949-
PN98.W64G46 1989   88-23203
809′.89287—dc19   CIP

Typeset in 11 on 13pt Garamond
by Downdell Ltd, Abingdon, Oxon.
Printed in Great Britain by
Billing & Sons Ltd, Worcester

Contents

Contents

Acknowledgements

I am grateful to Robert Detweiler for his encouragement and involvement in the initial stages of this project and Toril Moi for her help in the final stages. Donna Landry, Gerald MacLean, and William Beatty Warner offered emotional and intellectual support throughout; I have benefited from their shrewd advice on the structure and contents of the collection. A National Endowment for the Humanities Fellowship in 1987-8 is also gratefully acknowledged. Thanks are due to Ralph Cohen for permission to reprint Ellen Messer-Davidow's 'The Philosophical bases of feminist literary criticisms', and Jane Tompkins's 'Me and my shadow', both originally published in vol. 19 (Autumn 1987) of *New Literary History*. Philip Carpenter, my editor at Basil Blackwell, has been remarkably accommodating. I am also indebted to Susan Martin for meticulous copy-editing. My biggest debt is to the contributors, whose fine work is evident on every page.

Linda Kauffman
Chapel Hill, North Carolina
March 1988

Notes on Contributors

Michael Awkward is Assistant Professor of English and Afro-American Studies at the University of Michigan, Ann Arbor. His book, *Kissin'-Friends: Influence and Afro-American Women Novelists*, is forthcoming from Columbia University Press.

Joseph Allen Boone is Associate Professor in the English Department at Harvard University and is the author of *Tradition/Counter Tradition: Love and the Form of Fiction* (University of Chicago Press, 1987).

Barbara Christian is Professor of Afro-American Studies at the University of California, Berkeley. She is the author of *Black Women Novelists: The Development of a Tradition* and *Black Feminist Criticism: Perspectives on Black Women Writers* (Pergamon, 1985), and has published many articles on black women writers, Afro-American Studies, and Women's Studies.

Lee Edelman is Associate Professor of English at Tufts University. He is the author of *Transmemberment of Song: Hart Crane's Anatomies of Rhetoric and Desire* (Stanford University Press, 1987), as well as of essays on Elizabeth Bishop, John Ashbery, and lesbian and gay literary theory.

Frances Ferguson is Professor of English at Johns Hopkins University. She is the author of *Wordsworth: Language as Counter-Spirit* (Yale University Press, 1977) and *Solitude and the Sublime: The Aesthetics of Individuation* (Methuen, 1988). She also co-edited (with R. Howard Bloch) an issue of *Representations* on 'Misogyny, misandry, and misanthropy', (Fall 1987).

Linda Kauffman is Associate Professor of English at the University of Maryland, College Park. She is the author of *Discourses of Desire: Gender, Genre, and Epistolary Fictions* (Cornell University Press, 1986; 1988), and has published numerous essays and reviews on modern literature and feminist theory in such journals as *Signs, Criticism, Modern Fiction Studies,* and *Nineteenth Century Literature*. Her work-in-progress is *Special Delivery: Epistolary Modes in Modern Fiction*.

Gerald M. MacLean is Assistant Professor of English at Wayne State University. He is the author of *Time's Witness: Historical Representation in English Poetry, 1603-1660* and editor of the 1673 English translation of Poullain de la Barre's *The Woman as Good as the Man*. In 1988-9 he will be at Cornell University's Society for the Humanities, writing a book on feminism, materialism and deconstruction with Donna Landry.

Ellen Messer-Davidow teaches English and directs the Women's Studies Program at the University of Minnesota. Her essay is part of a book on *The Philosophical Bases of Feminist Literary Criticisms*, forthcoming from Oxford University Press.

Toril Moi directed the Women's Studies Program at the University of Bergen in Norway from 1985 to 1988. She is the author of *Sexual/Textual Politics: Feminist Literary Theory*, and editor of *The Kristeva Reader* and *French Feminist Thought*. She has published more than thirty articles on contemporary women writers and literary theory, and is presently writing a book on Simone de Beauvoir.

Timothy J. Reiss is Professor and Chair of the Department of Comparative Literature, New York University. He is the author of *The Discourse of Modernism* (1982, 1985) and *Uncertainty of Analysis* (1988).

David R. Shumway is Assistant Professor of Literary and Cultural Studies in the English Department of Carnegie-Mellon University. He is the current Director and founding member of GRIP, the Group for Research into the Institutionalization and Professionalization of Literary Studies. He is the author of *Michel Foucault* (Twayne, 1989), and is working on a book on the genealogy of American literature as an academic field from 1900 to the present.

Jane Tompkins is Professor of English at Duke University. She is editor of *Reader-Response Criticism: From Formalism to Post-Structuralism* (1980) and *Twentieth Century Interpretations of The Turn of the Screw* (1970). She is also author of *Sensational Designs: The Cultural Work of American Fiction 1790-1860* (Oxford University Press, 1985).

Patricia Yaeger is Head Tutor of the History and Literature concentration and Assistant Professor of English at Harvard University. She has published on Coleridge and Derrida in *SubStance*, on Welty and Bakhtin in *PMLA*, and on Kate Chopin in *Novel*. She is the author of *Honey-Mad Women: Emancipatory Strategies in Women's Writing* (Columbia University Press, 1988), and co-editor, with Beth Kowaleski-Wallace, of *New Feminist Readings of the Father* (Southern Illinois Press, 1988).

Introduction

Linda Kauffman

Within the American academy over the past twenty years, we have witnessed the flourishing of feminist publications, the recuperation of lost texts by women, the reconceptualization of the canon and literary history, and the development of interdisciplinary methods of feminist teaching and research. Yet some of the most prominent feminist literary critics nonetheless feel that the force of feminism has been consistently blunted. In 1979, Carolyn Heilbrun addressed the administrators of English Departments as follows:

> among all the changes of 'the life and thought of our age,' only the feminist approach has been scorned, ignored, fled from, at best reluctantly embraced ... Deconstruction, semiology, Derrida, Foucault may question the very meaning of meaning as we have learned it, but feminism may not do so.[1]

In 1980, Sandra Gilbert addressed the same forum, lamenting that while numerous new feminist journals had been established, and over a fifth of the panels at the Modern Language Association Conventions were now devoted to feminism, 'business goes on with the usual ferment over the new ideas of newly interesting men – Derrida, Foucault, Lacan, for instance – just as if no significant feminist transformations had taken place.'[2] But despite the fact that they each have a problematic (and quite different) relationship to feminism, neither Derrida, Foucault, or Lacan would deny that feminist transformations have taken place.[3] In fact, far from conducting 'business as usual', post-structuralist, marxist, and psychoanalytic theorists have a pervasive engagement with feminism. It has radically transformed the classroom experience; one simply cannot teach now without acknowledging the profound impact it has had on all our lives. Gilbert, however, identifies three forms of the massive denial of feminist criticism: indifference, apparently supportive tokenism, and out-right hostility. In 1983, Elaine Showalter exposed both the indifference and hostility of male compilers of surveys of modern criticism who consistently exclude feminism from their anthologies, and she simultaneously took Jonathan Culler and Terry Eagleton to task for what she saw as their appropriations of feminist criticism for critical theory. Showalter saw treachery in both the male erasure and the male embrace of feminism. She argued that feminism has 'worried too much already . . . about communicating with the white fathers, even at the price of translating its findings into the warp of their obscure critical languages'.[4] She also warned feminists to beware of a 'male theory' that would undermine the presumed authority and particularities of female experience. But Showalter confuses cause with effect, for rather than feminists 'translating' their findings, it is precisely the act of theorizing which has enabled them to frame the questions in ways that have radically altered our means of articulating perceptions of domination, subjugation, exploitation, and repression.

The efforts of Heilbrun, Gilbert, and Showalter to frame the issues of gender and theory in terms of female/male polarities resulted in antagonisms that were as simplistic as they were inevitable, for they ignored the complex and reciprocal interactions of feminist theory with critical theory. Those interactions are the subject of the essays in this volume. To assume that 'men theorize, women experience' is to remain trapped in the binary oppositions that theorists – whether explicitly feminist or not, whether male or female – have worked so hard to dismantle. Freud, Marx, Nietzsche and Saussure challenged our assumptions about what is 'natural' by examining the manifest and latent structures of the mind, of political economy, of philosophy, and of language. Derrida illuminated language's differences from itself; his critique of Western metaphysics – especially the desire to find a ground for being and an origin for languages – made possible the deconstruction of the centered subject. The notion of a fixed, unified sexual identity, as Lacan has shown, is as illusory as the myth of the unified subject. We have become aware of our construction as gendered subjects, in part because the symbolic order of language identifies us by the definitive opposition *man/woman*. Thus while the title of this volume posits a couple, *Gender and Theory*, and the book is arranged so that men respond to the essays of women and vice-versa, the structure is designed nevertheless to draw attention to such dichotomies in order to displace them by dissymmetry and dissonance. By enlarging the field of investigation, feminist theorists have revealed how elusive such terms are. To frame the debate as a dichotomy between gender versus theory or women versus men is to evade the fact that the conflict is really between an ossified and hardly liberal humanism and the theories – marxist, feminist, and/or poststructuralist – dedicated to demolishing it. Since feminist literary criticism is justly renowned for its capacity for self-reflexiveness and self-critique, one of the dilemmas it must perpetually confront is how to maintain its capacity for intervention. New strategies of subversion must continually be invented, and feminist theorists must remain committed to their sense of the irreducibility of difference, while being receptive to theoretical reconceptualizations of subjectivity, alterity, and identity.

If feminist criticism is to continue to exert the enormous impact during the next twenty years that it has had in the last twenty, it must constantly renegotiate its relationship to its own history, to the canon of traditional practices, and to the dominant intellectual discourses of the present age. *Gender and Theory* interrogates the interrelations of feminism and critical theory by reconceptualizing subjectivity in historically and culturally specific terms, insisting upon situating subjectivity within political contexts and practices. The essayists self-reflexively confront their particular positions in discourse and as subjects, fully aware that such gestures can easily become empty pieties. In addition to fracturing the models of the binary pair and the unified psyche, the essayists variously expose the limitations of pluralism as a theoretical practice.

My aim was to select essays that critically intervene and displace each other, effecting analytical crises and forcing new questions to be raised. For example, does the fact that the essays by Jane Tompkins and Barbara Christian complement one another constitute a reappearance of the same kind of humanism one finds in Gilbert, Heilbrun, and Showalter? Furthermore, since they both attack the role and function of theory itself, and argue for the necessity of preserving the author and the female subject, what difference(s) does race make? Another challenge concerns male voices: are those voices providing new methods of advancing feminism, or is that purpose inevitably drowned out by the all too familiar sound of masculinist appropriation?

The male control of discourse is a problem as old as feminism, one particularly apparent in the polemic of Mary Wollstonecraft. In Part I, 'Representing Philosophy', Timothy Reiss and Frances Ferguson examine Wollstonecraft's use of the idiom of the Enlightenment. The crux of their disagreement is whether this idiom, for all its apparent disinterested-ness, arguably perpetuates a patriarchal notion of rationality. Like Reiss and Ferguson, Ellen Messer-Davidow and David Shumway investigate the philosophical bases of feminist literary criticisms. Indeed, all four essayists in Part I focus on discursive practices, arguing that theoretical conceptions of language are vital in order to analyze how representation functions; to delineate the subtle differences within feminisms; and to assess the complex relations of discourse to power.

In Part II, 'The Body Writing / Writing the Body', we are asked to consider whether we have become so intimidated by the threat of being labelled 'essentialists' that we have lost sight of the specific body writing, or, conversely, whether we have returned to an earlier stage of feminist criticism that highlighted the primacy of individual experience. That is the crux of the debate between Jane Tompkins and Gerald MacLean. How does one's conception of how the body is socialized, sexualized, and politicized differ, depending on whether one argues as a pragmatist (Tompkins), a marxist-deconstructivist (MacLean), or a materialist who writes on post-structuralism and psychoanalysis (Moi)? How is the very construction of the problem further influenced by gender, race, and professional status – as well as by the same kinds of unconscious collusion with the dominant ideology that Reiss finds in Wollstonecraft? The same questions inform Joseph Boone's analysis of men's relation to feminism.

Part III, 'Transforming Texts and Subjects', emphasizes the appropriation and reappropriation of literary genres and traditions. Patricia Yaeger and Lee Edelman discuss the influence of French feminisms, psychoanalysis, and lesbian poetics on the female sublime, approached from the vantage point of political engagement. The impact of critical theory on the construction of the racial as well as the gendered subject is examined by Barbara Christian and Michael Awkward. Perhaps before one can endorse the Barthesian 'death of the author', one must first overcome the effects of centuries of silencing; confronted with that dilemma, what strategies do Afro-American feminist critics and literary theorists propose? In what ways are Afro-American theory and Afro-American feminism complementary, and in what ways are they antagonistic?

Far from striving for pluralistic consensus, these essays provoke controversy. Since the purpose is to liberate dialogue, I have drawn on a dialogic model for staging these discourses, for 'dialogism' dismantles the notion of two coherent subjects engaging in a reciprocal, balanced, one-on-one exchange. Since none of us is a coherent subject, we are always *beside* ourselves, in multiple senses. What is mistakenly defined as 'internal consciousness', for instance, is so imbued with external discourse that it calls into question the entire notion of a unified psyche.

Instead, the psyche itself should be understood as a boundary phenomenon, a 'social entity', continually in the process of interpreting ideological signs.[5] The contributors in this volume reconceptualize boundaries within the psyche and between self and other.

As if all these factors did not make the notion of dialogue complicated enough, each essay is 'dialogic' in another sense: it is followed by a response which demonstrates that another *logic* has been put into play, one that displaces and unsettles the initial argument, and reveals its unconscious resistances. Perhaps the most relevant model for this procedure is of a psychoanalytic *working through*: each essayist works through some of the most pressing theoretical problems in contemporary feminist and critical theory, and each respondent repeats the process, but with crucial differences which advance the argument in unexpected directions. This procedure, moreover, is not limited solely to each paired essayist and respondent: instead, the differences in their analyses lead other contributors to further interventions, and these debates spill over into the margins and the footnotes. For example, David Shumway challenges what he sees as the humanism of Ellen Messer-Davidow in ways that are similar to Gerald MacLean's critique of Tompkins. The limitations of methodologies that focus on individual identity are examined by Toril Moi and Michael Awkward, as well as by Shumway and MacLean. Joseph Boone's description of academic confrontations complements Lee Edelman's analysis of the sublime as a confrontational mode. Edelman's discussion of lesbian poetics, moreover, exposes the differences within feminisms. The opposition of gay men to phallic economies also alters the old binary oppositions. Patricia Yaeger's analysis of how modern American women writers appropriate the sublime mode can be contrasted to Michael Awkward's discussion of appropriative gestures in Afro-American literature and literary theory. In the construction of the volume as a 'whole', then, one never arrives at a point where one can fix – or has a fix on – the questions and answers; far from arriving at definitive solutions, the cumulative effect of reading and writing here is of resistance to certainty and stasis. One cannot find a point where premises can be taken for granted, or where arguments and conclusions can 'rest'.

Dialogism is the deployment not just of an alternative argument, or logic, but of an a-logic that contests the linearity, rationality, and objectivity of Western man and Western discourse. The theory of dialogism is complicated by the fact that each writer enters a pre-existing language system, which renders the concept of subjectivity linguistically as well as psychoanalytically inflected. Julia Kristeva is the theorist who has perhaps best helped us to recognize that we are multiply fractured between unconscious drives and symbolic language. As Kristeva points out, 'as soon as the insurgent . . . speaks, it gets caught up in the discourse allowed by and submitted to the Law.'[6] The contributors recognize their complicity in the very structures they are attempting to overthrow: structures of language and rhetoric, of contemporary critical theory, and of society's institutional apparatuses. Kristeva wonders whether in the women's movement there will be a:

> different relationship of the subject to discourse, to power? Will the eternal frustration of the hysteric in relation to discourse oblige the latter to reconstruct itself? Will it give rise to unrest in everybody, male or female? Or will it remain a cry outside time, like the great mass movements that break up the old system, but have no problem in submitting to the demands of order, as along as it is a new order? (p. 10)

In the attempt to establish different relationships to discourse and power, males and females in this volume share in the unrest. Their motives, however, cannot be identical, nor do those who share the same gender or race necessarily share the same motives. Since some feminists suspect that male feminists are merely donning a new costume, or invading the 'territory' in order to appropriate it for their own purposes, these essays remind us that feminism is neither a territory nor a passing fashion that one can wear or discard in order to dress for success. Instead, it is a political movement, one that requires of its participants considerable awareness of the subtleties of their positioning in discourse and their commitment to action. As Toril Moi argues, the question of whether men can be 'in' feminism is wholly irrelevant; the real question is whether they can be against patriarchy.[7]

The essays in this collection portray women and men in the process of theorizing, an activity which is essential if we are to understand how contemporary struggles are historically linked to domination and oppression. This is another crucial aspect of dialogism: it occurs between specific speakers at a particular time and place. That is why I wanted to provide a format for dialogic encounters in a specific historical moment, to capture the living mix of contemporary voices and the social organization of experience. The essays collectively demonstrate that neither gender nor theory, women nor men, feminism nor marxism, patriarchy nor capitalism can be conceived as monolithic formations. Such formulations merely disguise the specific operations of power and ideology. The question remains, as Kristeva notes, how to envision collective action without complacently submitting to another order. What is most distinctive about this volume is thus a sense of the urgency of these dialogic encounters and these analytical projects: projects which are theoretical because political and political because theoretical.

NOTES

1 Heilbrun 1979: 35.
2 Gilbert 1980: 20.
3 For Derrida's discussion of feminism and gender, see list of references below, and also Spivak's preface to *Of Grammatology* (1976: ix-lxxxvii) and Spivak 1983: 169-95. On Lacan's influence on feminism, see Rose 1986; Rose argues that while there is no 'denying . . . that Lacan was implicated in the phallocentrism he described', his views of femininity and female sexuality are profoundly significant for feminism: 'Lacan's writing gives an account of how the status of the phallus in human sexuality enjoins on the woman a definition in which she is simultaneously symptom and myth. As long as we continue to feel the effects of that definition we cannot afford to ignore this description of the fundamental imposture which sustains it', p. 81. Foucault (1980) discusses the impact of feminism, noting that:

> the real strength of the women's liberation movements is not that of having laid claim to the specificity of their sexuality and the rights pertaining to it, but that they have actually departed from the discourse conducted within the apparatuses of sexuality. . . . What has their outcome been? Ultimately, a veritable movement of de-sexualization, a displacement effected in relation to the sexual centering of the problem, formulating the demand for forms of culture, discourse, language, and so on, which are no longer part of that rigid assignation and pinning-down to their sex which they had initially in some sense been politically obliged to accept in order to make themselves heard. The creative and interesting element in the women's movements is precisely that.

He argues that American homosexual movements, in contrast, reduce everything to the order of sex, but 'the women don't. . . . Women on the other hand are able to have much wider economic, political and other kinds of objectives than homosexuals' (pp. 219-20).
4 Showalter 1983; see also Showalter 1981.
5 Bakhtin 1981; see also Emerson 1983.
6 Kristeva 1986: 10, hereinafter cited parenthetically in the text. Moi's translation.
7 Toril Moi, 'Men against patriarchy', ch. 8 in this volume.

REFERENCES

Bakhtin, Mikhail 1973. *Marxism and the Philosophy of Language*. Trans. Ladislav Matejka and I. R. Titunik, Studies in Language, vol. I. New York. [Written under the name of V. Volosinov.]

Bakhtin, Mikhail 1981. *The Dialogic Imagination: Four Essays*. Ed. Michael Holquist. trans. Caryl Emerson and Holquist. Austin: University of Texas Press.

Derrida, Jacques 1976. *Of Grammatology*. Trans. Gayatri Chakravorty Spivak. Baltimore: Johns Hopkins University Press.

Derrida, Jacques 1979. *Spurs: Nietzsche's Styles*. Trans. Barbara Harlow. Chicago: University of Chicago Press.

Derrida, Jacques 1982. 'Choreographies: an interview with Christie V. McDonald', *Diacritics* 12 (Summer): 66-76.

Derrida, Jacques 1987a. 'Women in the beehive', in *Men in Feminism*, ed. Alice Jardine and Paul Smith. New York: Methuen: 189-203.

Derrida, Jacques 1987b. *The Post Card: From Socrates to Freud and Beyond*. Trans. Alan Bass. Chicago: University of Chicago Press.

Emerson, Caryl 1983. 'The outer word and inner speech: Bakhtin, Vygotsky, and the internalization of language', *Critical Inquiry* 10 (Fall): 245-64.

Foucault, Michel 1980. 'Confessions of the flesh', in *Power and Knowledge: Selected Interviews and Other Writings 1972-1977*, ed. Colin Gordon. New York: Pantheon. [Originally published as 'Le Jeu de Michel Foucault', *Ornicar?*, 10 July 1977.]

Gilbert, Sandra 1980. 'What do feminist critics want? Or a postcard from the volcano', *ADE Bulletin* 66 (Winter): 16-24.

Heilbrun, Carolyn 1979. 'Feminist criticism: bringing the spirit back to English Studies', *The State of the Discipline: 1970s-1980s*. Special issue of *ADE Bulletin*, 62 (Winter): 35-8.

Kristeva, Julia 1986. 'From Ithaca to New York', in *The Kristeva Reader*, ed. Toril Moi. New York: Columbia University Press.

Rose, Jacqueline 1986. 'Feminine sexuality: Jacques Lacan and the école freudienne', in *Sexuality in the Field of Vision*. London: Verso. Repr. from *Feminine Sexuality - Jacques Lacan and the école freudienne*, ed. Juliet Mitchell and Jacqueline Rose, London: Macmillan, 1982; New York: Norton, 1983.

Showalter, Elaine 1981. 'The future of feminist criticism', in *Feminist Literary Criticism: A Working Paper for the National Humanities Center Conference*, Research Triangle Park, North Carolina, 21 March 1981: 65-81.

Showalter, Elaine 1983. 'Critical cross-dressing: male feminists and the Woman of the Year', *Raritan Review* (Fall): 130-49.

Spivak, Gayatri Chakravorty 1976. 'Translator's preface', to Derrida 1976.

Spivak, Gayatri Chakravorty 1983. 'Displacement and the discourse of woman', in *Displacement: Derrida and After*, ed. Mark Krupnick. Bloomington: Indiana University Press: 169-95.

Part I

Representing Philosophy

The essays in this section focus on the historical institutionalization of knowledge. They discuss various representations of philosophy, and ask us to consider what is at stake in those representations. What aspects of the philosophy of the Enlightenment led to the French Revolution, and what was the impact of feminism? What methodologies are most effective in reconstructing the strategies whereby the dominant discourse of Enlightenment reason assimilated dissenting voices and undermined their subversiveness? What effect do analyses of discursive practices have on material suffering and oppression? The implications of these questions are crucial for feminism: has it now achieved the status of a dominant discourse, or does it remain subversive and marginalized? What are the philosophical bases of feminist literary criticisms, and what subject matters should feminist literary critics focus on? Is any lasting change in the status of women possible without a more general theory of social transformation?

Mary Wollstonecraft's views of reason, nature, womanhood, liberty, justice, and revolution are the subject of the first two essays. In 'Revolution in bounds: Wollstonecraft, women, and reason', Timothy J. Reiss argues that within the dominant discourse of Enlightenment reason, women were depicted as naturally subordinate to men. Rather than breaking the bounds of this discourse, Wollstonecraft adhered to its norms and its values. Reiss examines the ways in which women internalize their oppression, and argues that Wollstonecraft never succeeded in resolving these issues, for a revolutionary theory cannot escape the constraints of its environment, except when the fundamental premises of the whole environment are thrown into question. Thus the very concept of universal justice is tied up with concepts of property, self-interest and public contract which underlie the inequalities and injustices Wollstonecraft protests against. Reiss draws parallels between Wollstonecraft's fundamental conservatism and Wordsworth's, and he compares her failure to secure women's rights with the failure of the French Revolution to secure human rights.

Frances Ferguson ironically entitles her essay 'Wollstonecraft our contemporary', because Reiss's Foucauldian analysis of Wollstonecraft's discourse prevents him from recognizing Wollstonecraft's shrewd political insights and radical achievements. She discusses Wollstonecraft's contributions to our understanding of gender by examining the relation of reason to pity. Ferguson disputes Reiss's emphasis on environment, noting that the role of representation is to make environment seem deterministic. She also takes issue with his representations of the French Revolution and Wordsworth. Rather than questioning the status of his own discourse, Reiss uncritically assumes that the post-modern perspective of contemporary critical theory is more radical; he thus reinscribes the very version of progress that he criticizes Wollstonecraft for endorsing.

Ellen Messer-Davidow's 'The philosophical bases of feminist literary criticisms' presents an overview of the major stages of feminist literary criticisms since the 1970s and discusses the relationship of feminist literary critics to the dominant intellectual systems of the modern age. How, she asks, do we structure knowledge when we are both inside and outside disciplines? How do we reconcile the narrow methodological demands of our specific disciplines with the broad interdisciplinary focus of women's studies? What subjects, methods, and epistemologies have men used in constructing reality and how can we reveal the artificiality of their constructions? As critics, we must self-reflexively emphasize the constructedness of our productions, our agencies and stances. Our real subject, she argues, is not literature, but the feminist study of ideas about sex and gender as expressed in literature and critical media. Messer-Davidow suggests ways of reconstituting knowledge from feminist perspectives by reconceptualizing our perception of feminist subject matters. This shift will lead to a 'rehumanized epistemology'.

In 'Solidarity or perspectivity?', David R. Shumway analyzes Ellen Messer-Davidow's essay and the responses to it, which originally appeared in *New Literary History* (Fall 1987). He disputes her analysis of the research tradition in literary studies and argues that knowledge is not structured as it is solely because of discursive practices or epistemology, but because of the current sexual, economic, and racial divisions of power and wealth. Thus in contrast to Frances Ferguson, who criticizes Reiss for writing from a Foucauldian perspective, Shumway enjoins Messer-Davidow to consider the Foucauldian implications of the relations of knowledge to power.

1
Revolution in Bounds: Wollstonecraft, Women, and Reason

Timothy J. Reiss

I know not how the Men will resent it to have their enclosure broke down, and Women invited to taste of the Tree of knowledge they have so long unjustly *Monopoliz'd*.

Mary Astell, 1694

Men that have not Sense enough to shew any Superiority in their Arguments, hope to be yielded to by a Faith, that, as they are Men, all the Reason that has been allotted to human Kind, has fallen to their Share.

Lady Mary Wortley Montagu, 1738

By 1792, when Mary Wollstonecraft published what has been called the manifesto of modern feminism, *A Vindication of the Rights of Woman*, most of its principal arguments had been aired for a good three centuries or more.[1] Christine de Pizan may have been an isolated early voice, but Agrippa, Marguerite de Navarre, Thomas Elyot, Marie de Gournay, and others were precursors of a considerable literature asserting women's rights to education, to positions of political and religious power, to all the material and spiritual benefits of civil society, and to freedom from men's domination. By the mid-seventeenth century many such arguments were based on a premise similar to Wollstonecraft's, that women possessed just the same rational powers as men. Indeed, in 1673, Poullain de la Barre argued that because these natural powers had remained uncontaminated in women by the violence inculcated in men by the (Hobbesian?) processes necessary for the implementing of civil society, the evolution of that very society now required that women take the leading roles. Society would otherwise destroy itself.

On Reason's subordinate

Poullain's assertively Cartesian argument was the last time anyone made so strong a claim about the equality of women's and men's reason for more than a century – save for Mary Astell, who, however, aims the very Cartesian arguments of Part II of *A Serious Proposal* (1697) toward encouraging woman to charity and piety, improving her status as wife and mother, and revalorizing the private sphere in general. Though many voices were raised throughout the eighteenth century in favor of educational opportunity for women, the idea of Enlightened reason excluded what it claimed as 'female' with increasing aggression, relegating it to its 'own' domain of sensibility, instinctual receptivity, nurturing protectiveness and childlike fancy.[2] These characteristics had always been among those considered 'feminine' by the Judeo-Christian tradition, but they had not always been seen as positive, or indeed even as descriptive of women's entire nature. From the late seventeenth century onward, however, they received an increasingly positive and exclusive valuation. By this exclusion of their contradictory characteristics, women could be included in the dominant culture, but marginally, either as passive consumers of that culture or as producers of their own sub-culture.

Once in place, this view of female sensibility had a curiously static quality. Part I of Astell's *Serious Proposal* (1694) argued a case for the purpose of women's education that differed very little not only from the contemporary views of Fénelon or Mme de Maintenon but also from those later put forward by Condorcet in 1791-2, or by Hannah More and Laetitia Barbauld around the same period. Nor do Perrault's ideas on women's place in the home (1694) differ from those urged by Dr Gregory in the 1770s.

Before discussing this process of excluding women from the developing dominant culture of seventeenth- and eighteenth-century Europe, one caveat: these considerations concern almost exclusively a very restricted group of chiefly middle-class women. We must beware of letting them stand in for 'Woman'.[3] Yet while the importance of these discussions may indeed be disproportionate, it is real, for they enable us better to understand both the functioning of a dominant Enlightenment culture that remains by and large our own, and the nature of its disenfranchisement of women.

It is also important to insist upon the point that women were not entirely excluded from that dominant culture. To do so might well have created as fearsome a group as the poor of nineteenth-century industrial cities - London's outcasts or Paris's dangerous classes. Rather, women were incorporated as second-class participants; as such they could be controlled and dominated. In 1777, Hannah More described women's necessarily subsidiary role in the culture of Enlightened reason:

Women have generally quicker perceptions; men have juster sentiments. Women consider how things may be prettily said; men, how they may be properly said. In women (young ones at least), speaking accompanies and sometimes precedes reflection; in men, reflection is the antecedent. Women speak to shine or to please; men, to convince or confute. Women admire what is brilliant; men what is solid. Women prefer an extemporaneous sally of wit, or a sparkling effusion of fancy, before the most accurate reasoning, or the most laborious investigation of facts. In literary composition, women are pleased with point, turn, and antithesis; men, with obser- vation, and a just deduction of effects from their causes. Women are fond of incident, men, of argument . . . .

In short, it appears that the mind in each sex has some natural kind of bias, which constitutes a distinction of character, and that the happiness of both depends, in a great measure, on the preser- vation and observance of this distinction.[4]

More's estimate disagreed only slightly from La Bruyère's opinion that women were either children or ornamental objects existing for men's titillation, a view he had expressed in his *Caractères* in 1688-92. In fact so prevalent did this strain of thought remain throughout the eighteenth century and so clearly sexist was it, that one is not surprised to see Richard Polwhele use the very remarks just quoted from More to footnote his violently antifeminist poem, *The Unsex'd Females*, which he wrote in 1799 in reaction to Wollstonecraft.[5] Thus it is clear that the years between La Bruyère and More saw little change. Indeed, from the fight about women's role and status that accompanied the Querelle des Anciens et des Modernes during the last twenty years of the seventeenth century until well into the twentieth, some more or less extreme version of this view became standard in law as in literature, in social reality as in the cultural discourse that apprehended it.

More's view of the female mind as incapable of sustained attention, as ornamental rather than logical, superficial not deep, anecdotal not analytical, suitable for the invention of fanciful fictions but unable to philosophize or to think with clarity, is the precise counterpart of La Bruyère's opinion. Another century later, such views received their satirical come-uppance:

It is sometimes stated that as several women of genius in modern times have sought to find expression for their creative powers in the art of fiction, there must be some inherent connection in the human brain between the ovarian sex function and the art of fiction. The fact is, that modern fiction being merely a description of human life in any of its phases, and being the only art that can be exercised without special training or special appliances, and produced in the moments stolen from the multifarious, brain-destroying occupations which fill the average woman's life, they have been driven to find this outlet for their powers as the only one presenting itself.[6]

Between the strong demands on behalf of women and reason characteristic of the first half of the seventeenth century and the understanding that human 'nature' is largely the creation of social action and the result of particular socializing practices that characterizes the twentieth, there lie three centuries throughout which every effort was made in the dominant discourse to depict women as naturally subordinate to men because lacking those very qualities essential to the dominance of the culture in which they might therefore participate but which they could never hope to direct or lead.

At the same time it is important to emphasize the fact that this debate respecting the status of women, the origins of which lay in the late seventeenth century, was 'not about their exclusion from culture, but about their exclusion from certain functions *within* that culture. The difference is important: within culture, women, like other excluded participants, are reduced to passive recipients; were they rejected outside culture, they could become its active opponents.'[7]

The young Wollstonecraft began by echoing such reactionary views. They are apparent, for example, both in her 1787 *Thoughts on the Education of Daughters* and her 1789 anthology, *The Female Reader*. In the last, she drew as many extracts from such writers as James Gregory and Anna Barbauld as she did from less reactionary sources, while the views she set forth in its preface would have been familiar to Hannah More. Woman must learn to speak, to read, and to think well, but not 'to obtrude her person or talents on the public'.

Wollstonecraft did not cling long to these opinions. In the phrase qualifying the one just quoted from this early work she already hinted at what was to come. Woman is not to obtrude only 'when necessity does not justify her and spur her on'. Could a growing sense of women's exclusion from culture and social activity provide such necessity? The deceptively mild assertion with which she concluded her preface indeed implied something of the kind: 'as we are created accountable creatures we must run the race ourselves.'[8] Already, too, this overt acceptance but implicit rejection of women's cultural subordination provides both a foretaste of Wollstonecraft's eventually unsuccessful struggles to resolve these complex issues and an explanation of the violently abusive reaction to Godwin's *Memoirs*, published in 1798.

The incorporation of women within culture in a subsidiary position but from whence various demands could be urged, the seemingly conditional acceptance of such subordination, and the growing demand that men justify their domination and aggression, are processes explaining, I think, both why Wollstonecraft's contentions could be perceived as menacing, and why they remained nonetheless limited. She did not see herself as a member of a totally deprived class seeking to be included in the fold (she is not, *pace* de Beauvoir, some 'Other'). Rather was she trying to readjust the order of beneficiaries, so to speak, in the dominant order. For this very reason she had no difficulty seeing other groups as candidates for exclusion. We need not be surprised, but we should thus be armed against taking Wollstonecraft for something she is not. Zillah Eisenstein has already warned us against this.[9] But it deserves more attention: not in order to belittle Wollstonecraft's achievement (hardly possible at this late date), but rather to contribute to the understanding in general of how a dominant discourse can absorb dissenting voices and recuperate apparent subversion, and in particular to discover why such strong feminist voices as those of Mary Wollstonecraft and her contemporaries Catherine Macaulay, Mary Hays, and Mary Ann Radcliffe, writing during the revolutionary years at the turn of the eighteenth century, achieved little or no immediate effect.

Two explanations offer themselves. At one level, ineffectiveness was connected with the seemingly trivial and obvious fact that such alternative ways of understanding as the materialist social explanation just quoted from Olive Schreiner were unavailable to Wollstonecraft and her contemporaries. As most of this essay will seek to show, such a constraint meant they were forced to adhere to the norms of the very reason whose oppressive dominance was the object of their attack. The result was a failure that Wollstonecraft, for one, appeared to recognize – at least implicitly. At another level, no doubt, the defeat had to do with the very nature of the 'revolutionary years' themselves. And it is to this last issue that I shall turn first, in order to provide the historical context out of which the discourse and its opposition arose.

Revolution within the limits of Reason alone

On 14 July 1789, the Bastille fell to an angry Parisian crowd. The event was scarcely of major military importance in the Revolution: although its fall could be heralded as the sign that Louis XVI had lost his capital, it was not until 1880 that 14 July was decreed the National Holiday of the French Republic. It is perhaps not irrelevant that this occurred just nine years before the erection of the Eiffel Tower was equally symbolically to confirm the free Republic's burgeoning prosperity, founded on the back of a repressive industrialization, nor that the horrific depression of 1880 may have made such a positive symbol necessary. The Bastille's fall may well symbolize less the democratization of the French state than it does the bourgeoisie's creation of the conditions for industrialization and its own wealth.

'Oh wond'rous power of words,' Wordsworth exclaims, 'how sweet they are / According to the meaning which they bring!' (*The Prelude* [1805], VII.121-2). For factual ambiguity has little enough to do with the symbolic clarity ascribed to such events, and one may well agree with those historians who have argued that the Revolution did not rupture French (or European) history. It doubtless remade it in the sense that more people were enabled to participate in the benefits of Whiggish history, and it certainly quite altered the form of political discourse in France, providing it (precisely) with a *symbolic* moment of break and seeming new departure. France was catching up with England, even going so far eventually as to create a constitutional monarch. But by no means was everyone to participate in this expanding access to the benefits of industrial capitalism. For women, in particular, no Bastille, symbolic or otherwise, was to fall.

For Mary Wollstonecraft, however, the Bastille had quickly become both a personal and political symbol. As early as 30 October 1786, upon her arrival at the Kingsboroughs' castle in Mitchelstown, Ireland, where she was to be governess, she had written to her sister, Everina: 'I entered the great gates with the same kind of feeling as I should have if I was going into the Bastile [*sic*].' On 19 November 1789, she complained to her friend and protégé, George Blood, that he had not written: 'you were not shut up in the Bastile [*sic*].' [10] For Wollstonecraft, the image depicted to perfection women's bondage. In the posthumously published *Maria*, her eponymous heroine explains how 'marriage had bastilled me for life', and how, once a man has left his wife, he is free but for the small allowance whose payment 'is thought sufficient to secure his reputation from taint', whereas a woman who leaves her husband 'is despised and shunned'. 'Such is the respect', she added, 'paid to the master-key of property!' [11] In the novel, Maria's lament may also be taken as a commentary upon Jemima's tale, when she had earlier related how misery and rejection led her 'from absolute necessity' down the path away from publicly-approved morality to her position as keeper of the 'poor wretches' now confined in the insane asylum. [12] Interestingly, this tale is almost a precise fictional depiction of the conditions Mary Ann Radcliffe inveighs against in *The Female Advocate*. Such confinement is indeed emblematic of the failure to discover a way to change the actual status of women, and these problems are clearly tied, for Wollstonecraft, to the hope of the Revolution.

Just as women's position did not change, and as feminist voices fell silent in the trap of Enlightened Reason's dominance, so too the Revolution in France merely confirmed Reason's iron hold on the social order. We should not indeed be lured into the belief that European history suddenly made some qualitative leap into difference. The reaction of one important Romantic may be helpful in understanding this, especially because he took up some of the issues on which Wollstonecraft also focused. In a text much abused by critics, Wordsworth did indeed exclaim: 'Bliss was it in that dawn to be alive. / But to be young was very heaven!' (*The French Revolution as it appeared to enthusiasts at its commencement* [1804]). In the *Prelude*, from which I quoted earlier, he had apostrophized:

> Oh! most beloved Friend, a glorious time
> A happy time that was; triumphant looks
> Were then the common language of all eyes:

> As if awak'd from sleep, the Nations hail'd
> Their great expectancy . . .
>
> (*Prelude*, VI.681-5)

Some read this as an outpouring of ardent revolutionary fervour, as a fundamental questioning of what they have fondly seen as a yoke of oppression being cast aside by the only truly revolutionary literary movement in our tradition – one shortly crushed by unwonted government censorship (as though such censorship had not been endemic for the previous century and a half of 'literature'). For women, at least, the Revolution represented no such release from servitude. In this same poem, Wordsworth gave voice to the prevailing ideology of women's place in the cautionary tale of 'Mary of Buttermere', the Maiden 'in her cottage Inn', who overwhelms the poet with 'delight' and 'admiration of her modest mien, / And carriage, mark'd by unexampled grace', a lady of 'discretion', of 'just opinion', of 'female modesty', 'patience', and the rest. Above all, she merits approbation because 'her new-born Infant, fearless as a lamb' now 'sleeps in earth'. All this she manages despite 'betrayal' by 'a bold bad Man'. And now 'happy are they both / Mother and Child!' (*Prelude*, VII.321-60).

This praise of Mary (whose name is hardly irrelevant, with her child 'fearless as a lamb') is of course linked with Romanticism's idealization of nature: 'The Spirit of Nature was upon me here; / The Spirit of Beauty and enduring life / Was present as a habit' (*Prelude*, VII.736-8). Shades of Shaftesbury, one might say. And this is the Wordsworth who, in the same year as writing the first version of *The Prelude*, in *The Recluse* relates how:

> On Man, on Nature, and on Human Life,
> Musing in solitude, I oft perceive
> Fair trains of imagery before me rise,
> Accompanied by feelings of delight
> Pure, or with no unpleasing sadness mixed . . .
>
> (*The Recluse*, 754-8)

Here we find the same nostalgia for a lost wholeness with Nature, with the Divine presence of some untrammelled absolute Justice (oh, happy Mary with her dead child in her pauper's cottage), as Goldsmith urged in *The Traveller* and *The Deserted Village*, two other poems often co-opted by left-wing critics with small sense of history. Those only are astonished by Wordsworth's later addition to *The Prelude* of fulsome praise for Burke ('Genius of Burke! forgive the pen seduced / By specious wonders . . .', VII.512ff.) who ignore what the disagreeable sentimentality of the wondrous Mary of Buttermere leads up to – the poet's journey to Cambridge and the discovery of female emancipation and/or prostitution:

> It was but little more than three short years
> Before the season which I speak of now
> When first, a Traveller from our pastoral hills,
> Southward two hundred miles I had advanced,
> And for the first time in my life did hear
> The voice of Woman utter blasphemy;
> Saw Woman as she is to open shame
> Abandon'd and the pride of public vice.
> Full surely from the bottom of my heart
> I shuddered; but the pain was almost lost,
> Absorb'd and buried in the immensity
> Of the effect: a barrier seemed at once
> Thrown in, that from humanity divorced
> The Human Form, splitting the race of Man
> In twain, yet leaving the same outward shape.
> Distress of mind ensued upon this sight
> And ardent meditation . . .
>
> (*Prelude*, VII.412-29)

He manages, however, to overcome this horror: 'afterwards / A milder sadness on such spectacles / Attended; thought, commiseration, grief / For the individual, and the overthrow / Of her soul's beauty' (429-33).

That it is difficult to tell whether Wordsworth is speaking of emancipation or prostitution is not surprising – and on at least one occasion, as we will see, a similar problem arises in Wollstonecraft herself. The conflation is typical of contemporary opinion (more so in France, perhaps, than in England), which tended to make small distinction between the authority and self-possession implied by the first and an unconfined sexuality of which prostitution was but the extreme. This is the case throughout the entire eighteenth century and well into the nineteenth. Referring to Hume and Grimm as representative, Elizabeth Fox-Genovese remarks: 'Female authorship – with all the authority the term implies –

was more or less explicitly assimilated to female sexuality, and both were discouraged.' Such male writers, she adds, now including such as Rousseau and Restif de la Bretonne, 'were appalled by what they viewed as the lawlessness and unruliness of at least some eighteenth-century [French] women. They saw a pervasive failure of delicacy and modesty; they shuddered at female sexual license; they reproved women's intrusion into intellectual and political life.'[13]

Richard Polwhele's poem *The Unsex'd Females* (1799) is simply a belated and vulgar version of such views: on the one hand he lamented the new woman's 'imperious mien', 'dismissal' of 'the heart', and her claim of 'mental energy', on the other he deplored her lack of 'decorum', her surrender to 'Passion's fire', and (this with some salaciously obscene lip-smacking) her readiness to expose 'in full view, the meretricious breast'.[14] Less vulgar, Wordsworth's poem echoed views of this kind. But the poet's attitude toward women is evidently not limited to one poem, whose supposed revolutionary context simply makes it so much clearer. We might take, for example, Wordsworth's romanticized cottage spinners in the poem 'Nuns Fret Not': 'Maids at the wheel . . . / Sit blithe and happy'. When we consider that women spinners earned only an eighth as much as their male counterparts, that hand-loom weavers worked between fourteen and sixteen hours a day, that the poet dismissed the idea of women operating power machines, we realize that this poetry was far from innocent.[15] Such views shed new light on Mary of Buttermere, as they also make us understand that the idealization of the women in their cottages close to Nature is a way of concealing the harsh realities that forced the Jemimas and the women spoken of by Mary Ann Radcliffe into a life of crime and prostitution. Woman close to nature, nurturing and protective, was also a counter to the Enlightenment prescription of a rational, logical man. Wollstonecraft took on Rousseau over just that issue, as he depicted the relationship between men and women in *Émile*.

Yet these views, like Burke's *Reflections* (1789) and the opposition expressed in texts such as Wollstonecraft's 1790 *Vindication of the Rights of Men*, or Tom Paine's *Rights of Man* of the same year, were all, of course, reactions to the Revolution and, more particularly perhaps in the English context (though this does not apply to Paine), to fears that another revolution might occur north of the Channel. All were caught up in the same singular process of Enlightenment of which the Revolution itself was one very physical manifestation. And just as women were ultimately excluded from the benefits of the Revolution itself, so they found themselves the embodiment of anti-Enlightenment ideology. It was this difficulty which, I would maintain, ultimately prevented Wollstonecraft from arguing a truly revolutionary case – that is, for a change in the order of the dominant discourse itself. Rather, she argued *within* Enlightenment rhetoric, for the extension of equality without regard (at least) to gender. Wollstonecraft was asserting women's right to catch up with men, in the same manner as Tom Paine (for example) argued that the enfranchisement of the dispossessed – whether colonials, the poor, or the aged – must catch up with that of the proprietors. It was, always, a matter of the right to participate in the system, not of the need to change it.

*The perennial attempt to answer the question: Is human reason
continually improving?*

The English provoker of fears that the revolutionary 'plague' (as Burke called it) might spread across the Channel was Dr Richard Price. I may take a moment to glance, however rapidly, at a little of his work with some confidence in the utility of doing so, not only because he was the proximate cause of Burke's diatribe against the French Revolution, but also because he was Wollstonecraft's close friend and supporter at a particularly crucial time, when she first opened her school at Stoke Newington and began to practice certain of her just-forming ideas on education. The foundations of his arguments are no more startling or new than are Wollstonecraft's, and, indeed, are entirely typical of an era stretching from the late seventeenth century almost to the present.

On 4 November 1789, in commemoration of the Glorious Revolution, the preacher delivered 'A Discourse on the Love of Our Country'. It provoked a considerable furore. In this celebrated pamphlet, Price set out to show, on the basis of an argument from onto- to phylo-genesis, that love of country inevitably leads to love of one's neighbor – and thence to a kind of individualistic love of the world, of humankind. I am reminded of nothing so much as Defoe's assertion, made a little over half a century earlier, at the beginning of his *Serious Reflections* [on *Robinson Crusoe*]: 'The World, I say, is nothing to us, but as it is more or less to our Relish: All Reflection is carry'd Home, and our Dear-self is, in one Respect, the End of Living.' In Price's words:

With this view, I must desire you to recollect that we are so constituted that our affections are more drawn to some among mankind than to others, in proportion to their degree of nearness to us, and our power of being useful to them. It is obvious, that this is a circumstance in the constitution of our natures which proves the wisdom and goodness of our Maker; for had our affections been determined alike to all our fellow-creatures, human life would have been a scene of embarrassment and distraction. *Our regards,* according to the order of nature, *begin with ourselves; and every man is charged primarily with the care of himself.* Next come our families, and benefactors, and friends; and after them, our country. We can do little for the interest of mankind at large. To this interest, however, all other interests are subordinate. The *noblest principle in our nature is the regard to general justice*, and that good-will which embraces all the world. . . .[16]

This 'justice' had figured importantly in earlier writings in the tradition. In his *Philosophical Rudiments* (1651), Hobbes had written that the concept of justice had provided him with the fundamental axiom enabling a scientific study of civil society and an understanding of the passage out of the state of nature: it is the very foundation of the political contract. In his 1650 preface to *Gondibert*, George Davenant used the concept of justice to explain his argument concerning the poetic establishment of society. A quarter of a century later, Thomas Rymer used the term 'poetical justice' to denote the alliance between the moral, rational and aesthetic orders of the world – more precisely, perhaps, their identity.

It may be Burke, perchance, who brought this concept of justice to its rhetorical paroxysm. Concluding his series of speeches in the impeachment proceedings against Warren Hastings in the 1790s, the Honorable Member first reminded the Lords of their precarious situation (thinking here of the French contagion), and then expatiated in his best preacherly manner:

There is one thing, and one thing only, which defies all mutation, – that which existed before the world, and will survive the fabric of the world itself: I mean justice, – that justice which, emanating from the Divinity, has a place in the breast of every one of us, given us for our guide with regard to ourselves and with regard to others, and which will stand, after this globe is burned to ashes, our advocate and accuser before the great Judge, when He comes to call upon us for the tenor of a well-spent life.[17]

The apocalyptic tone and notion of justice as the divine ethical guiding principle of the world reflect not only Price, but an entire century of thought and action: for that justice is as common to Mandeville's idea that the service of private self-interest is morally useful to the whole of civil society as it is to Rousseau's elaboration of the relation between the individual and the general will. One still finds it in Hegel's *Philosophy of Right* (1821). Indeed, throughout the whole period from the late seventeenth century until the libertarian claims of our own day, it has remained the primary ethical justification for the articulation of general social action upon individual interest. In the present time, John Rawls's *Theory of Justice* (1971) springs readily to mind.

In his 1795 'Thoughts and Details on Scarcity', Wollstonecraft's adversary Burke thus typically asserted that we should feel only gratitude toward 'the benign and wise Disposer of all things, who obliges men, whether they will or not, in pursuing their own selfish interests, to connect the general good with their own individual success.'[18] This view was held as much by Price as by Defoe, as much by Mandeville as by Wollstonecraft's friend and eventual husband, William Godwin, whose *Enquiry Concerning Political Justice* (1793) argues at great length in favor of a civil association founded entirely on the absolute freedom of every individual. And in her Scandinavian letters (1796), Wollstonecraft similarly remarks that growth of mind and stimulation of human industriousness requires that the faculties be 'sharpened by the only thing that can exercise them, self-interest'.[19]

It should scarcely surprise us that Wollstonecraft adopted these principles, and ascribed them to women. Indeed, in the following case, she has borrowed almost verbatim from Price: 'Speaking of women at large, their first duty is to themselves as rational creatures, and the next, in point of importance, as citizens, is that, which includes so many, of a mother.'[20] What is interesting in such a claim, however, is the way in which citizenship has been narrowed to motherhood. When Samuel Richardson, for example, placed a similar argument in a woman's mouth, he does not appear to have made such a limitation. In his analysis of *Clarissa*, Christopher Hill has recorded an affirmation of just this relation of self to world. He cites the heroine's explanation of her behavior to Miss Howe, as arising 'principally from what offers to my own heart;

respecting, as I may say, its own rectitude, its own judgment of the *fit* and the *unfit*; as I would, without study, answer *for* myself *to* myself, in the *first* place; to *him* [Lovelace] and to the *world*, in the *second* only. Principles that *are* in my mind; that I *found* there; implanted, no doubt, by the first gracious Planter: which therefore *impel* me, as I may say, to act up to them . . . let others act as they will by *me*.'[21]

Writing as a woman, using the means of the dominant discourse at the same time as querying some of its most oppressive aspects, Wollstonecraft's situation is at once more ambiguous, more complicated and more conflicted than the masculine one which Richardson could give *his* heroine. Wollstonecraft was partly under the blinding sway of an ideology imposing marriage and motherhood as a woman's duty, and her difficulty was to put those citizenship 'duties' in terms that would not deny the equality of reason and social function. The only terms available for such affirmation were the Enlightenment ones Price and others offered: 'Reason', she wrote, 'is . . . the single power of improvement; or, more properly speaking, of discerning truth. Every individual is in this respect a world in itself' (*VRW*, 142). And she linked the expansion outwards from self, to family, to nation, to the idea of progress and the development of the rational understanding: 'the grand actions of the heart, particularly the enlarged humanity which extends to the whole human race, depend more on the understanding, I believe, than is generally imagined.' Thus, while the underdeveloped Norwegians had got only as far as the ability to consider their families, progress would augment the capacity of their reason: 'which I conceive will always be the case, till politics, becoming a subject of discussion, enlarges the heart by opening the understanding' (*Letters*, 63n, 64).

Quite clearly here we can see precisely the same conceptual scheme as in Price, Burke, or Godwin: the idea of the uniqueness of the individual is the primitive statement, so to speak, out of which will be elaborated all subsequent statements – in this case forming a society in every way customary. And if I put the matter in these idealist and disembodied terms, the reasons are deliberate. Arguing her case in this manner forced Wollstonecraft to make motherhood the primary function of woman as social being, as 'citizen', despite her own actual and stated experience of the subordinate status this *necessarily* imposed on women, not seldom taking the form of a moral and intellectual brutalizing of the mind, when it did not lead to real physical brutality. Situating the statement of individuality first, Wollstonecraft found the distinguishing *human* characteristic to be the familiar one of reason, and the distinguishing *female* characteristic to be that of childbirth.

The sentence about motherhood quoted from *A Vindication of the Rights of Woman* repeated a preoccupation of the 1787 *Thoughts on the Education of Daughters*: 'a woman may fit herself to be the companion and friend of a man of sense, and yet know how to take care of his family.' The use of the adjective 'his' is obviously not anodyne: 'to prepare a woman to fulfil the important duties of a wife and mother, are certainly the objects that should be in view during the early period of life.' [22] Even when, much later (in *VRW*), she raised the family to a kind of ideal form – where woman and man are equal – the home arrangement will remain the woman's primary function: and that must remove her from the public sphere in which *social* reason more clearly operates. Indeed, in *VRW*, she insisted on something like the need for *social* differences even as she argued a lack of natural ones, though she failed to explain why such difference is necessary: 'women, I allow, may have different duties to fulfil; but they are *human* duties, and the principles that should regulate the discharge of them, I sturdily maintain, must be the same' (*VRW*, p. 139).

Groundwork of the Critique of Moral Education

Wollstonecraft was aware of this contradiction as early as the publication of *Thoughts*, commenting at the outset on the necessary imperfection of certain rational educational projects: 'To be able to follow Mr. Locke's system (and this may be said of almost all treatises on education) the parents must have subdued their own passions, which is not often the case in any considerable degree' (*Thoughts*, pp. 11-12). The moral and conceptual dilemmas into which the contradiction led become clearer when, at the conclusion of the work, we see its author commenting on the dangers confronting the 'young innocent girl when she first enters into [the] gay scenes' of public places, in tones akin to those used later by Wordsworth in the *Prelude*. 'She would often be lost in delight,' wrote Wollstonecraft, 'if she was not checked by observing the behaviour of a class of females who attend those places.' 'What a painful train of reflections do then arise in the mind, and convictions of the vice and folly of the world are prematurely forced on it. It is no longer a paradise, for innocence is not there; the taint of vice poisons every enjoyment, and affectation, though despised, is very contagious' (*Thoughts*, pp. 158-9).

It is not clear to me here whether she was speaking of prostitutes or of those idle wealthy women whom she despised and constantly castigated. Perhaps she had both in mind. What does seem clear is that her remark positively cried out for an elaboration examining the social conditions that forced women into such situations, although she herself might not necessarily be aware of such a need. In fact, critics and biographers of Wollstonecraft frequently dismiss the *Thoughts* as a rather conservative early work, where Wollstonecraft was simply testing a number of ideas, many of which she will later discard.

If she was speaking of prostitutes, however, the 1792 *Vindication* moderated her earlier disapprobation. Here she described the perils faced by 'those unfortunate females who are broken off from society', frequently through no fault of their own: 'Asylums and Magdalens', she went on, 'are not the proper remedies for these abuses. It is justice, not charity, that is wanting in the world!' In Wollstonecraft's view, such situations were caused by an education that trained women to remain subordinate to men:

> Losing thus every spur, and having no other means of support, prostitution becomes her only refuge, and the character is quickly depraved by circumstances over which the poor wretch has little power. . . . Necessity never makes prostitution the business of men's lives; though numberless are the women who are thus rendered systematically vicious. This, however, arises in a great degree from the state of idleness in which women are educated, who are always taught to look up to man for a maintenance, and to consider their persons as the proper return for his exertions to support them. (*VRW*, p. 165).

This passage appears clearly to equate the woman who idles in marriage with the prostitute, and may be viewed as a commentary on the equation suggested in *Thoughts*, at the same time as explaining the scorn with which she regarded such women as Lady Kingsborough, her mistress when she worked as a governess in Ireland.

She did not sustain so sympathetic a handling of the question. Indeed, as far as I know, the paragraph just quoted is unique in Wollstonecraft's writing. She more readily adopted the earlier tone:

The shameless behaviour of the prostitutes, who infest the streets of this metropolis, raising alternate emotions of pity and disgust, may serve to illustrate this remark [that bashfulness is not modesty but only ignorance]. They trample on virgin bashfulness with a sort of bravado, and glorifying in their shame, become more audaciously lewd than men, however depraved, to whom this sexual quality has not been gratuitously granted [!], ever appear to be. But these poor ignorant wretches never had any modesty to lose, when they consigned themselves to infamy; for modesty is a virtue, not a quality. No, they were only bashful, shamefaced innocents; and losing their innocence, their shamefacedness was rudely brushed off: a virtue would have left some vestiges in the mind, had it been sacrificed to passion, to make us respect the grand ruin. (*VRW*, p. 228)

Not only did she now hold these women responsible for their own situation ('they consigned themselves to infamy'), but she appeared to view women, unlike men, as having a 'sexual quality gratuitously granted', thus echoing one of the eighteenth century's more unsavory assertions about women. No longer did she even hint at the earlier suggestion of male responsibility. Her obvious confusion on this issue was not shared by all her contemporaries who addressed these questions, however. A brief discussion of the ideas of her little-known peer, Mary Ann Radcliffe, suggests that other commentators were untroubled by the popular condemnation of prostitution.

In *The Female Advocate* (1799), Radcliffe elected to stress the dominant discourse's own claim to plead for equality of opportunity for the downtrodden. Most especially, she put the case for women who had been forced into prostitution by poverty, by orphan- or widowhood, or simply by the lack of access to work endemic to the condition of middle-class feminine 'gentility' (a situation frequently adumbrated by Wollstonecraft). With derisive irony Radcliffe contended that men, who claim themselves more powerful than women, should therefore protect them just as (and because) they assert the right to: 'I contend not with the Lords of the creation for any other privilege than that protection which they themselves avow to be the real rights of women.'[23] She did not question men's dominance, but urged they should therefore do their utmost to help those they called the weaker sex: 'as women seem formed by nature to seek protection from man, why, in the name of justice, refuse the boon?' (*FA*, p. 404: the opposition between the particular, 'women', and the general, 'man', itself seems infused with a certain mockery). All who refuse to give support should 'appear and show cause, why they are entitled to oppress these poor women, in order to enjoy indolence and ease' (*FA*, p. 468). Her sarcasm could become ferocious as she argued that those who assert the right to dominance must accept the responsibility accompanying it. The biting irony underscored the thought that both are equally unjustifiable: 'Nor is there the smallest danger, when once the business is commenced, that the deep penetration and humanity of the guardians of the common weal will ever be baffled in so laudable a pursuit' (*FA*, p. 467).

As in Wollstonecraft's case, no doubt, this attack on the dominant masculine-oriented ideology and rhetoric did not go beyond the demand that women have access to the same advantages and benefits. Radcliffe did not propose any different order of activity or discourse (even if we suppose that possible). The ironic demand for men's protection in fact amounts to a demand for access to the advantages and privileges long enjoyed by men: 'then is it not highly worthy the attention of men, men who profess moral virtue and the strictest sense of *honours* to consider in what mode to redress those grievances! For women were ultimately designed for something better, though they have so long fared otherwise' (*FA*, p. 409). The value-system remains that of Enlightened rationalism. 'In the name of reason, justice, and truth' (*FA*, p. 463) was a constant refrain, representing a familiar view of human reason, whose claimed equality but actual partiality received suitably ironic attention from Radcliffe: 'as it is not expected a female can have much knowledge in judicature [due to improper education], I go upon the grounds of common sense and reason, and not activated by any other motive than a wish to see happiness prevail' (*FA*, p. 465).

In Radcliffe's work, her ridiculing of the properness of male domination produced something akin to our contemporary notion of gender: the idea that much or most of what we perceive as sexual difference is socially produced. At one point, for example, she accused men of taking from women even those jobs that are properly theirs, asserting that in this way they deprived women even of the last poor barriers between them and complete destitution: 'For can it be termed either manly, honourable, or humane, to oppress industry and helpless innocence, and place them under the absolute necessity of sacrificing their virtue, their happiness, and everything they hold dear, at the shrine of the avaricious, *and* (for the sake of distinction) *effeminate tradesmen?'* (*FA*, p. 426; Radcliffe's emphasis). Her use of the term 'effeminate', as the parenthetical qualification indicates, is intended both in a literal sense (taking women's jobs, they are 'becoming' female) and in a rather different way: such jobs, the last resort of women, are so designated in a masculine system. This thought provoked her to further sarcasm, to a 'joke', as she called it: 'suppose no lady would suffer herself to be served, in the shops of these effeminate traders, by any of the short clothed gentry, would it not be a means of compelling all those who chuse to carry on the tragi-comic farce, to effect the business under the disguise of gown and petticoat? (*FA*, p. 428: I am reminded of Cynthia Ozick's joke about sexual difference being marked by a choice between two long cloth tubes or one short one).

Her sense that the status of the sexes was socially specific did not prevent Radcliffe from viewing her own society as otherwise superior. Thus she could not understand how efforts were made 'by the humane friends of liberty' on behalf of 'the poor slaves' (*FA*, p. 469), when nothing was done for members of their own society. The slave, after all, was in her view less human than a member of rational society. (The idea that the greater maturity of rational society placed it ahead of others was of course perfectly in line with a familiar Kantian view of what the Enlightenment was.) And within this better society, Radcliffe argued that British women should take their proper full place:

> The slave is little acquainted with the severe pangs a virtuous mind labours under, when driven to the extreme necessity of forfeiting their virtue for bread. The slave cannot feel pain at the loss of reputation, a term of which he never heard, and much less knows the meaning. What are the untutored, wild imaginations of a slave, when put in the balance with the distressing sensations of a British female, who has received a refined, if not a classical, education, and is capable of the finest feelings the human heart is susceptible of? A slave, through want of education, has little more refinement than cattle in the field . . . . (*FA*, p. 469)

One may doubtless argue that since 'the poor unfortunate women of our nation' were themselves seen as laboring 'under the very worst kind of slavery' (*FA*, p. 470), their full participation in the dominant discourse would *reasonably* precede that of 'the African', whose lack of refinement was due to ignorance and 'want of education' - which, after all, was the reason why British women could not participate either in certain kinds of discussion.

Clearly, Radcliffe never questioned the correctness of the dominant discourse. Rather, she addressed the matter of who 'owned' it. Her concern was in fact with everyone's gradually maturing accession to the one *right* form of discourse: rational, just, true, commonsensical. What *was* unusual was Radcliffe's ferocious argument that men's claim to equality depended on the assertion of women's (and others') *in*equality: she was thus implying that gender difference was a matter of discourse.

In some of these areas I think it fair to say that she went some way beyond her better-known contemporary. Wollstonecraft's arguments also concerned access to the privileges enjoyed by (some) men in a society whose organization presupposed inequality for all, be they male or female. That is certainly why she did not pursue the matter of prostitution into the thickets of social and political conditions, why she is unconcerned, for example, with matters of class, and why she makes no bones about maintaining the received understanding of self, subject, individual, and relations between many such. *Thoughts* may be a slightly conservative early work, but the assumptions underlying it never changed. The distinctly un-Lockean statement about the nature of the Subject with which she began *Thoughts* remained the basis of both *Vindications* as well as of her two novels: 'It is, in my opinion, a well-proved fact, that principles of truth are innate. Without reasoning we assent to many truths; we feel their force, and artful sophistry can only blunt those feelings which nature has implanted in us as instinctive guards to virtue' (*Thoughts*, p. 13). By nature, then, the mind is endowed with a 'beautiful simplicity' (*Thoughts*, p. 14). In the *Vindication of the Rights of Men*, Wollstonecraft similarly wrote: 'What is truth? A few fundamental truths meet the first enquiry of reason, and appear as clear to an unwarped mind, as that air and bread are necessary to enable the body to fulfil its vital functions.'[24]

Truth, simplicity, beauty, natural reason, and motherhood for women . . . One is reminded not only of Descartes, but of the later ethical and moral tradition flowing with scarcely a break from Boileau and Shaftesbury, through Hutcheson, Hume, Adam Smith, Beattie and Reid, to Keats, Shelley and beyond, linking Nature, Truth, Beauty and Justice as the metaphysical dwelling-place of the human individual.

I do not intend my argument that Wollstonecraft failed to go beyond her peers as a criticism of her. Indeed, one may well argue that women, including Wollstonecraft, must occupy a situation wholly equal to men's before we all can take on the more general project of changing society and its concept. [25] I am simply warning again that Wollstonecraft should not be made anachronistically into something she was not. Moreover, the question really is whether lacking a more general project of transformation, *any* change in practical status of *any* individual within society is possible. Such things do not alter separately, of course, and it is certainly the case that Wollstonecraft and her circle thought the American and French Revolutions *did* herald such general transformation. History has shown *us* that to a large extent they were mistaken in that belief, and reading their texts in the light of subsequent history can show us *why* the persistence of pre-Revolutionary dominant patterns of thought inevitably meant they *would* be wrong: such patterns comprised their way of thinking as well as that of everyone else.

Idea for a feminist history with a cosmopolitan purpose

In addition to her conviction that certain qualities were innate in individuals (marking her and his Humanity), Wollstonecraft also argued that people were products of a socio-cultural environment. In some sense she applied this even to motherhood. When speaking of breast-feeding and the 'maternal feeling', she wrote that she was of the 'opinion, that maternal tenderness arises quite as much from habit as instinct' (*Thoughts*, p. 4). [26] Like the inconclusive discussion of prostitution, this 'quite as much' begs for pursuit, for it clearly leads to the matter of biological determinism. In point of fact, one logical term of Lockean sensationalism could have led directly to such a questioning: if one assumes a human rationality common to the whole race (without further specification), as Locke did, if one then postulates that this rationality is a female as much as a male quality, as Wollstonecraft did, and if one further supposes reason activated only from the exterior through the senses, then when such rationality is taken as the fundamentally unique principle of *all* human action – *as* human – it follows that all such action is *always* the result of external conditions. To think of it as 'male' or 'female' is secondary to its being rational and human, and that last judgment is possible only by virtue of some external ('natural' or 'social') stimulus – a fact true both of the action and of the judgment.

The Humean conclusion could be avoided only by positing the existence of some kind of 'governor' (what in French is called a '*patron*', thus allowing an entirely suitable wordplay - recalling 'his' family), taking the form, for example, of innate truths and instinct. Thus what Wollstonecraft had cast out the front door returned through the back: in this case taking the form of the biological determinism present in the maternal feeling. Thus on the one hand she asserted in *A Vindication of the Rights of Woman*: 'I here throw down my gauntlet, and deny the existence of sexual virtues, not excepting modesty. For man and woman, truth, if I understand the meaning of the word, must be the same . . .'; while on the other she immediately went a long way toward picking her gauntlet up again: 'Women, I allow, may have different duties to fulfil; but they are *human* duties, and the principles that should regulate the discharge of them, I sturdily maintain, must be the same' (*VRW*, p. 139). Human, rational duties they may be, but they are also and equally female duties as opposed to male. *Access* to the dominant order may be achieved by women, but their participation will always and necessarily be different in some ways. And where may that not lead?

Once that is said, we must also recognize that this apparent logical flaw permitted Wollstonecraft to protest that oppressing women distorted and brutalized her right to the *same* place in the sun enjoyed by men - a right due them as equal partners in the species called 'human'. As she wrote in *Maria*, her aim was to expose 'the misery and oppression, peculiar to women, that arise out of the partial laws and customs of society', and especially out of marriage (as we have seen elsewhere). In a letter used by Godwin to preface this posthumously published novel (1798), she observed:

> For my part, I cannot suppose any situation more distressing, than for a woman of sensibility, with an improving mind, to be bound to such a man as I have described for life; obliged to renounce all the harmonizing affections, and to avoid cultivating her taste, lest her perception of grace and refinement of sentiment, should sharpen to agony the pangs of disappointment . . . These appear to me (matrimonial despotism of heart and conduct) to be the Peculiar Wrongs of Woman, because they degrade the mind.[27]

This is very far from the irony of the 'Advertisement' preceding her other novel, *Mary*: 'In an artless tale, without episodes, the mind of a woman, who has thinking powers is displayed. The female organs have been thought too weak for this arduous employment; and experience seems to justify the assertion. Without arguing physically about *possibilities* - in a fiction, such a being may be allowed to exist.' [28]

The story related in *Mary* is indeed an animadversion against the kind of marriage into which the fictional heroine had entered with Charles, and from which death alone could release her, but it is not in any way a questioning of the institution of matrimony itself or of the fundamental duty (and instinct) of maternity. Mary may finally be obliged to cut herself off from both social and family life, and to take refuge in her self, looking to death as a welcome relief, but this is the consequence of a bad, forced marriage, not of the institution (whose improvement Wollstonecraft sometimes appeared to view as a real possibility). Again: the dominant order is not *wrong*, it simply does not always function as it should.

When the French Revolution broke out a year after the publication of *Mary*, the potential for a general transformation of society existed in Wollstonecraft's mind. But by the time of *Maria*, ten years later, little had changed, save the darkening of Wollstonecraft's vision. By then, as we shall see, it was almost as if Wollstonecraft had become aware that *no* alternatives were available. Indeed, thinking about transforming the order had become as impossible as the transformation itself. She may have become more fiery, more 'emancipated' even, but her inability to push beyond conventional assumptions meant that in fact she differed little from those other women 'who had been forming public opinion during the crucial years in which liberal views were gaining ground'. These included such as Anna Barbauld and Hannah More, of whom Erna Reiss justly comments that they 'accepted the old conventional idea of womanhood'. So they 'were quite content to sink the personality of woman entirely in that of man, to accept it as her mission in life that she should be not complementary but ancillary to him.' [29] Again, the terms of the discussion proffer their constant subtle trap.

In 1790, Wollstonecraft took on Burke, defending the French Revolution by opposing the bright flame of 'liberty, civil and religious', and the idea of the 'social compact' seemingly consummated in France, to 'the demon of property' still passionately defended across the Channel (*VRM*, pp. 7-8). The first two are the fundamental social marks of the free, rational human individual. The third is her scornful characterization of the system Burke was trying to protect from contagion:

I perceive, from the whole tenor of your Reflections, that you have a mortal antipathy to reason; but, if there is anything like argument,

or first principles, in your wild declamations, behold the result: -that
we are to reverence the rust of antiquity, and term the unnatural
customs, which ignorance and mistaken self-interest has consoli-
dated, the sage fruit of experience: nay, that, if we do discover
some errors, our *feelings* should lead us to excuse, with blind love,
or unprincipled filial affection, the venerable vestiges of ancient
days. These are gothic notions of beauty - the ivy is beautiful, but,
when it insidiously destroys the trunk from which it receives
support, who would not grub it up? (*VRM*, 9-10)

Burke's attempt to maintain a system in distortion is thus dismissed as
passionate, irrational, and, in sum, 'unmanly'. The tables are neatly
turned.[30] In Wollstonecraft's view, a human truth - the tree trunk -
underlay custom: paralleling, if you will, the innate truths underlying
perceived sensation. It allowed correction but not transformation. What
Wollstonecraft failed to acknowledge, however, was that the choice of
truths characterized and particularized a socio-cultural environment,
composing its reality. Not surprisingly, Wollstonecraft's views were those
of her time - and they included certain claims about women's condition
that she did not (could not?) set out to change.

Thus Wollstonecraft's grubbed-up ivy differed little from Robinson
Crusoe's rejection of the paternal yoke, done in order to *repeat* his
father's mercantile success *for himself*. Unlike Wollstonecraft's Burke,
Crusoe did not suffer from unprincipled filial affection. In her view,
modern Western society, like that of Swift's Yahoos, had degenerated
from its original accord with liberty and contract. The ivy's removal
restored that pristine association. Although repetition seems to have
given Wollstonecraft some assurance of human stability, one begins to see
in such an argument the dangers of a nostalgia to which in fact she would
eventually abandon her thought. Like Mme de Lafayette's Princesse de
Clèves, she sought women's access to that restored social compact on a
basis of full equality. However, she overlooked or ignored the fact that it
was a *particular* compact: the one Hobbes had shaped from his earlier
notion of 'justice'. Attacking Burke's 'love of church', Wollstonecraft
noted that she would not bother about the details of his arguments and
invectives, aiming only at the 'foundation': 'on the natural principles of
justice I build my plea for disseminating the property artfully said to be
appropriated to religious purposes, but, in reality, to support idle tyrants,
amongst the society whose ancestors were cheated or forced into illegal
grants' (*VRM*, p. 125).

These natural principles of justice, we saw, are what link the individual with the community. They also (as I suggested in mentioning not only Hobbes, but also Davenant and Rymer) permit the articulation of human reason with the laws of nature, the verisimilitude of literature with the truth of the world, the moral imperatives of individual sensibility with the ethical rules placed in nature by the Divinity. (This last assumption was of course picked up by Mary Ann Radcliffe.) These principles mark mature reason, order, and judgment, and are the very signs of that human maturity which, for Kant ('What Is Enlightenment?'), are the essential characteristics of progress. In respect of its treatment of such principles, it could be argued that a novel such as *Jacques le fataliste* was one of a kind (in France): for it queried in its own terms the dominance of that very lawful Reason of which the novel is one idealized manifestation. That could be done meaningfully only once. In the English tradition it was achieved by Diderot's model, *Tristram Shandy*, the novel Viktor Shklovsky characterized as the most typical of all, just because it bared the rational principles of novelistic composition.

Wollstonecraft's view, however, was rather different. To her, *Shandy* represented, on the contrary, the immaturity of rampant fancy, opposed to judgment. *That*, not its self-examination, was rather the reason why it could not be repeated (at least in its own language):

> though it may be allowed that one man has by nature more fancy than another, in each individual there is a spring-tide when fancy should govern and amalgamate materials for the understanding; and a graver period, when those materials should be employed by the judgment. For example, I am inclined to have a better opinion of the heart of an *old* man, who speaks of Sterne as his favorite author, than of his understanding. There are times and seasons for all things: and moralists appear to me to err, when they would confound the gaiety of youth with the seriousness of age; for the virtues of age look not only more imposing, but more natural, when they appear rather rigid. (*VRM*, p. 141)

Burke and all he represented and favored belonged to that passionate spring-tide. The times, his opponent argued, were now beyond it. Political and social maturity demanded the restoration of the original compact in all its pristine rationality.

Again, we see these same terms: judgment, reason, seriousness, rigidity, justice, truth, and so on. If, in the light of this, one counts the number of times Wollstonecraft used the adjective 'manly', it quickly becomes clear that it is neither a device linked to the pseudonymity of the first edition of *A Vindication of the Rights of Man*, nor simply an irony. It marks a specific mode of thought. Nor can one here make use of the ludicrous concept of 'penis envy' - itself a product of the same discursive dominance, and one all too frequently invoked, directly or indirectly, in biographies of Wollstonecraft, whether by men or women. (To me, such references are akin to remarks comparing her to a serpent or a hyena.)

But then, I have no wish to belittle her achievement. On the contrary. I suggest that a revolutionary thought cannot escape from the constraints of its environment except under conditions where the *whole* environment is in doubt. If we may judge from the deeper despair of *Maria* (written during the period of her personally happy relations with Godwin), Wollstonecraft herself was not unaware of such constraints. There is little startling in that, except for those who strive to displace statements from one historical environment into a different one. She would be the first to warn against doing that, and *A Vindication of the Rights of Man* is one long assertion of the ease with which such attempts, such displacements, can be refuted: its one constant underlying argument is that because matters have been done in some way since time long past is not only *not* a reason for so continuing them, but may well create the need for more abrupt change. Burke, she wrote at one point, was so absurd as to suggest that the French should have looked to illustrious ancestors, rather than to present frailties. This might, she wrote with scorn, be good advice when addressed to a young painter: 'but, in settling a constitution that involved the happiness of millions, that stretch beyond the computation of science, it was, perhaps, necessary for the Assembly to have a higher model in view than the *imagined* virtues of their forefathers; and wise to deduce their respect for themselves from the only legitimate source, respect for justice' (*VRM*, pp. 99-100) - and of course, common reason and innate truths.

Wollstonecraft herself thus dismissed Burke on the grounds of anachronism. For the same reason, we could not now base a revolutionary appeal on a call to universal justice. She could, however, for that concept was long and deeply embedded in the dominant discourse, so that its use as an argument to urge women's access to men's privilege was at once understood and perceived as a threat (making her a 'hyena in petticoats', according to Horace Walpole). By the same token, it could not actually *be* revolutionary. As we have seen, the very concept of universal justice is entirely tied up in concepts of property and possession, self-interest and public contract, individualism and equality, and the rest, which underlie the very *in*equalities and injustices Wollstonecraft is querying. One wonders what she would have thought of the conservative turn made later in life by Godwin: perhaps simply that it was the inevitable result of the kind of despair of ineffectiveness expressed in *Maria* - that or suicide (as she intimated there).

The failure of Reason in the return of nature

For Wollstonecraft, the alternative then became not something new, but Wordsworth's and Goldsmith's cry of back to nature: 'This sight I have seen; - the cow that supported the children grazed near the hut, and the cheerful poultry were fed by the chubby babes, who breathed a bracing air, far from the diseases and the vices of cities. Domination blasts all these prospects . . .' (*VRM*, pp. 148-9). 'Cheerful poultry'?! Is this now the 'Nature and Reason' which in Burke's 'system, are all to give place to authority' (*VRM*, p. 157)? Well, no, of course not. But the nostalgic impulse once again makes clear the contradiction inevitable in a revolutionary project that cannot but be elaborated from within the dominant system, but which finds itself quite isolated, in the sense that its search for transformation is denied by a surrounding stability whose founding principles are the same.

As before, Wollstonecraft was quite clear that this *was* a nostalgia. In a short piece first published in the *Monthly Magazine* of April 1797 and reprinted ʟy Godwin the next year in the *Posthumous Works*, she explored the question of 'Poetry and Our Relish for the Beauties of Nature'. Commenting that contemporary taste for nature seemed derived rather from poetry than from direct observation, she continued:

I was led to endeavour, in one of my solitary rambles, to trace the cause, and likewise to enquire why the poetry written in the infancy of society, is most natural: which, strictly speaking (for *natural* is a very indefinite expression) is merely to say, that it is the transcript of immediate sensations, in all their native wildness and simplicity, when fancy, awakened by the sight of interesting objects, was most actively at work.[31]

This was to repeat Macpherson's claims for Ossian and the by-now commonplace eighteenth-century view of Homer. But it also repeated her own argument in *A Vindication of the Rights of Men* about the relation of fancy to immaturity, as it deliberately associated both with beauty and nature. The poet who can recapture 'the image of his mind, when he was actually alone, conversing with himself, and marking the impression nature had made on his own heart', is able then to speak to us 'the language of truth and nature with resistless energy' (PBN, p. 171). 'In a more advanced state of civilization,' she continued, 'a poet is rather the creature of art, than of nature' (PBN, p. 172). Fancy had by then become 'shrivelled by rules' (*idem*). These later writers are no longer 'the first observers of nature, the true poets' (PBN, p. 173).

This change in poetry accompanied a corresponding evolution in non-poets. 'Most people' will turn to poetry rather than to nature, because they lack 'a lively imagination', and because 'the poet contracts the prospect, and, selecting the most picturesque part in his *camera*, the judgment is directed' (PBN, p. 174). While Wollstonecraft's age had replaced fancy by judgment, poetry was also preferred to direct observation of the world because people would rather accept a traditional taste before exploring fresh vistas (*idem*). As she had angrily written ten years earlier: 'I am sick of hearing of the sublimity of Milton, the elegance and harmony of Pope, and the original, untaught genius of Shakespeare. These cursory remarks are made by some who know nothing of nature, and could not enter into the spirit of these authors, or understand them' (*Thoughts*, pp. 52-3). The nostalgic impulse was thus a deliberately chosen one – presented both as belonging to a more excellent past and as necessary to the transformation of modern culture and society: 'in the present state of society, the understanding must bring back the feelings to nature, or the sensibility must have such native strength, as rather to be whetted than destroyed by the strong exercises of passion' (PBN, p. 174). This claim may well be compared to that made by William Morris a century later: and both took it entirely seriously. Sadly for Wollstonecraft's prescriptions for women's equal rights, at least once it inclined her to the view that there was nothing social whatever about maternal sentiment, that it was completely natural and biological. For example in 1796 she wrote of her daughter: 'you know that as a female I am particularly attached to her – I feel more than a mother's fondness and anxiety' (*Letters*, p. 55).

The conflict of concepts

In Wollstonecraft's case, this nostalgic response was tantamount, I feel, to an expression of genuine and profound despair. Yielding to it in 1797, she turned away from the very impulse that began her most celebrated work, the *Vindication of the Rights of Woman*. There, the nature metaphor stood quite precisely for what had to be *refused*, whereas reason and judgment were the auspicious signs. Nature - an unhealthy nature, to be sure - was a sterility to be overcome only by reason:

> The conduct and manners of women, in fact, evidently prove that their minds are not in a healthy state; for, like the flowers which are planted in too rich a soil, strength and usefulness are sacrificed to beauty; and the flaunting leaves, after having pleased a fastidious eye, fade, disregarded on the stalk, long before the season when they ought to have arrived at maturity. One cause of this barren blooming I attribute to a false system of education, gathered from the books written on this subject by men who, considering females rather as women than human creatures, have been more anxious to make them alluring mistresses than affectionate wives and rational mothers; and the understanding of the sex has been so bubbled by this specious homage, that the civilized women of the present century, with a few exceptions, are only anxious to inspire love, when they ought to cherish a nobler ambition, and by their abilities and virtues exact respect. (*VRW*, p. 79)

It may be said that this bad nature was produced by false education just as poetry produced a restrained and controlled nature in the later text. Maybe so. But the point is that in the *Vindication of the Rights of Woman*, Wollstonecraft assumed that fine nature and human reason were on the same side, together creating a more perfect woman. This view was the typical 'manly' one of the Enlightenment. Elsewhere she tied exactly such an alliance to the concept of civilization as progress to maturity: those who have 'traced [the] progress' of civilization, she declared, will know that it makes use of reason so as to enable 'us to retain the primitive delicacy of our sensations'. In this example, the ability to enjoy the kind of sensuous experience known to the first poets was joined with a notion of advanced reason in a way directly opposed to the slightly later writing looked at a moment ago. Here, 'in that state of society in which the judgment and taste are not called forth, and formed by the cultivation of the arts and sciences, little of that delicacy of feeling and thinking is to be found characterized by the word sentiment' (*Letters*, pp. 20-1). This view of rational nature runs throughout the letters from Scandinavia, and the Kantian tone of the following passage, for example, is unmistakable (though expressed in somewhat Burkean language): 'Nature is the nurse of sentiment, - the true source of taste; yet what misery, as well as rapture, is produced by a quick perception of the beautiful and sublime, when it is exercised in observing animated nature, when every beauteous feeling and emotion excites responsive sympathy, and the harmonized soul sinks into melancholy, or rises to extasy, just as the chords are touched, like the aeolian harp agitated by the changing wind' (*Letters*, p. 58).

Indeed, the possible loss of this alliance is the very reason for the anxiety expressed with regard to her daughter. Her concern proceeded from reflection 'on the dependent and oppressed state of her sex', which meant she might be 'forced to sacrifice her heart to principles, or principles to her heart'. As a mother she promised to 'cultivate sensibility, and cherish delicacy of sentiment' in her daughter, in constant fear lest her simultaneous unfolding of 'her mind' would in fact provoke an inward conflict, making her 'unfit for the world she is to inhabit' (*Letters*, p. 55). Such a struggle would be internalized, but created by the abusive masculine order of things. We can easily see from such a remark how Wollstonecraft would envisage the right inclusion of women in the social order as feeding the very process of Enlightenment: 'The world requires, I see, the hand of man to perfect it; and as this task naturally unfolds the faculties he exercises, it is physically impossible that he should have remained in Rousseau's golden age of stupidity' (*Letters*, p. 87).

The word 'physically' is important here, denoting not simply the thought that the evolution *is* actually a physical one, but her inclusion, in the idea of general improvement, of conditions of labor and matters concerning the economic relations of production (*idem*). These are nonetheless always understood as a linear growth toward maturity - all quite typical of Enlightenment reason, as is the nature/reason bond itself. It cannot therefore function as a revolutionary ax. Its inability to become such an instrument, seemed to lead Wollstonecraft toward a conception of nature opposed to reason: to make of it some kind of healing balm for the withered soul of modern humanity. In the *Vindication of the Rights of Woman*, reason was supposed to repair the 'faded' leaves of a false nature by providing proper nourishment. Five years later, in the *Monthly Magazine* article, nature would heal a fancy that reason has 'shrivelled': false reason, perhaps, but the point there is that none other was available.

Right reason would mean that women would no longer be 'treated as a kind of subordinate beings', that they be considered 'part of the human species', endowed as much as men with 'improvable reason' (*VRW*, p. 80). If 'good sense' is the widespread distinction of humanity – as Descartes had it – then women (as Poullain had observed) share it by definition. The theory itself allows for no exceptions. But that is a little like the idea of the equality of humankind in general: as we have seen, only a certain kind of individual is equal, and indeed a more universal underlying inequality is essential to the concept's very maintenance. Relying upon such concepts is of course the source of all Wollstonecraft's contradictions. In a sense this is revealed by the way she spoke of the transformation in question, as she wrote of the 'exclamations against masculine women', even as she 'corrects' herself: 'if it be against the imitation of manly virtues, or, more properly speaking, the attainment of those talents and virtues, the exercise of which ennobles the human character, and which raises females in the scale of animal being, when they are comprehensively termed mankind, all those who view them with a philosophic eye must, I should think, wish with me, that they may every day grow more and more masculine' (*VRW*, p. 80).

At one level, however, the contradiction is a hidden one. Hidden, because the discourse to which Wollstonecraft seeks access for women did not state the premise of exclusion. On the contrary, it denied it. In the overt terms of its thinking such access was not merely possible but actually attainable. Oddly contradictory as these terms were at one level, they remained the only ones available. Wollstonecraft would have been entirely pleased by the praise offered by John Adams after reading her *French Revolution* of 1794: that she was 'a Lady of a masculine masterly understanding'. Indeed, he was actually doing no more than echoing the beginning of her own preface to that work: 'the revolution in France exhibits a scene, in the political world, not less novel and interesting than the contrast between the narrow opinions of superstition, and the enlightened sentiments of masculine and improved philosophy.'[32]

When Wollstonecraft rejected 'sickly delicacy' in favor of 'simple unadorned truth', and 'false sentiment' for 'natural emotions', seeking an education to prepare 'a rational and immortal being for a nobler field of action' (*VRW*, p. 82), she was choosing the traditional female/male sets of oppositions. They were, again, the only available option. That they were immediately perceived as a very real and profound threat at once to male privilege and to the place allotted to women by such privilege was clear from the reaction of people like Walpole and More, with their epithets of 'hyena' and 'serpent', as well as by the vituperation that only grew warmer after her death. In every way they were reminiscent of the scorn heaped some 200 years earlier on the head of another woman writer, Marie de Gournay, by a male literary group of supposed innovators and their aristocratic women supporters. At the beginning of the eighteenth century Eliza Haywood had more than once remarked on 'that tide of raillery which all of my sex, unless they are very excellent, indeed, must expect when once they exchange the needle for the quill'.[33]

Wollstonecraft made her appeal to that coercive male privilege itself: 'I presume that *rational* men will excuse me for endeavouring to persuade [women] to become more masculine and respectable.' And in any case, she adds reassuringly, real difference in 'bodily strength must render them in some degree dependent on men in the various relations of life' (*VRW*, p. 83). And so we return to biological determinism. She went yet further: 'Let it not be concluded that I wish to invert the order of things. I have already granted that, from the constitution of their bodies, men seem designed by Providence to attain a greater degree of virtue. I speak collectively of the whole sex; but I see not the shadow of a reason to conclude that their virtues should differ in respect to their nature' (*VRW*, p. 109). Maybe so, but this concession (which there is no reason to believe ironic) was enormous. Not only did it assume society as it was to be on the right path toward the wisest constitution, but it allowed that measure of actual inequality already claimed by men. It simply said the inequality was too great, not that it was essentially wrong. That is why she added that the adjustment must not be all one-sided: 'let men become more chaste and modest' (*VRW*, p. 84). How far these terms were ingrained may be seen in the following throwaway line: 'sometimes virtue and its shadow are at variance. We should never, perhaps, have heard of Lucretia, had she died to preserve her chastity, instead of her reputation' (*VRW*, p. 245). The comment exemplifies that internalization of oppression Wollstonecraft elsewhere castigated with insistence. (At a rather different level, she argued that the Terror was a temporary failure due to the French having lived so long under tyranny - it, too, had become internalized.)

The demand, then, was always to equality of treatment and situation. And these would be those already existing in society, based on the same premises taken as characteristic of legitimate and right human society wherever and whenever it be found. As she remarked in her dedication to Talleyrand:

Contending for the rights of woman, my main argument is built on this simple principle, that if she be not prepared by education to become the companion of man, she will stop the progress of knowledge and virtue; for truth must be common to all, or it will be inefficacious with respect to its influence in general practice. And how can woman be expected to co-operate unless she knows why she ought to be virtuous? unless freedom strengthens her reason till she comprehends her duty, and sees in what manner it is connected with her real good. If children are to be educated to understand the true principle of patriotism, their mother must be a patriot [think of this word's etymology]; and the love of mankind, from which an orderly train of virtues spring, can only be produced by considering the moral and civil interest of mankind; but the education and situation of woman at present shuts her out from such investigations. (*VRW*, pp. 86-7)

The argument thus became concerned with correcting a flaw 'subversive of morality' (*VRW*, p. 87) in society as it is, not with transforming such society. Wollstonecraft insisted this was so. She simply wanted to extend to the excluded half of the human race rights and benefits already enjoyed by men, and which they frequently use to oppress women. Thus she sought to deploy in favour of women, 'the very arguments which [men] use to justify [their] oppression' - to deploy them, contrary to men's usage, 'to promote their happiness'. For, she asked: 'who made man the exclusive judge, if woman partake with him of the gift of reason?' (*VRW*, p. 87). As it was, women 'may be convenient slaves, but slavery will have its constant effect, degrading the master and the abject dependent' (*VRW*, p. 88). She did not deny that in the present state of society, men had succeeded in causing women to internalize their oppression: 'still the regal homage which they receive is so intoxicating, that until the manners of the times are changed, and formed on more reasonable principles, it may be impossible to convince them that the illegitimate power which they obtain by degrading themselves is a curse, and that they must return to nature and equality if they wish to secure the placid satisfaction that unsophisticated affections impart' (*VRW*, p. 103).

To avoid this result, education must make sure girls never 'be allowed to imbibe the pernicious doctrine that a defect can, by any chemical process of reasoning, become an excellence' (*VRW*, p. 126). Such had been the consequence of 'the language of men, and the fear of departing from a supposed sexual character has made even women of superior sense adopt the same sentiments' (*VRW*, p. 143). 'Considering the length of time that women have been dependent,' she retorted to Rousseau, 'is it surprising that some of them hunger in chains, and fawn like the spaniel? "These dogs", observes a naturalist, "at first kept their ears erect; but custom has superseded nature, and a token of fear is become a beauty" ' (*VRW*, p. 179). 'Indignantly', she cried, 'have I heard women argue in the same track as men, and adopt the sentiments that brutalize them, with all the pertinacity of ignorance' (*VRW*, p. 202).

Toward the correction of authoritarian individualism

The basic principles of humanity for Wollstonecraft are reason, virtue, and knowledge, the second two flowing from the right exercise of the first – and these look extraordinarily like the three Kantian *Critiques*, of pure reason, practical reason, and judgment. The equation between Enlightenment and maturity seen earlier is also Kantian. And these three principles comprise Wollstonecraft's 'rights and duties of man' (*VRW*, p. 91). She argued that all reasonable people recognize that the best society and wisest 'constitution is founded on the nature of man' (*VRW*, p. 92), and maintained that they agree by and large on what that nature is. She thought however that because society had been misshapen by piecemeal growth, many changes were necessary to align it with its own ideal. Present society was therefore a deviation from truth and a distortion of human nature, not because it was wrong in any essential way, but because it had erred: just as, as I suggested earlier, the Europeans, and even more the Yahoos, had wandered from the right path indicated by the Houyhnmnms (in Gulliver's fourth voyage). The correction for this error was not radical change but simply a more orderly version of the same.[34] In fact Wollstonecraft made this point in her rejection of Rousseau's arguments about the state of nature as perfection (though as we have seen she was constantly tempted by a similar nostalgia). She wrote: 'Rousseau exerts himself to prove that all *was* right originally: a crowd of authors that all *is* now right: and I, that all will *be* right' (*VRW*, p. 95).

Progress followed an orderly path toward legitimacy and perfection; the question concerned not a directional change in the path, but decisions as to where humanity was currently situated upon it, and how far it could continue along it. Thus the founding principles themselves indicated that within society any power based wholly on command and obedience, on profound distinctions of mastership and subordination – from that of an absolute prince to that functioning within the army, the navy or the clergy – was a threat to a society founded on rational equality: as society 'becomes more enlightened', it 'should be very careful not to establish bodies of men who must necessarily be made foolish or vicious by the very constitution of their profession' (*VRW*, p. 98). It was, she concluded, 'the pestiferous purple which renders the progress of civilisation a curse, and warps the understanding' (*VRW*, p. 99). Such an argument may have appeared revolutionary to the eighteenth century, but it was quite simply a more logical application of the principles upon which the (imaginary) British constitution 'claimed' to rest, and a statement of facts taken to underlie the Revolution in France (which the English were beginning to regard with some fear, though the Terror was yet to come). That is why she always emphasized the desire for equality, not power. In Wollstone-craft's words: ' "educate women like men," says Rousseau, "and the more they resemble our sex the less power they will have over us." This is the very point I aim at. I do not wish them to have power over men; but over themselves' (*VRW*, p. 154). Or again: 'It is not empire, – but equality, that [women] should contend for' (*VRW*, p. 204).

Finally, that this *was* the case, and that in theory actual social order *did* correspond to these principles in Wollstonecraft's eyes, is suggested by her argument that the proper education to inculcate sound principles is essentially social: 'Men and women must be educated, in a great degree, by the opinions and manners of the society they live in' (*VRW*, p. 102). Unless these corresponded in some way to the sought-for ideal, such a statement would be nonsensical. Even though in actual practice, these principles remained imperfect and ultimately required that 'society be differently constituted', nonetheless they were not so far distant from the right social order that human beings may not, through them, 'become virtuous by the exercise of its own reason' in addition (*VRW*, pp. 102-3). For, after all, however imperfect the present manifestation, things must –

inevitably – go in the right progressive direction. The different constitution of which Wollstonecraft speaks is a melioration not a new instauration, and its local habitation is actually the presence of an order just for all-humanity and echoed in the original three principles: 'surely there can be but one rule of right, if morality has an eternal foundation, and whoever sacrifices virtue, strictly so called, to present convenience, or whose *duty* it is to act in such a manner, lives only for the passing day, and cannot be an accountable creature' (*VRW*, p. 120).

That eternal rule of right reason, virtue, and knowledge is the source of all progress, when humanity heeds it, rather than those desires that depart from it. Then, 'as sound politics diffuse liberty, mankind, including woman, will become more wise and virtuous' (*VRW*, p. 122). This was the belief in progress always implicit in her work on the French Revolution, an event she considered (even through and after the Terror): 'the natural consequence of intellectual improvement, gradually proceeding to perfection in the advancement of communities, from a state of barbarism to that of polished society, till now arrived at the point when sincerity of principles seem to be hastening the overthrow of the tremendous empire of superstition and hypocrisy, erected upon the ruins of gothic brutality and ignorance' (*Revolution*, vii-viii). Political revolution was entirely parallel to the sexual, and education for women as for men must be 'the first step to form a being advancing gradually towards perfection' (*VRW*, pp. 142-3).

Torn between the inevitable trap of the very discursive order she initially sought to escape and a nostalgic return to some vague concept of a kind of 'wholeness' with nature, Wollstonecraft bodied forth the problems, some of the traps, and some of the traces of resolution to be confronted by future feminisms. Ultimately, as Mary Poovey has observed, she was unable to escape the tyranny of the 'bourgeois' premises she was forced to use. As Poovey writes: 'in doing this her voice hesitates and finally falters into silence.' Wollstonecraft concluded by placing some hope in 'feminine' ideals of sensibility, nurture, and so forth, but at the same time she was always aware how much those ideals were themselves dependent upon familiar liberal values and of the extent to which she was caught up in conflict and contradiction: 'she cannot relinquish the individualistic values tied up with the sentimental structure itself.' Like many others, she was unable to 'abandon the ideal of "true sensibility," even after she had recognized that the romantic expectations endemic to such sensibility were agents of the very institutions she was trying to criticize.'[35] Wollstonecraft never completely accepted the retreat backwards into some kind of asocial nature, nor was she able to see any order but that of possessive individualism and authoritarian liberalism. In the fragment she left of *Maria*, unable to choose between concluding with her heroine's suicide or with a somewhat forlornly utopian prospect of hope, Wollstonecraft admirably summed up her own awareness of the snares she had spent her life trying to avoid and the meshes from which she was finally unable to disentangle herself.

NOTES

1 I wish to record my profound thanks to Patricia J. Hilden for her generously attentive reading of this essay. Though she will certainly continue to disagree with some of my assertions and analyses, she has enabled the excision of errors, the calming of wild generalization, and above all the clarification of jumbled argument.

2 Condorcet, for instance, was to write in 1790 that women 'are not guided by men's reason, it is true, but they are by their own', 'Sur l'admission des femmes au droit de la cité', in Condorcet, *Oeuvres*, ed. O'Connor and Arago, 1847-9: X.125. (Cf. his remark: 'women are superior to men as to the soft and domestic virtues', ibid.: X.124). Mary Poovey has provided an interesting study of the relation between such ideologically inscribed characteristics and the developing structure of the middle-class home, with its increasing separation from what is taken to be the productive workplace and emphasis on a 'nurturing' aspect (1984: esp. 3-113).

3 The danger of such assimilation has frequently been observed. Kate Millett long since pointed out, for example, the hypocritical nature of such use of the term 'woman': 'It is necessary to realize that the most sacrosanct article of sexual politics in the period [the nineteenth century], the Victorian doctrine of chivalrous protection and its familiar protestations of respect, rests upon the tacit assumption, a cleverly expeditious bit of humbug, that all women were 'ladies' - namely members of that fraction of the upper classes and bourgeoisie which treated women to expressions of elaborate concern, while permitting them no legal or personal freedoms' (Millett 1970, repr. 1977: 73).

4 More *Essays*, 1847: II.335-6.

5 Polwhele 1974: 36-7n.

6 Schreiner 1978: 158.

7 Reiss 1983: 168. The matter is treated in greater detail in Reiss 1987.

8 Wollstonecraft, *The Female Reader (1789)*, intro. Ferguson, 1980; v, xv.

9 Eisenstein 1981.

10 Wollstonecraft, *Collected Letters*, ed. Wardle 1979: 120, 185.

11 Wollstonecraft, *Maria or The Wrongs of Woman* intro. Ferguson, 1975: 103, 106. Margaret Kirkham has argued that in *Mansfield Park*, rather veiled references to the Bastille are partial evidence of Jane Austen's expression of a feminism similar to Wollstonecraft's - who would also be its source. In that novel, Kirkham writes, 'Maria [Bertram] sees Sotherton as "a dismal old prison," and, as she sends

Rushworth off to fetch the key for the iron gate through which she wishes to pass with Crawford, quotes Sterne's starling which, imprisoned in the Bastille, sang, "I can't get out, I can't get out"' Kirkham 1986: 37). While the last remark is accurate enough, Maria is not responsible for the first, but Rushworth himself (Jane Austen, *The Complete Novels*, n.d.: 500, 529). Fortunately, Kirkham's entire argument is more solidly based than this inaccuracy might suggest, though it is always risky, of course, (a) to take so widely available a symbol as the Bastille as evidence for the particular influence of one author, and (b) to interpret so vague and readily obtainable a phrase as 'a dismal old prison' as referring precisely to the Bastille.

12 Wollstonecraft, *Maria*, intro. Ferguson, 1975: 55. Jemima's tale occupies pp. 52-69 in this edition.

13 Elizabeth Fox-Genovese, 'Introduction', in Spencer 1984: 4.

14 Polwhele, *The Unsex'd Females. A Poem*, intro. Luria, 1974: 7, 13, 15.

15 For these last remarks I am indebted to an unpublished paper by Claire Collins.

16 Price *Discourse*, 1790: 12; my italics.

17 Burke, *Works*, 1867: XII.395-6.

18 Ibid.: V.141.

19 Wollstonecraft, *Letters Written during a Short Residence in Sweden, Norway, and Denmark*, ed. Poston, 1976: 48. Henceforth cited as *Letters*.

20 Wollstonecraft, *A Vindication of the Rights of Woman*, ed. Kramnick, 1975: 257. Henceforth cited as *VRW*, followed by page reference.

21 Hill 1958, repr. 1964: 391-2. The reference is to Richardson, *The Works*, ed. Mangin, 1811: VIII.105.

22 Wollstonecraft, *Thoughts on the Education of Daughters: With Reflections on Female Conduct, in the Important Duties of Life*, 1787, repr. 1972: 56, 58. Henceforth cited as *Thoughts*.

23 Radcliffe, *The Female Advocate*, intro. Luna, 1974: 398. Henceforth cited as *FA*.

24 Wollstonecraft, *A Vindication of the Rights of Men (1790)*, intro. Nicholes, 1960: 37. Henceforth cited as *VRM*.

25 It is well known that when she wrote *The Second Sex* and for many years after, de Beauvoir believed the transformation of society to be the most urgent project, on the grounds that it would bring women's full emancipation with it. Only in the early 1970s did the failures of Western marxism convince her that complete social change, if not quite utopian, was certainly far off, while women's equality was a realizable project.

26 This, too, in point of fact, may be understood as a 'Cartesian' thought. For Descartes, virtue as a habit and social intercourse as customary were both ideas going virtually without saying. One finds them also in Marie de Gournay (who also seems to make a distinction equivalent to that of sex and gender).

27 'Author's Preface' to *The Wrongs of Woman: or, Maria. A Fragment*, in Wollstonecraft, *Mary. A Fiction* and *The Wrongs of Woman*, ed. Kelly, 1976: 73-4.

28 Ibid.: xxxi.

29 Reiss 1934: 3-4.

30 I owe this remark to Kathryn Kirkpatrick, who is elsewhere elaborating a view of *VRM* and *VRW* based upon some of its implications.

31 Wollstonecraft, 'Poetry and Our Relish for the Beauties of Nature', in *A Wollstonecraft Anthology*, ed. Todd, 1977: 171. Henceforth cited as PBN.
32 Wollstonecraft, *An Historical and Moral View of the Origin and Progress of the French Revolution and the Effect It Has Produced in Europe*, intro. Todd, 1975: v. Adam's praise is quoted by Todd in her introduction, p. 14. Henceforth cited as *Revolution*.
33 Dedication to *The Fair Captive* (1721), quoted by Horner 1929-30: 22.
34 On this, see ch. 11 of my *Discourse of Modernism* (1982).
35 Poovey, 1984: 108.

REFERENCES

Austen, Jane n.d. *The Complete Novels*. New York: Modern Library.
Beauvoir, Simone de 1952. *The Second Sex*. Trans. H. M. Parshley. Repr. New York: Vintage, 1971. [1st French edn, 1949.]
Burke, Edmund 1867. *Works*. Revised edition, 12 vols. Boston: Little, Brown.
Condorcet, A.-N. Caritat de 1847-9. *Oeuvres*. Ed. A. Condorcet O'Connor and M. F. Arago. 10 vols. Paris: Firmin Didot.
Eisenstein, Zillah 1981. *The Radical Future of Liberal Feminism*. New York and London: Longman.
Hill, Christopher 1958. 'Clarissa Harlowe and her times', in his *Puritanism and Revolution: Studies in Interpretation of the English Revolution of the 17th Century*. Repr. New York: Schocken, 1964.
Horner, Joyce M. 1929-30. *The English Women Novelists and Their Connection with the Feminist Movement (1688-1797)*. Smith College Studies in Modern Languages, vol. 11, nos. 1, 2, 3. Northampton, MA: Smith College.
Kirkham, Margaret 1983. *Jane Austen, Feminism and Fiction*. Repr. New York: Methuen, 1986.
Millett, Kate 1970. *Sexual Politics*. Repr. London: Virago, 1977.
More, Hannah 1847. *Essays on Various Subjects Principally Designed for Young Ladies*, in *The Works*, vol. II. 7 vols. New York: Harper.
Polwhele, Richard. *The Unsex'd Females. A Poem*, and Mary Ann Radcliffe, *The Female Advocate. Or, an Attempt to Recover the Rights of Women from Male Usurpation*. [Facsimile edition.] Intro. Gina Luria. New York and London: Garland, 1974.
Poovey, Mary 1984. *The Proper Lady and the Woman Writer*. Chicago and London: University of Chicago Press.
Poullain de la Barre, François 1673. *De l'égalité des deux sexes*. Repr. Paris: Fayard, 1984.
Price, Richard 1790. *A Discourse on the Love of Our Country*, delivered on 4 November 1789, at the Meeting-House in the Old Jewry, to the Society for commemorating the Revolution in Great Britain. London & Boston: Edward J. Powars.
Radcliffe, Mary Ann. *The Female Advocate. Or an Attempt to Recover the Rights of Women from Male Usurpation*. [See Polwhele.]
Reiss, Erna 1934. *Rights and Duties of Englishwomen: A Study in Law and Public Opinion*. Manchester: Sherratt & Hughes.

Reiss, Timothy J. 1982. *The Discourse of Modernism*. Repr. Ithaca and London: Cornell University Press, 1985.

Reiss, Timothy J. 1983. 'Classical criticism and ideology', *Papers on French Seventeenth-Century Literature*, 10, no. 18.

Reiss, Timothy J. 1987. 'Corneille and Cornelia: reason, violence, and the cultural status of the feminine. Or, how a dominant discourse recuperated and subverted the advance of women', *Renaissance Drama*, n.s. 18. Ed. Mary Beth Rose. Evanston, IL: Northwestern University Press.

Richardson, Samuel 1811. *The Works*. Ed. Rev. Edward Mangin. 19 vols. London: William Miller & James Carpenter.

Schreiner, Olive 1978. *Women and Labour*. [1911.] Pref. Jane Graves. London: Virago.

Shklovsky, Viktor 1971. 'Sterne's *Tristram Shandy:* stylistic commentary', in *Readings in Russian Poetics*, ed. Ladislav Matejka and Krystna Pomorska. Cambridge, Mass.: MIT Press: 57. [Originally published in 1917 as 'Art as technique'.]

Spencer, Samia I. (ed.) 1984. *French Women and the Enlightenment*. Bloomington: Indiana University Press.

Wollstonecraft, Mary 1960. *A Vindication of the Rights of Men (1790)*. Intro. Eleanor Louise Nicholes. Gainesville, FL: Scholars' Facsimiles & Reprints.

Wollstonecraft, Mary 1972. *Thoughts on the Education of Daughters: With Reflections on Female Conduct, in the Important Duties of Life* (1787). Clifton, NJ: Augustus M. Kelley.

Wollstonecraft, Mary 1975. *An Historical and Moral View of the Origin and Progress of the French Revolution and the Effect It Has Produced in Europe* (1794). Intro. Janet M. Todd. Delmar, NJ: Scholars' Facsimiles & Reprints.

Wollstonecraft, Mary 1975. *Maria or The Wrongs of Woman*. Intro. Moira Ferguson. New York and London: Norton.

Wollstonecraft, Mary 1975. *A Vindication of the Rights of Woman*. Ed. Miriam Brody Kramnick. Harmondsworth: Penguin.

Wollstonecraft, Mary 1976. *Letters Written During a Short Residence in Sweden, Norway, and Denmark*. Ed. Carol H. Poston. Lincoln and London: University of Nebraska Press.

Wollstonecraft, Mary 1976. *Mary, A Fiction* and *The Wrongs of Woman*. Ed. Gary Kelly. London: Oxford University Press.

Wollstonecraft, Mary 1977. 'Poetry and Our Relish for the Beauties of Nature', in *A Wollstonecraft Anthology*. Ed. Janet M. Todd. Bloomington and London: Indiana University Press.

Wollstonecraft, Mary 1979. *Collected Letters*. Ed. Ralph M. Wardle. Ithaca: Cornell University Press.

Wollstonecraft, Mary 1980. *The Female Reader (1789)*. A facsimile reproduction with an intro. by Moira Ferguson. Delmar, NJ: Scholars' Facsimiles & Reprints.

Wordsworth, William 1956. *Selected Poetry*. Ed. Mark Van Doren. New York: Modern Library.

Wordsworth, William 1970. *The Prelude, or Growth of a Poet's Mind (Text of 1805)*. Ed. Ernest de Selincourt, new ed. Stephen Gill. Repr. London: Oxford University Press, 1975.

2
Wollstonecraft Our Contemporary

Frances Ferguson

Timothy Reiss confronts Mary Wollstonecraft's writing by pointing to its impossibility - the impossibility of its being understood and effective. It was, Reiss contends, a product of its age, an epiphenomenon of the dominant discourse to such a degree that it could only proceed in terms of claims about essential values - reason, justice, liberty. Thus, it could never adequately represent a genuine alternative to the very Enlightenment configurations that contributed to women's powerlessness. Instead of reconceiving the basic terms, then, Wollstonecraft merely proposed that the empire of these terms be increased to include the unenfranchised. She settled for access.

As Reiss sketches in his position, however, he must adopt a curious tone. It is not really Wollstonecraft's fault that she does not break free of the dominant discourse, he indicates, but he pursues an ongoing comparison of Wollstonecraft's views with contemporary accounts of gender - as if to suggest a standard by which to judge her positions. He takes it to be axiomatic that Wollstonecraft herself does not really speak in these writings and that the dominant discourse of the Enlightenment speaks her. And yet he never addresses the adequacy of the discourse in which he is speaking, the contemporary standard by which he judges and exonerates, disparages and forgives. If his generally Foucauldian analysis enables him to see the limitations of Wollstonecraft's perspective, it does not enable him to specify what the 'genuinely radical' looks like. Nor does it enable him to escape a rather bizarre variation on the Enlightenment account of progress as he continually suggests that whatever 'we' believe in the present is, somehow, better than what it was possible to believe before. While Reiss is scornful of the Enlightenment account of maturity and progressive self-development, he repeatedly reinvents a version of progress in assuming that the modern possibility of seeing the formal conditions of representation laid bare is itself an appropriate entelechy, a more radical gesture.

Reiss's discussion presents an account of the mutually contradictory reactions to Wollstonecraft's writings, but passes over what position Wollstonecraft might have seen herself to be adopting. And the paradox of the reception of Wollstonecraft's writings is, for him, that they were both familiar in their line of argument and, at the same time, unheard, in not being taken seriously enough to produce any significant changes in the status of women. On the score of familiarity, he points to the fact that Christine de Pizan, Agrippa, Marguerite de Navarre, Thomas Elyot, Marie de Gournay, and others 'were precursors of a considerable literature asserting women's rights to education, to positions of political and religious power, to all the material and spiritual benefits of civil society, and to freedom from men's domination' (p. 11). Thus, Wollstonecraft's general position was not unheard of; it was, however, unheard, in that it effected no 'change in practical status of *any* individual within society' (p. 31). By arguing 'within Enlightenment rhetoric – for the extension of equality without regard (at least) to gender,' Wollstonecraft, in Reiss's view, foregrounded the 'matter of the right to participate in the system', not that 'of the need to change it'. Thus, although her contemporaries and Wollstonecraft herself saw her position as radical, Reiss – and we – can see that it did not represent a revolutionary position but merely the temporary appearance of one, and that in fact 'prevented Wollstonecraft from arguing a truly revolutionary case – that is, for a change in the order of the dominant discourse itself' (p. 21).

One might be tempted to take such an account of Wollstonecraft as critical, but Reiss explicitly states that he does not mean it to be:

> I do not intend my argument that Wollstonecraft failed to go beyond her peers as a criticism of her. . . . I am simply warning again that Wollstonecraft should not be made anachronistically into something she was not. Moreover, the question really is whether lacking a more general project of transformation, *any* change in practical status of *any* individual within society is possible. (pp. 30–31)

But if Reiss does not intend his argument as a criticism of Wollstonecraft, he does intend it as a criticism of Enlightenment thought as it was formulated by such figures as Wollstonecraft and Thomas Paine, who, like other progressive thinkers, argued for the extension of freedom to an ever-increasing number of people on the basis of 'pre-Revolutionary dominant patterns of thought' (p. 31). For them, as Reiss indicates, human reason and human rights were inevitably correlated with one another, in that reason provided the capacity for one person to acknowledge the rights of another, to imagine the similarity of all reasoning creatures. Basically, then, Reiss rejects the 'dominant discourse' of the late eighteenth century because it postulated reason and freedom as origin and endpoint of a teleological argument that could *only* conceive the rights of some as *merely* providing an instance of the rights of all. While Wollstonecraft claimed women's rights as a subset of human rights, Reiss would have had her – along with other late eighteenth-century writers – overthrow such essentialist and universalist claims. Where Wollstonecraft saw reason promulgating a recognition of similarity between men and women, Reiss finds the recognition of difference more compelling.

Thus, he treats the French Revolution as a case study in how the abstract recognition of similarity may end, in practice, in differential effects. Aligning the French Revolution with its claims to universalize individual liberty with Wollstonecraft's concern to claim individual liberty for women, Reiss adverts to Wordsworth's recollection of his early enthusiasm for the Revolution and the sense that 'the Nations hail'd / Their great expectancy' (*Prelude*, VI.684-5). On the one hand, he suggests, the Revolution disappointed many, including those like Wordsworth whose positions developed in the direction of conservatism and those who saw it as insufficiently revolutionary. On the other, it disappointed women in particular, because women continued to live as if immured in a personal Bastille of confining institutions. If the logic of these claims does not come clear, we may begin to see that the direction of Reiss's discussion relies less upon tracing out an argument than upon identifying issues and themes that have the formal similarity of having had the same name at some time. Thus, if Reiss escapes a naive belief in reason and its ability to induce coherence, he ends up committing himself to an associational mode in which the formal fact of naming – and the repeating of names – has an extraordinary prominence. Specifically, Reiss's emphasis on the repetition of words and names by a variety of persons creates a text that is by definition more available to a later interpreter than to the persons who actually wrote those words and names. Since no one can imagine that Wordsworth, say, is 'responsible' for Wollstonecraft's or Kant's use of the word 'reason', any more than that Kant moves because Wollstonecraft decides to walk across a room, the account that Reiss implicitly gives of the dominant discourse is that it identifies itself by repeating names and words. But if the interpreter does not seem to be claiming regulatory authority in constructing the discourse, she/he has an inevitably prominent role in allowing a formerly dominant discourse to reveal itself. And the project of reading past texts becomes one focused less on origin – what they thought – than on endpoint – what we think of it.

Reiss has laid out a structure in which the parallelism between women's claims in particular and more general claims on behalf of humans seems to involve a suspect adherence to reason as an innate human characteristic. Thus, although he establishes the kind of parallelism between human rights and women's rights that enables him to suggest that the French Revolution disappointed men and women alike, he clearly wants the parallelism to imply a contrast, in which women were more disappointed than others. But the complications of Reiss's argument continue to appear, as he instances Wordsworth's account of the tale of 'Mary of Buttermere' (*Prelude*, VII.321-60) as 'disagreeable sentimentality' over 'the wondrous Mary of Buttermere' and as 'nostalgia for a lost wholeness with Nature, with the Divine presence of some untrammelled absolute Justice' (p. 18).

Implicit in Reiss's account at this point is the perception that the analogy between human nature (and its inevitable and inalienable rights) and nature can be converted from a principle of equality into a justification for inequality if nature is taken to fall differentially upon men and women. And Reiss takes Wordsworth's conservatism to fall particularly harshly on women in the passage in which Wordsworth travels to Cambridge and, in Reiss's account, discovers 'female emancipation and/or prostitution' (p. 19). Reiss cites the passage as participating in a 'conflation [that] is typical of contemporary opinion . . . which tended to make small distinction between the authority and self-possession implied by the first [emancipation] and an unconfined sexuality of which prostitution was but the extreme' (p. 19). But the two examples from Wordsworth – that of Mary of Buttermere and the woman passed on the road to Cambridge – are not nearly so continuous as Reiss takes them to be, and in ways that pertain directly to the question of self-possession. For the point of the Mary of Buttermere story is that Mary has achieved a modesty that makes the details of her personal sexual history irrelevant, that she seems a Maiden – and this in spite of the fact that Wordsworth invented a child that his life model for the story never had, as if to underscore the fact that her having produced a child would provide a clear sign of her previous sexual activity. Thus, Wordsworth's testimony about her would seem to acknowledge less horror at emancipated women than respect for the possibility that Mary's account of her own actions has greater standing than any external, or societal, view of them. In fact, a similar issue emerges in his description of the prostitute (or emancipated woman) when he speaks of how the sight of the woman 'Abandon'd' to 'open shame' causes him something like an interpretative confusion: 'a barrier seemed at once / Thrown in, that from humanity divorced / The human Form, splitting the race of Man / In twain, yet leaving the same outward shape' (*Prelude*, VII.424-7).

We may imagine that Wordsworth might have seen an emancipated woman and taken her for a prostitute; since his poem only attempts to record his reading of his observations, it makes little sense to affirm or deny their accuracy. The central point of the passage, however, is to register a moment of recognition in which he sets down the fact that apparent similarity (the similarity of appearance that enables him to identify all human beings as human beings) may yield equivocal values. One may look human and be good, one may look human and be bad. Moreover, one's appearances may be appropriated for the purposes of other people's viewing. Where Reiss takes Wordsworth's description of the Maiden of Buttermere to be a nostalgically elaborated agrarian vision in which women remain natural, I take him to be addressing the horror of theatrical representation that arises in the city as individuality is acted out as someone else's fantasy. In Book VII of *The Prelude*, Wordsworth describes his experiences of London and introduces Mary of Buttermere's story. Mary has the same kind of accidental, fragile, and temporary celebrity that someone like murderer Gary Gilmore had before he was executed, and Wordsworth relates Mary's story with the same kind of proprietary small-town pride that someone from Utah might feel reading Norman Mailer's book about the Gilmore case, *The Executioner's Song*. For what Wordsworth disapproves of is not the possibility, as Reiss suggests, that women might be sexually active, but that the display of Mary's victimization represents an illegitimate appropriation of her life. To have married a bigamist is to have been betrayed, it is to see oneself as the victim of someone else's desire to produce effects in a conspicuously unequal manner, because the representative function of the marriage oath applies differently to the monogamous wife and the bigamous husband. But Wordsworth specifically does not suggest that he admires Mary for being so gullible and primitive as to have been a target for a bigamist. He speaks, rather, of her 'discretion':

> Her just opinions, delicate reserve,
> Her patience, and humility of mind
> Unspoiled by commendation and the excess
> Of public notice – an offensive light
> To a meek spirit suffering inwardly.
>
> (*Prelude*, VII.311-15)

And the language of sexual melodrama ('"a bold bad man"') that Reiss quotes as Wordsworth relates his having seen Mary's story enacted is language that the poet has specifically distanced himself from by using quotation marks (in the 1805 version; he drops the phrase entirely in the 1850 version). Far from defending Mary's honor or naturalness – or virtue as the essential nature of woman – Wordsworth merely acknowledges the fact that the theatrical appropriation of Mary's story in the rhymed melodrama *Edward and Susan, or The Beauty of Buttermere* does not redress the injury that the bigamist did to her but rather adds insult to it.

Much like Rousseau in the *Lettre à d'Alembert sur les spectacles*, the Wordsworth of Book VII contemplates the possibility that the city, through the sheer pressure of its myriad activities for a multitude of people, might cause one to have to represent oneself so often and so variously to others that one would lose track of oneself. Thus, he surveys a number of characters, as if to size up the real or potential impact of their environment upon them. Between mentioning Mary of Buttermere and recalling the time he had seen the prostitute on the road to Cambridge four years earlier, he speaks of a very small boy he has seen in London, a child young enough to have been able to speak comprehensibly for only six months (in the 1850 version; twelve months, in the 1805). Next to his conspicuously painted mother and surrounded by 'chiefly dissolute men / and shameless women' (VII.360-1), the boy seems 'A sort of alien scattered from the clouds' (l.350), someone as yet untouched by his society, 'Like one of those who walked with hair unsinged / Amid the fiery furnace' (ll.369-70).

To assemble the various examples – the staging of the story of Mary of Buttermere, the sight of the young boy who seems like an alien from the clouds, and the glimpse of the blasphemous woman – is to see the basic point that Wordsworth would make about the theatricalization of persons in the city – that the process of aging comes to seem like the ongoing displacement of innate individual characteristics by environment. And if many commentators have taken the blasphemous woman as a prostitute, one could certainly argue that they were, even if mistaken on grounds of sexual morality, accurate in recognizing Wordsworth's descriptions as tending toward a portrait of the kind of self-alienation that is slavery, the selling of oneself into the status of property.

This is to say that Reiss's concern for 'self-possession' is as important to Wordsworth as it is to Reiss; to say, that is, that the collection of examples he employs may be too obsessively involved with self-possession – but not that it repudiates self-possession. For I think that Wordsworth takes the woman on the road to be a prostitute not because of her display of self-possession, but precisely because of her lack of it. He is using prostitution as a variant of the situations of Mary of Buttermere and the deprived child, situations in which one's self-possession has been appropriated by other people long before one could conceivably be in the position of being able to lay claim to it.

I am dwelling on Wordsworth here both because Wordsworth represents for Reiss the more retrograde and embarrassing aspects of Wollstonecraft's politics and because I think that Reiss misidentifies Wordsworth and Wollstonecraft in similar ways, as he points to their distance from politically acceptable views in the late twentieth century. In the effort to avoid making Wordsworth and Wollstonecraft into what they were not – that is, late twentieth-century feminists – Reiss allows a real, though comparatively minor, difference (over the meaning of prostitution) to overwhelm a similarity that is more important (on the score of women's right to as much – and as little – self-possession as men have). Thus, while Reiss may see prostitution as a version of emancipation because any individual ought to have the right to sell herself or himself whenever she/he pleases, both Wordsworth and Wollstonecraft regard prostitution with a horror that both Reiss and I register. Yet where Reiss reads that horror as a version of censure, I read it as a version of pity.

When Wollstonecraft does censure, moreover, her very vehemence accords respect by insisting that individual women are accountable for their behavior. Thus, in *A Vindication of the Rights of Men* she writes with fear and loathing of other women, certain corrupt and aristocratic women who command the torture of black slaves. Although Wollstonecraft may offend our contemporary desire for female solidarity in castigating these women, the essential point of her entire discussion is not to suggest, as Reiss would argue, that the Enlightenment discourse of innate reason and justice of necessity makes man the norm – or ideal type – against whom woman must always appear as an inferior version. Rather, her account suggests the precariousness of sustaining the characteristics that are culturally posited as givens; women may 'be' affectionate, but women deprived of the benefits of education cannot sustain even their apparently innate goodness:

> But without fixed principles even goodness of heart is no security from inconsistency, and mild affectionate sensibility only renders a man more ingeniously cruel, when the pangs of hurt vanity are mistaken for virtuous indignation, and the gall of bitterness for the milk of Christian charity. (*VRM*, p. 111)

Thus, aristocratic women who are supposedly innately good and affectionate act with ironic cruelty. Trying to delude themselves about the inferiority of their status in relation to men, they require a display of their superiority to black slaves. They demand that the suffering of slaves be made conspicuous to them, as if torture could be marshalled for the purpose of theatrical entertainment:

> Where is the dignity, the infallibility of sensibility, in the fair ladies, whom, if the voice of rumour is to be credited, the captive negroes curse in all the agony of bodily pain, for the unheard of tortures they invent? It is probable that some of them, after the sight of a flagellation, compose their ruffled spirits and exercise their tender feelings by the perusal of the last imported novel. - How true these tears are to nature, I leave you [Burke] to determine. (*VRM*, p. 111)

In what is one of the shrewdest political insights of late eighteenth-century writing, Wollstonecraft then links Burke's politics in his *Reflections on the Revolution* with the aesthetic position of his *Enquiry into the Origin of Our Ideas of the Sublime and Beautiful*. Burke's account of what is *naturally* pleasing in women involves, she argues, the same kind of tendentious statement about women's nature that leads him repeatedly to define nature and natural rights in terms of property and the holding of real estate. For Burke's entire tendency in the *Reflections* is to make all individuals epiphenomena of property in land and to minimize individual rights while maximizing an individual's responsibilities to represent his land. And if this involves making property in land look like nature, Burke is entirely happy to do so.

For Wordsworth and Wollstonecraft the standing and utility of nature are quite different from what they are for Burke. Thus, although there is no doubt but that they continually worry the concept of nature, they are specifically committed to the possibility of a conception of nature that opposes it to property. And from that perspective someone like Wordsworth can engage in a dialogue with the natural landscape that repeatedly tries to imagine that there is a human nature not entirely derived from culture. For Wollstonecraft, however, the natural scene is, if anything, even more charged than it is for Wordsworth, because she specifically presents the individual contemplating a natural scene as renewing a sense of value that is not dependent on the value judgments of other people. As Reiss mentions, she is interested in sublime nature rather than in paintings of nature precisely so that nature should be the occasion of a confrontation with one's sense of oneself - without the intervention of cultural formulations of nature.

Reiss's point, of course, is that Wollstonecraft's effort to avoid such things as cultural formulations is her problem. You can't, he seems to say, either be understood by or overthrow the dominant discourse if you remain within the Enlightenment orbit of reason and individualism, because that is to imagine not just that we can choose between reason and irrationality but that the opposition between those two terms will ever allow us to choose anything but reason. That is, Wollstonecraft may carve out a language in which gender is not innate or fixed by redeploying 'manly' traits and 'feminine' traits so that it becomes clear that men frequently rely upon 'feminine' behavior and women compete in the 'manly' pursuit of virtue, but even to reallocate those traits by gender - and thus to indicate the limits of the cultural assumptions implicit in the notion of, say, 'manly' virtues - does not seem to approach the position that Reiss implicitly wants Wollstonecraft to occupy. Thus it is that Reiss can concede that Wollstonecraft frequently moves toward an understanding of gender in cultural terms that is congruent with current accounts, but that she can never do enough in this regard. The Enlightenment's very effort to think through notions like those of justice, nature, individuality, and community hopelessly entangles the individual with society in a way that keeps replicating past inequities by always rationalizing them.

These natural principles of justice, we saw, are what link the individual with the community. They also . . . permit the articulation of human reason with the laws of nature, the verisimilitude of literature with the truth of the world, the moral imperatives of individual sensibility with the ethical rules placed in nature by the Divinity. . . . These principles mark mature reason, order, and judgment, and are the very signs of that human maturity which, for Kant ('What is Enlightenment?'), are the essential characteristics of progress. In respect of its treatment of such principles, it could be argued that . . . *Jacques le fataliste* . . . queried in its own terms the dominance of that very lawful Reason of which the novel is one idealized manifestation. . . . In the English tradition it was achieved by Diderot's model, *Tristram Shandy*, the novel Viktor Shklovsky characterized as the most typical of all, just because it bared the rational principles of novelistic composition. (p. 35)

The passage quoted above seems to me particularly interesting because it follows Wollstonecraft's lead in suggesting the political implications of aesthetic judgments. And while Reiss implies that the limitations of Wollstonecraft's aesthetic judgments mirror the limitations of her political (or epistemological) judgments, it is at least worth registering not only that Wollstonecraft prosecutes such a line of argument about Burke's *Reflections*, but that this insight represents a signal departure from Paine's more widely disseminated reply to Burke, *The Rights of Man*. This is to say that I think that the dominant discourse of the Enlightenment for Reiss seems dominant almost to the point of absurdity – so dominant that he can neglect the contours of Wollstonecraft's position in an effort to get on to a stance that would be genuinely forward-looking – which would be, apparently, twentieth-century structuralist and post-structuralist aesthetics.

Implicit in Reiss's entire discussion is a rampant 'presentism' that involves suggesting that Wollstonecraft would have held our views of gender, our views of the dominant discourse, if she could have – that is, if she had not been born too soon and thus could have helped herself. But I think that Reiss is mistaken in his suggestion that the perspective of the present offers a politically saving vision of the limits of Enlightenment reason. For while it occasionally sounds as if the dominant discourse is merely a technological skill that enables one to address problems better (as when he excuses Wollstonecraft on the grounds that Olive Schreiner's socialism was not available to her), and as if Wollstonecraft would have turned out better work if she had had a word processor or a microwave oven, it seems to me that her work directly addresses a continuing tension between feminist theory and structuralist and post-structuralist theory. For like Andrea Dworkin, Susan Brownmiller, and Catharine MacKinnon, Wollstonecraft points to what seems to her like a virtually ineradicable physical difference between men and women – most men's superior physical strength in comparison with most women's. In the end, Reiss sees Wollstonecraft as a naively essentialist feminist; she may argue, he says, that the possibility of education for women indicates that gender is only culture-deep, but she ends by suggesting that women are marked by motherhood while men are marked by reason. This view seems to me fundamentally mistaken, because I think that Wollstonecraft tries to reconceive the culturally determined sexual division of reason and pity. Although both reason and pity are versions of identification, Wollstonecraft is preoccupied with the habits that make reason appear to be a version of identification with forces superior to oneself and pity to be a version of identification with forces inferior to oneself. Both kinds of identification may come to feel innate, but Wollstonecraft's whole point is that neither one is. Thus she argues that reason should learn to imitate pity, should learn to read the similarities of reason that link men and women. While Dworkin, Brownmiller, and MacKinnon hold that the difference in relative physical strength between men and women inevitably vitiates the possibility of culture being anything but a social representation and enforcement of violence against women, Wollstonecraft would employ reason to bridge that difference. And if she thus manifests a naive faith in reason, one can at least see the force of the illusion of individuality and autonomy for her. For that illusion is bound up with the claim that a woman's own account of herself might have greater standing than someone else's account of her. It is to say that Galatea may well be part of an ineluctable schema of appearances but that she may, nonetheless, begin to speak.

REFERENCES

Burke, Edmund 1968. *A Philosophical Enquiry into the Origin of Our Ideas of the Sublime and Beautiful*. Ed. J. T. Boulton. Notre Dame: University of Notre Dame Press.

Burke, Edmund 1982. *Reflections on the Revolution in France*. Ed. Conor Cruise O'Brien. Harmondsworth: Penguin.

Wollstonecraft, Mary 1975. *A Vindication of the Rights of Woman*. Ed. Carol H. Poston. New York: W. W. Norton.

Wordsworth, William 1970. *The Prelude, or Growth of a Poet's Mind* (Text of 1805). Ed. Ernest de Selincourt, new ed. Stephen Gill. Repr. London: Oxford University Press, 1975.

3

The Philosophical Bases of Feminist Literary Criticisms

Ellen Messer-Davidow

Feminist scholars in all fields have asked about our posture toward the dominant male intellectual traditions – are we[1] to confront them or dismiss them, borrow from them or criticize them? The collective feminist wisdom is divided on this subject as on so many others. Myra Jehlen, for instance, urges us to find some way of engaging 'the dominant intellectual systems directly and organically' lest we segregate ourselves in an enclave of women's studies or, worse, jettison ourselves off the world.[2] Conversely, Deborah Rosenfelt argues that 'only in autonomous programs can Women's Studies continue its evolution toward disciplinary status and achieve its full intellectual and political promise.'[3] The problem they are discussing, manifested organizationally by the relation of Women's Studies programs to the departments that populate universities and colleges, concerns the way we traditionally structure knowledge. It is a crucial problem because we find ourselves awkwardly situated; we are, according to the authors of *Feminist Scholarship: Kindling in the Groves of Academe, of* the disciplines in using their methods and correcting their knowledge, but we are *outside* them in aspiring to interdisciplinary study.[4]

Meanwhile, in literary study feminist critics are similarly ambivalent. Some continue to borrow, either purposefully or unwittingly, from traditional schools – archetypal, marxist, structuralist, psychoanalytic, semiotic, deconstructive, and hermeneutic, to name a few. Enjoying the smorgasbord, they reassure us that we can select the useful elements of these approaches, 'while discarding the biases'.[5] Others fear that the enterprises of writing and thinking, let alone criticism, are so thoroughly infected by patriarchal ideology that women can achieve expression only through a new female biolanguage or rebellious silence.[6] The dilemma appears to be that we cannot do with traditions and cannot do without them.

It is time to clarify our place in the domain of *literary* study where feminists suffer greatly the anguish of divided allegiance.[7] I believe that feminist literary critics who borrow uncritically borrow troubles mainly because our two endeavors are fundamentally incompatible. To support my contention, I treat our relation to literary study as a matter that needs to be deliberated at the level of research tradition, not the particular schools that compose it. My aim is to suggest a way of reconstituting knowledge that evolves from feminist perspectives. My method is to use a framework that places traditional and feminist literary criticisms on a single plane of analysis. It shows how feminist literary criticisms can be differentiated from traditional ones and how they can be integrated theoretically with the feminist criticisms proceeding in other fields.

The framework comprehends diverse theories and practices by specifying their philosophical bases: their *subject, subject matters, methods of reasoning*, and *epistemology*. The *subject* of literary study is everything that can be said about literature. In a given criticism, however, a critic does not discuss the totality of literature, an unmanageable subject, but chooses some aspect of it, a *subject matter* such as the author, reader, form, representation, or linguistic medium. Discussing a subject matter, a critic employs *methods of reasoning* such as differentiating, integrating, using principles, seeking cause, inferring between parts and wholes, and making analogies.[8] These methods refer to, derive from, apply, connect, and explain subject matters already formulated. Differentiation separates literature from other recognized subjects. Integration binds literature to subjects, such as language, behavior, politics, or myth, framed in certain ways and ready to inform critics about literature. A principle applied in a criticism articulates a proposition derived from previous instances, while a principle induced arises from an assemblage of instances intuited, at least, to have a significant relationship. Causality of an agent and effect, like inference between a part and a whole, relates previously recognized entities.

The choice of subject matters and methods refracts a criticism. By selecting different subject matters (the form of a work and its linguistic medium), two critics pursue distinct criticisms; they may belong to different schools (neo-Aristotelian and deconstructive) or the same one (structuralist). By applying different methods of reasoning (differentiating and integrating) to a subject matter (the linguistic medium), two critics pursue distinct criticisms: one considers literary language unique, the other a type of signification. Explicitly, then, discussions of literature, whether theoretical or practical, are determined by the *subject matter selected* and the *methods of reasoning exerted upon it*.

Thus far I have suggested classifying literary criticisms by their choice of a subject matter inflected by the reasoning exerted upon it. Now I want to shift to an overview. The subject matters and methods are constitutive elements of the predominant research tradition in Western literary study. A research tradition binds theoretical and practical work by specifying an *epistemology*, which, to quote the philosopher Larry Laudan, provides '*a set of general assumptions about the entities and processes in a domain of study, and about the appropriate methods to be used for investigating the problems and constructing the theories in that domain*'.[9] Implicitly, the epistemology of traditional literary study indicates the entities that exist in that domain – authors, works, audiences, representations, and media – and the methods used to investigate them – differential, integral, principled, causal, inferential, and analogical thinking. Boundaries are an important feature of these entities; maintaining them is what the methods do. Thus the epistemology of traditional literary study, as of other disciplines, separates ontology, epistemology, and technique: what exists from what is known, the knowers from the knowing, the knowing from the known, the human agents from the knowledge they produce. How do traditional thinkers construe these elements?

In both literary and scientific endeavor, the knowers – scholars, critics, scientists – extricate themselves from the methods, objects, and especially results of inquiry. The knowers can vanish into anonymous objectivity, or stand aside as disinterested critics and impartial spectators, or congeal into an authoritative 'we', or diversify into a company of pluralists. As knowers recede behind their methodologies, existence and knowledge loom large and autonomous. Existence consists of things separated from other things by inherent boundaries, subject to orderly change or combination, and abstractable from their contexts, while knowledge consists of representations of existence whose accuracy can be verified. The assumption about knowing in such a domain might be stated thus: the form of a chiefly independent reality can be abstracted and represented through the media of inquiry (statements, formulae, images, models) in a principled way. The passive voice of my statement faithfully obscures the human agents who abstract and represent.

Passages from Leonard B. Meyer's essay 'Concerning the sciences, the arts – AND the humanities' illustrate these epistemological assumptions. About existence, he says: 'The phenomena – planetary motions, molecular structures, economic behavior, and the like – are not themselves derived from, and consequently cannot refer to or be *about*, anything else. They neither disclose nor propose. They exist.'[10] He assumes that knowledge is an abstract representation of an objective existence: 'Scientific theories consist of propositional statements of hypotheses expressing and explaining recurring and orderly relationships found in the world of natural events, social behavior, and human action. They are general in that they refer to classes or types; they are abstract in that they account for only some attributes of the natural world' (p. 166). Artworks, he continues, possess the 'integrity and autonomy character-istic of natural phenomena' (p. 181), but as unique entities they do not lend themselves to classification and abstraction. Aesthetic theories 'are less coherent, rigorous, and well confirmed than scientific ones' because of the complexity of artworks, their variability, and the difficulty of studying creative and affective processes (p. 202). Meyer typically separates existence, knowing, and knowledge, attributing problems in knowing and knowledge to the objects of study; the characteristics of artworks and processes, he says, make them less amenable than natural phenomena to theoretical ways of knowing. He does not, however, consider the agency of scientists and humanists.

Discussing epistemology, I employ two concepts: *agency* and *stance*. *Agency* refers to ourselves and others as knowers, instrumental not only in producing knowledge but also in designing domains of study. It calls attention to our power as knowers, whether or not we recognize it. *Stance* refers to the relation of knowers to the other entities in a domain of study. It calls attention to how we position ourselves with regard to methods of knowing, subjects of investigation, and knowledge produced. Traditional literary scholars and critics seldom assume the stance of radically detached objectivity taken by natural scientists, because they cannot hide their agency when they are individuals writing prose with voice rather than a team using statistics. Nor do they take the stance of mastery assumed by social scientists, because they conceive of literary works as unique entities that resist control and homogenization. But they do take stances: critical uniformity, which imposes a single perspective; pluralism, which allows diverse technical, but not personal, perspectives; and self-dramatization, which creates an illusion of personal perspectives.[11]

Borrowing troubles

Tutored in the literary research tradition, feminist critics have borrowed not only its particulars but also its fundamentals - its subject, subject matters, methods of reasoning, and epistemology. We have assumed, indiscriminately I think, that literature is our subject, and with that decided we have perforce embraced the rest. Discussing gender under these circumstances, we are in trouble.

The most numerous feminist criticisms treat authors: women writers, conditions of female authorship, female creative processes, and expressions of female consciousness. Elaine Showalter, who coined the term 'gynocritics' to denote the 'study of women *as writers*', takes this approach in *A Literature of Their Own*, which examines the socio-economic conditions of British women writers and the expressions of their self-awareness. Reasoning integrally, she uses the concept of 'sub-culture' to sketch a tradition of feminine, feminist, and female literature.[12] Karen Keener and Catharine Stimpson observe the effects of social repression on authorial expression. Keener mentions the homophobic attitudes, censorship, institutional harassment, and ostracism that impede the writing, publishing, and studying of lesbian literature. Stimpson explains that the cultural yoking of lesbianism and deviancy forced lesbian self-awareness into special literary modes: stifled writing, encoded writing, narratives of damnation, romantic and realistic narratives of rebellion, and recently narratives of development, affirmation, and celebration.[13] Similarly, Alice Walker, Barbara Smith, Lorraine Bethel, Ann Allen Shockley, Erlene Stetson, and Margaret Walker document the astonishing creativity of black female authors under such oppressive conditions as enforced illiteracy, educational deprivation, virulent racism, stunning poverty, and neglect by white male, and sometimes white feminist, publishers.[14] Recent studies and anthologies celebrate the expression of black female identities by historical and contemporary black women writers.[15]

Early reader-centered criticisms took a distinctively political tone. In a now classic essay, Lillian Robinson defines feminist criticism as 'criticism with a Cause', 'ideological and moral criticism', 'revolutionary' criticism, whose aim - alleviating the oppressive effects of literature on women - entails not only interpreting and evaluating literary works but also transforming the institutions of literature, criticism, and education. In her aptly titled book, *The Resisting Reader*, Judith Fetterley argues that the 'major works of American fiction constitute a series of designs

on the female reader', among them denigration, exclusion from a liter-
arily defined humanity, and self-alienation. 'Literature', she asserts
analogically, 'is political', and 'power is the issue in the politics of
literature, as it is in the politics of anything else' - power to disable female
readers.[16] Many criticisms now use psychology and psychoanalysis to
delineate male and female reading.[17]

Originally, feminist criticisms analyzed representation. While early
studies criticized the inaccurate and deprecating images of women in
male-authored literature, more recent ones treat representation in female-
authored works. Annis Pratt's *Archetypal Patterns in Women's Fiction*
discloses that women's novels, like men's, portray development in
society, but that female development 'is thwarted by our society's
prescriptions concerning gender' and 'disrupted by social norms dictating
powerlessness'. In 'The thieves of language: women poets and revisionist
mythmaking', Alicia Ostriker selects contemporary women's poetry that
revises patriarchal myths and values. Recognizing that the challenge to
gender stereotypes must be followed by reconstruction, she herself
presents what she praises in poetry - a reconstituted literary reality.[18] By
treating race, class, and gender, Trudier Harris's *From Mammies to
Militants: Domestics in Black American Literature* and Barbara Christian's
essays on black female characters emphasize the cultural specificity of the
objects and manners of representation.[19]

Criticism that focuses on the linguistic medium is increasingly popular
among feminists who borrow, undoubtedly because it is the masculinist
criticism of the moment in Europe and the United States. Of the French
feminist writings denominated *l'écriture féminine*, many ruminate
analogically on sexuality and textuality. Demonstrative rather than
explanatory, they attempt to dismantle the messages of the dominant
'phallologocentric' discourses and to 'embody' female identity in a
language that originates in womblike darkness, flows from its creator like
her body fluids, and diffuses rhythmically like her multiplicitous sexual
pleasure.[20] Criticisms here employ less compelling imagery. Dorin
Schumacher regards a text as an entity of potential meaning and criticism
as the process of constructing that meaning. A critic, she asserts, reads for
a literal understanding of the text, but also imposes meaning on it by
selecting an interpretive model, often gender-linked, and seeking an
extended meaning for the words of the text as they relate to the model.
Annette Kolodny argues that we learn and use those interpretive strategies which allow us to read well the male works that we traditionally

have read well. She recommends that instead of judging female-authored works we 'ascertain the adequacy of any interpretive paradigm to a full reading of both male and female writing', thereby astutely shifting the critical focus from works to interpretive processes. [21] While French feminists seek a female manner and medium for encoding messages, American ones examine strategies for decoding. Both, however, work hard to engender the literary medium.

One finds little feminist criticism of a strictly formal nature. Feminists have complained that in focusing narrowly on the work – its form or structure – a critic abstracts it from human conditions, including gender. Indeed the claim has some validity, for in treating formal properties rather than authors, readers, or characters and in using differential reasoning to separate form from such analogues as behavior, politics, or myth, a critic does seem to dehumanize literature. In formal criticisms, our references to gender look suspiciously like foreign matter we imported into the literary discourse, whereas we do have grounds for discussing the subject when we treat authors, readers, and characters, entities to whom, after all, gender traits may be imputed. But gender traits do not rightfully characterize literary forms and language, notwithstanding the astonishing number of traditional and feminist critics who bestow these traits on them. [22] We can, of course, think anything we like, but our ontology specifies that people and literary works exist as distinct orders. Nevertheless, the recalcitrance of formal approaches in feminist criticism, as I suggest later, is greatly exaggerated. [23]

Feminist critics who borrow these traditional subject matters necessarily encounter intractable problems. For instance, they make divergent judgments about a work – its formal excellence but moral repugnance, its exemplary effects but artistic flaws, its ideological purity but creative restraints, its freedom of authorial expression but loathsome values. The many debates that feminist critics have conducted on which of these judgments should receive primacy cannot, of course, be decided. [24] Traditional literary criticisms produce divergent judgments of a work simply because focusing on a particular subject matter compels a particular type of evaluation: form criticisms tend to judge the crafting of a work, author criticisms the creative virtuosity and sincerity, reader criticisms the quality of the effect or response, representation criticisms the mode and authenticity of the work, linguistic criticisms the efficacy of communication or adequacy of interpretation. The objects of evaluation and the standards are built into the subject matters, and, except for a pluralistic tolerance of all comers, no literary metastandards exist in this scheme to mediate among them.

Feminist critics' antipathy toward formal criticisms for precluding discussions of gender, their endowment of the linguistic medium with gender traits, and their insertion of gender into discussions of authors, readers, and characters confirm trouble in borrowing the traditional subject. Gender is so conspicuous in feminist criticisms precisely because it is not a recognized aspect of literature. While traditional critics probe their subject of literature, feminist critics juggle a version of Virginia Woolf's tenuously coupled subject of women *and* literature. To traditionalists, the first part of it is tediously intruded; to us, it is not yet integrated.

The wildly discrepant judgments about women and literature made by feminists and traditionalists reveal more trouble in borrowing the subject. We charge traditional critics with devaluing everything female in literature: female authors and readers, works written by and for women, portrayals of female experiences, styles and genres thought to be feminine, and such roles as patron and editor when they are performed by women. They retort (if they do at all) that most women's literature is already judged glaringly deficient by the standards that affirm 'great' and 'near-great' (male) literature and that we take the untenable position of opposing social ideals to literary standards. We ourselves accept this formulation of the problem when we debate what we call a work's aesthetics and its politics. On the one hand, as literary critics we want to affirm, as Wayne Booth declares, that 'art works exist as valued achievements of a high order.' [25] On the other hand, as feminist critics we want to affirm that the equitable disposition of people is a valued achievement of a high order. The tension surfaces agonizingly when these two allegiances clash and we are forced to pass judgment, say, on Milton's great epic. But 'great' in what sense? If we weren't thinking about gender while thinking about literature, we wouldn't be torn between the excellent crafting of a work and the pernicious effects of its ideology. We wouldn't be torn, I submit, between conflicting evaluations arising from two distinct subjects.

Borrowing traditional methods, feminists borrow more troubles. Methods of reasoning - differential, integral, principled, causal, inferential, and analogical - function referentially in a bounded universe. They refer to entities already formulated by the research tradition and, more importantly, they do *not* refer to entities that are excluded by it. [26] Employing these methods, feminist literary critics are in danger of accepting not only particular formulations but also the traditional construal of reality, another male construction. ' "Representation of the world" ', Catharine MacKinnon quotes Simone de Beauvoir, ' "like the world itself, is the work of men; they describe it from their own point of view, which they confuse with the absolute truth." The parallel between representation and construction should be sustained: men *create* the world from their own point of view, which then *becomes* the truth to be described.'[27] Insofar as methods uncritically introduce into our work aspects of male-created reality, they subvert our task of transforming it.

Dorin Schumacher illustrates this problem at the interpretive level. A traditional critic, she says, who wants to support his male-centered rendering of a text, 'has a wide selection of critical ideas from which to choose' – Freudian or Jungian psychologies, Christian or classical ethics, myriad histories, political and economic theories, traditions in the arts. All these 'philosophies include in themselves the masculinist idea of man as self, or normative, and woman as other, or deviant', naturally affirming his interpretation. But a feminist critic 'cannot apply these ideas to the text without first challenging the basic masculinist assumptions behind them; in other words, challenging the weight of Western tradition' (p. 34). Thus, integral and analogical methods of reasoning, which illuminate literature by referring it to an analogue, partake of a closed system. They expedite references to aspects of the male-created reality to confirm the masculinist apprehension of literature, which further bolsters the male-created reality.

Differential reasoning that functions within the male-created reality while disavowing its definition of female only paints an obverse portrait. For instance, some French feminists argue that woman is not what men think she is. They define her as opposite or apart from the male definition, thus unintentionally substantiating what men have been saying all along: woman is other. In their formulation, she is other in relation not to men but to the male definition of her. Also reasoning differentially, radical feminists in this country valorize the traits that men use to degrade women, thus affirming the male definition, but not evaluation, of what is female. The referential quality of integral, analogical, and differential methods does not preclude their use by feminists, but it does restrict our choices of analogues for literature (or anything else) to alternative constructions of reality.

While inference among parts and wholes presents similar referential problems, causal and principled reasoning brings the additional troubles of oversimplification. The linking of cause and effect works best with few variables, demonstrable relationships, and a domain of study that lends itself to compartmentalization. Literature resists tidy analysis, critics say. The manifestations of gender and literature, which feminists scrutinize, are even less simple, demonstrable, and discrete, but a compulsion to show cause has sent many traditional and feminist critics on a hunt for the determinants of literary sex differences. [28]

If causal reasoning is a simplistic method leading to inadequate results, literary principles often are the simplistic results of inadequate methods. Principles, as statements of laws, doctrines, or truths about literature, are derived from and explain instances. Increasingly, feminist literary critics maintain that traditional principles of style, form, and period, as well as creativity and response, were derived from pools of works written and studied primarily by men of similar cultural circumstances. For instance, the editors of *The Voyage In: Fictions of Female Development* explain that concepts of development are 'colored by many interrelated factors, including class, history, and gender'. [29] By examining culturally diverse fictions of female development, they hope to revise the principles derived from the eighteenth-century German *Bildungsroman* and its androcentric successors. Such principles have a limited scope that is mistaken for a generic or universal one. Still, they are efficacious. Principles derived from the literature that stocks traditional canons and histories act to admit like works to, and dismiss unlike ones from, these records. Reinforcing both their own authority and that of the chosen works, they maintain a closed system of literature.

If methods of reasoning refer to aspects of the male-created reality, a function that supports the traditional apprehension of literature, then the closed system, as Catharine MacKinnon says about women's oppression generally, 'is, finally, neither demonstrable nor refutable empirically' - because, of course, there is no other system so long as we remain within this one. By confronting a closed system with its methods, MacKinnon believes, we expose 'the reality to be criticized' (p. 542). I believe we must delineate all the elements - subjects, methods, and epistemologies - men have used in constructing their reality to show it for the artifact it is. Feminists are writing about the dynamics of literary study as a closed system. Deborah Rosenfelt's 'The politics of bibliography: women's studies and the literary canon' discloses how scholars devised bibliographic taxons and criteria that screen women's writings from literary canons and scholarship, while circularly authorizing canonicity, scholarship, and bibliography. Paul Lauter's 'Race and gender in the shaping of the American literary canon: a case study from the Twenties' reveals other factors - 'the professionalization of the teaching of literature, the development of an aesthetic theory that privileged certain texts, and the historiographic organization of the body of literature into conventional "periods" and "themes"' - in the maintenance of a closed system.[30]

Borrowing from literary epistemology, feminists preclude our endeavor. The central issue is that we cannot accept traditional assumptions about the agencies and stances of knowers. Objectivity conceals the existence of knowers' agencies, stances, and perspectives. Uniformity imposes a single stance and perspective on knowers. Pluralism admits knowers with diverse investigative, but not personal, perspectives. Self-dramatization creates the illusion of knowers with personal perspectives. Knowers who assume these stances do not view sex, race, class, and affectional preference as basic variables in literary study; they are mostly white, middle class, heterosexual men who, in looking at each other, do not see diverse circumstances. They work with what they have. Contingently, Adam Smith was right when he said in *The Theory of Moral Sentiments* that 'all the subjects of science and taste, are what we and our companion regard as having no particular relation to either of us. We both look at them from the same point of view.'[31] This principle applies only when knowers of homogeneous circumstances assume a common stance to organize inquiry.

When critics ignore their agencies and stances in literary study, certain troubles are logically predictable. First, if they obscure their agency, they *perceive* its products - canons, histories, theories, curricula, and accounts of sex differences - to be objective rather than constructed, scholarly rather than polemical, intellectual rather than social, when they are only objectified. Borrowing this assumption, feminists cannot credibly propose to change the organizing constructs of literary study. Second, once these products are removed from their human agents and granted autonomy, they appear to possess intrinsic validity and merit. Borrowing this assumption, feminists cannot credibly challenge the standards that uphold literary study. Third, without human agents, the cultural affiliations of sex, race, class, affectional preference, and other circumstances that bear on knowing are irrelevant. Borrowing this assumption, feminists cannot discuss the issues that interest us about literary study.

Last, without building cultural self-awareness and diversity into their perspectives, critics experience such distortions as centricity (the male as focal point, the female as marginal), exclusivity (the male as all, the female as absent), subjectification (the male as subject, the female as moldable object), and isolation (the male as self, the female as other). For feminists, the failure to incorporate agencies into the domain of study precludes the requisite of our criticism, feminist perspectives. Without them, we make no feminist criticisms. More devastatingly, when we adopt traditional perspectives, the consequences to us are the marginalization, negation, objectification, and alienation of our female selves in the service of a critical self.

A related trouble is that traditional literary epistemology inculcates a dehumanization not only of agents but of subject. As Fraya Katz-Stoker puts it: 'An atmosphere was created in which one was taught to treat and teach literature as if it were unattached to anything else in the world. The words *literature, poetry*, and *art* conjure up images of bubbles floating in a cloudless, Platonic sky.'[32] The objectifying of literature by itself does not cause the trouble. To study a subject, we must objectify it conceptually and linguistically, and to do that we arbitrarily bound and name it. 'The *boundaries* of a system', Alfred Kuhn explains, 'are not inherent characteristics of the things, but of the kind of problem facing the person who is studying or dealing with the system.'[33] If we are studying a muscle cell, the cell wall is the boundary of the system, but if we are studying range of motion the muscles fall within the system.

Traditional critics have dexterously, if not always cognizantly, altered the boundary of *literature* to suit their needs. *Literature* encloses as its prime entities the author, work, audience, universe, and medium, each one surrounded by a boundary that critics adjust when, for instance, they focus singly on the author, work, or reader and then refocus on them together as the sender, medium, and receiver of a message. But adjusting the boundaries of entities within a system is not the same as expanding the system's boundary. Historically the boundary of *literature* has shrunk: in eighteenth-century England, *literature* comprehended almost all printed and many oral works; in the nineteenth century, it narrowed to *belles lettres*; under New Criticism, it enshrined a group of texts which the principles of intrinsic criticism separated from non-literary matter. Modern literary critics assiduously denounced extra-literary activity and defended against the incursions of historical, psychological, and sociological critics as if they were (to use their imagery) on a border patrol to protect literary territory from foreign accession.[34]

Now culture critics are permeating the boundaries of literary entities – by providing sociologies of authorship and literary genesis, social analyses of conventions, descriptions of the culture of reading, historical accounts of representation, and theories of texts embedded in linguistic systems, to name a few. But if the traditional literary entities of author, work, reader, representation, and linguistic medium now appear in the domain of study with cultural penumbras, the literary system has not yet admitted the entities and processes that most concern feminist literary critics – our own human ones.

The troubled borrowings of feminists from traditional literary criticisms point to the unsuitability of the subject, subject matters, methods, and epistemology for us. The location of the difficulties in the constitutive elements of the literary research tradition highlights the improbability of reconciling our endeavor with one that is fundamentally incompatible.

The philosophical bases of feminist literary criticisms

What I am deducing is the idea that feminist literary criticisms have a subject of their own, subject matters that are aspects of that subject, an enlarged methodological repertoire, and a rehumanized epistemology. The subject of feminist literary criticisms appears to be not literature but the feminist study of ideas about sex and gender that people express in literary and critical media. The elements that compose this proposition – *sex and gender, ideas about, in literary and critical media, people express, feminist study of* – require explanation.

Sex refers to those features thought to differentiate biologically between people classified as male and female, and gender to those features thought to differentiate culturally. These natural and cultural dimensions of humanity have been discriminated with the development of modern disciplines, especially the social sciences, since the seventeenth century. Feminist thinkers, such as Mary Wollstonecraft and Charlotte Perkins Gilman, used cultural analysis to defend against the ideology of divine determinism that informed conservative moral philosophies in the eighteenth century and against the ideology of biological determinism that succeeded it during the nineteenth century. Nevertheless, I am disposed to argue that this distinction, for all its usefulness then and today, is not a valid one here.

I use the phrase *ideas about sex and gender*, rather than *sex and gender* alone, to emphasize that both phenomena are constructions and for three more reasons. The obvious one is that *ideas about*, not personal traits of, sex and gender appear in literary and critical works, which themselves consist of various ideas and forms expressed in linguistic media. Correlatively, it is *ideas about* sex and gender that people express in their behaviors: for instance, authors in their creating and audiences in their responding. In short, artworks, language, and behavior, like clothing, curricula, games, and governments, all serve as media for expressing sex/gender ideas. Some feminist critics mistakenly think that sex/gender traits characterize a creative process, product, or response – and so feminists may characterize them, but this approach only aids the masculinist project of arranging media to convey sex/gender schemes.

Furthermore, I use *ideas about* because it is mainly the ideas, not the traits, whose existence can be verified at this time. We know how the ideas come to exist and function. People *think* sex/gender traits exist; then they single out these traits, rather than those of metabolism, interpersonal style, eye color, or moral conduct, in order to establish the fundamental categories of human nature, structure relationships, assign roles, bestow values, dispense privileges, and otherwise order the complexities of life. Sex/gender ideas are in plentiful supply. Actual traits are not. What traits are alleged (for example, genetic make-up, reproductive physiology, long bone growth, hemispheric specialization), whether their range is greater within or between the sexes, the extent to which physiology, psychology, and culture reciprocally mesh in producing them, and how appropriately they serve as indicators of human nature remain to be clarified. Much that has passed for scientifically established 'fact' about sex traits, feminists contend, is invalidated by the androcentric perspectives and misogynistic values that have warped the choice of subjects, problems, methods, and designs in research.[35] Putative sex traits have a large ideational component. Gender traits, of course, originate in idea, not matter.

The most important reason for referring to *ideas about*, not traits of, is to make crucial corrections in epistemology. The moment we accept the traditional framing of this matter – that is, male and female, sex and gender, fact and supposition, actuality and idea – we have no way out of the system we want to change. The mistake of many feminists, in my opinion, is to accept the categorization itself and to adjust the formulaic attributions within it by reassigning traits to male and female, valorizing female and devaluing male, or shuffling male and female roles. Such, for instance, is the approach taken by much French feminist criticism, radical feminist criticism, and feminist literary criticism that, as Carolyn Heilbrun remarks, embroiders the 'analogy between pens and penises, between wombs and creativity'.[36] I recommend not that we cease to investigate sex and gender but that we understand them to be man- or woman-made classifications of people and existence that are dispensable despite their apparent tenacity. Research shows that there are diverse, not two, combinations of sex chromosomes, genitalia, secondary character- istics, and behaviors. Some investigators believe that people who do not conform to one of the two sex/gender classes are anomalies.[37] Conversely, I submit that the many instances of sexual 'abnormality', along with the 'deviations' from normative gender identities and erotic preferences, which are recorded in scientific and other literatures, are a function of the inadequacy of the categorization itself. If we must think about people in terms of sex/gender, we can contrive a more accurate scheme than 'class *m*, class *f*, and misfits', and discern ourselves as its makers. But even this remedy, if it is based on fact and actuality, is not radical enough.

Facts and actualities are elusive, I think, because they are illusory. Recognizing our instrumentality as knowers, we can blur the distinctions between male and female, fact and supposition, actuality and idea, dissolving these categories as we search for others to order life. Doing so, we begin to see that we invented not only the particular facts and actualities, as we did the suppositions and ideas, but also the designations themselves of these modes. My reference to *ideas about*, then, is meant to convey the arbitrary nature of sex/gender classification: the categories of male and female, their applications to existence, and the evidence marshaled in their behalf, like the traits that inconsistently mark them from one culture to another, are fabricated by us.[38]

Feminist literary critics study ideas about sex and gender that people express *in literary and critical media*. For instance, Eve Kosofsky Sedgwick's *Between Men* analyzes literary representations of a homo- social system of relations, a continuum of 'male friendship, mentorship, entitlement, rivalry, and hetero- and homosexuality', in which women are the exchangeable property that cements bonds among men. Mary Poovey's *The Proper Lady and the Woman Writer* describes how the ideology of propriety, which inculcated female self-effacement, was filtered through personal histories and transformed into style in the works of Mary Wollstonecraft, Mary Shelley, and Jane Austen. Linda Woodbridge's *Women and the English Renaissance* reinterprets works relevant to the controversy over women, showing which genres prescribe gender ideologies, which express authorial misogyny or feminism, which describe the lives of women and men, and which sport with gendered literary conventions.[39] These feminists study sex/gender ideas expressed in literary representations, styles, and modes. But the ideas are expressed in other media: for instance, economies, dance steps, human development, furniture, jurisprudence, and gestures. What distinguishes feminist literary critics from feminists working in other fields, I shall argue later, is mostly medium.

The remaining elements of the subject of feminist literary criticisms – *people express* and *feminist study of* – insert us into the model. People express ideas about sex and gender; feminist literary critics study them. Furthermore, we study them self-reflexively. We contemplate our agencies: that is, ourselves selecting a subject of inquiry, framing it, and producing knowledge from our particular feminist perspectives. Some traditional critics ponder their agency *in* inquiry, but they generally disregard the influence of their cultural circumstances (especially a sex, race, and affectional preference) *upon* inquiry.[40] Building our agencies into the model, we ensure that an epistemological commentary accompanies the knowledge we make.

To determine the subject matters of this subject, I must again adjust the philosophical model applied to literary study. Our subject matters can be: (1) ideas about sex/gender in themselves, analyzed formally, comparatively, and historically; (2) people who conceive, articulate, use, or otherwise embody these ideas, as well as their inventive and expressive processes; (3) the effects these ideas have on people individually and collectively; (4) the media of language, literature, and criticism where these ideas are expressed, as well as the associated processes; and (5) our self-reflexive feminist study of subjects, subject matters, methods, and epistemologies.

The adjustments and the reasons for them are apparent. First, the literary research tradition omits self-reflexive agencies and perspectives, which I introduce here as the fifth subject matter. Next, the literary research tradition specifies a mimetic conception of works as representations of an objective universe. Because I believe that a feminist research tradition is not served by distinctions between representations and reality, supposition and actuality, idea and fact, I omit this subject matter as *ours*. We can, however, discuss how others express these dichotomies under the first and fifth subject matters: for instance, we can analyze historically what Milton and Darwin say about inherent sex traits, or reveal the epistemological assumptions of scientists engaged in sex differentiation research.

A final adjustment concerns an assumption about feminist subject matters. They appear to be discrete entities, whereas I mean them to be a dynamic system suspended only on paper. Similarly, in a given discourse a traditional literary critic appears to expound one subject matter and a feminist literary critic to flit among several. These impressions are created by the different assumptions but identical constraints that order the two domains of study. Traditional literary critics envision bounded literary entities, and we envision sex/gender ideologies circulating through mutable human systems. To explain them we stop the action. Stopped action, like discrete subject matters, is not an intrinsic quality of the phenomena we study but a requirement of the agents who study them – a concession to the temporal limitations of our understanding and language. In time we can build a synchronous account of our subject matters as we glissade among them and turn upon ourselves.

For instance, in a chapter of *The Madwoman in the Attic* titled 'Milton's bogey: patriarchal poetry and women readers', Sandra Gilbert and Susan Gubar quote Virginia Woolf's perplexing comment from *A Room of One's Own* that 'to resurrect "the dead poet who was Shakespeare's sister" . . . literate women must "look past Milton's bogey".'[41] Attempting to discover who or what was Milton's bogey, since Woolf does not explain, they examine her 1918 diary, finding comments on *Paradise Lost* that are diffident, humble, and nervous in contrast to her confident judgments about Sophocles and Byron. From such clues, they decide that Milton's bogey is 'his cosmology, his vision of "what *men* thought" and his powerful rendering of the culture myth that Woolf, like most other literary women, sensed at the heart of Western literary patriarchy. The story that Milton, "the first of the masculinists" [here they quote Woolf], most notably tells to women is of course the story of woman's secondness, her otherness, and how that otherness leads inexorably to her demonic anger, her sin, her fall, and her exclusion from that garden of the gods which is also, for her, the garden of poetry' (p. 191). The effect of Milton's patriarchal poetry on the women who read it is to inhibit their imaginations. Of inhibition, Gilbert and Gubar find evidence not only in Woolf's diary, but also in *A Room of One's Own, Orlando, Between the Acts*, and *The Voyage Out*. Less subtle, they claim, are the effects on other women writers such as Elizabeth Barrett

Browning, Charlotte Brontë, and Christina Rossetti, whose works revise *Paradise Lost*. Concerning subject matters, Gilbert and Gubar trace sex/gender ideas as they circulate from author to text to reader/author to text, along the way transformed from the ideas of the patriarch into those of the protesters. Feminist literary criticisms like these connect rather than compartmentalize their subject matters.

The chief requirement for self-reflexive feminist criticism and especially for formal, comparative, and historical analyses of sex/gender ideas is to understand dichotomous thinking about human nature. I propose that when traditionalists think about two categories of people, *m* and *f*, these maneuvers occur:

a *The first differentiation establishes two categories and names them* m *and* f. There are other ways to categorize. We can vary the number of categories and their temporality, making flexible, not permanent, assignments of people to them.

b *The next differentiation ascribes the traits that sort people into* m *and* f. Traditionalists need some traits – it matters little what they are even though they may be convincingly rationalized – to differentiate people and maintain the two-category system. They need specific traits (strength and weakness) to enforce specific relations (dominance and submission) between people and categories. The ascribed traits may vary in locus (innate or acquired), cause (divinely implanted or socially induced), and effect (restrictive or empowering).

c *A third differentiation bestows positive and negative values on* m *and* f *and their traits*. Feminists believe that traditionalists value the male and devalue the female, but persuasive determinists of every age praise the traits they want women to adopt, raising them above the ruder traits, but not the persons, of men. Similarly, French and radical feminists reverse the values, but seldom the traits, of the sexes.

d *Another differentiation sets the focus on* m *and* f. Traditionalists situate the male exclusively or centrally and the female, if not absent, marginally to literary and other endeavors. Many feminists focus centrally or exclusively on the female, a technique that allows us to recover women's lives and works and to correct androcentric perspectives. But we need to employ a double, relational focus on sex/gender like the one I am describing now.

e *The next differentiation standardizes* m *and/or* f. Traditionalists make the male the norm – the pattern for a group, the model for humanity, the standard of quality. Focusing exclusively on the male, they make it the norm by default. If they construe the male as the norm for a male population, the standardization effaces race, class, and other specificities, or if for humanity, the standardization effaces sex/gender. They incorrectly extrapolate a human norm from a homogenous population when they derive models of psychological development from male subjects, of linguistic competence from male speech, of genre from male-authored works. More perversely, focusing centrally on the male, they may make it the human norm by a democratic logic that converts majority into quality and female marginality into deviance. As psychological studies show, traditionalists consider male traits normal and healthy, but female ones unhealthy and childlike. Here the confusion of male-specific with human-generic modulates into (mis)judgments of moral salubrity, lending the standardization prescriptive and punitive force.

f *Another differentiation indicates the relations of* m *and* f. Instead of dominance and submission, some feminists envision males and females relating through reciprocal empowerment and some envision separation.

g *A further differentiation confers perspectives on individuals categorized as* m *and* f. A man who thinks traditionally about sex/gender views himself as self and a woman as other, undoubtedly because he experiences his self (whether as feelings and thoughts or as a complex identity) and infers differentially, as the dichotomous system requires him to do. In this perspective, which subjectifies the self and objectifies the other, he is reinforced by others like him. A woman who accepts the traditional view of woman as other is self-alienated. Feminists must not embrace the self/other dichotomy in claiming our selfhoods, but develop a perspectivity that confers selfhood all around.

h *The final differentiation secures the system*. In order to secure the two categories, traditionalists make a third category; it subsumes all those deviants from *m* and *f* whose unclassified existence would undermine the dichotomous structure of the system.

An understanding of dichotomous thinking about human nature must be based not on tentative analyses like mine but on formal, comparative, and historical studies of gender ideology.[42]

For instance, a double, relational focus on sex/gender informs Annette Kolodny's complementary studies, *The Lay of the Land* and *The Land Before Her*, which examine how men and women cast their experiences and ideas of the American landscape. Men, she shows, use metaphors of erotic domination to describe a virgin continent they would penetrate, master, and possess; women use metaphors of domesticity to describe a frontier garden they would cultivate. Similarly, in 'The mythic mannish lesbian: Radclyffe Hall and the New Woman', Esther Newton argues that Hall's depiction of Stephen Gordon as a 'mannish' lesbian repudiates only the female sexuality, but not the logic, of heterosexual ideology. By dichotomizing the sexes and conflating sexuality and gender identity, the ideology dictates that a woman who rejects passive, heterosexual femininity for active homosexuality must be masculine.[43] Such analyses are needed for all the subject matters of feminist literary criticism.

Methods of reasoning determine 'the logic of the philosophic system as a whole ... the derivation of one proposition from another'.[44] But feminists in many fields believe that methods also determine the other fundamentals of study. In 'Feminism and science', Evelyn Fox Keller suggests 'that method and theory may constitute a natural continuum, despite Popperian claims to the contrary ... because of the recurrent and striking consonance that can be seen in the way scientists work, the relation they take to their object of study, and the theoretical orientation they favor.'[45] Writing on political theory, Catharine MacKinnon argues that the method selected determines each theory's vision of reality, which is to say in my terms that the method of reasoning determines a criticism's framing of its subject. 'Clearly', she declares, 'there is a relationship between how and what a theory sees .... Method in this sense organizes the apprehension of truth; it determines what counts as evidence and defines what is taken as verification' (p. 527).

I agree that method influences the choice and framing of the other fundamentals in a domain of study, but not unilaterally. Determinative force rebounds among the subject, subject matters, methods, and epistemology so that the subject of study as we conceive it influences the reasoning we apply, influences the subject of study as we conceive it, influences.... This reciprocity allows us to infer how we derive propositions from how we conceive a subject. To begin the inference, what are the features of our subject as we conceive it? And next, what methods of reasoning do these features imply?

Feminist social scientists conceive of our subject much as I recommend we do in literary study – as complex sex/gender ideologies circulating through cultural systems. For instance, Nancy Chodorow describes the subject of her book *The Reproduction of Mothering: Psychoanalysis and the Sociology of Gender*: 'I argue that the sex-gender system is a social, psychological, and cultural totality. We cannot identify one sphere as uniquely causal or constitutive of the others. You cannot understand the social organization of gender apart from the fact that we are all psychologically sexed and gendered, that we do not have a self apart from our being gendered. My book also argues that we cannot understand the psychology of men and women apart from the social organization of gender in which this psychology is produced.'[46]

Analogously, we could say that the sex/gender system is a literary, critical, and cultural totality. We cannot understand literature and its study apart from the fact that we as authors, scholars, and critics are gendered, nor can we understand ourselves apart from the cultural organization of gender that produces us. William W. Morgan asserts that the tradition of making and studying literature, 'like the governmental, religious, educational, economic and social traditions of which it is a part, has operated by and large according to male norms and has excluded, distorted or undervalued female experience, female perceptions, female art, and female scholarship and criticism.' He continues: '*Insofar as it presents itself as a history, analysis, and evaluation of human literary activity*, everything that we know as the literary cultural tradition is, simply, wrong; it is a history principally of male activity, analyzed and evaluated according to male perceptions and norms' (pp. 810-11; author's emphasis). His description of his subject resembles Chodorow's description of hers: the prominent feature of both is their systemic quality.

Traditional methods of reasoning grasp details but cannot comprehend a system. Our methods of reasoning perform various functions that are suited to analyze and approximate systems: they specify subject matters, trace patterns among them, and represent our agencies.

Literary critics are able to universalize the entities they study by ignoring the cultural particulars that differentiate them; we must avoid this error. Objecting to the presumptuous use of 'feminist critics' when only white ones are mentioned, Mary Helen Washington declares that 'black women are searching for a specific language, specific symbols, specific images with which to record the myths of their history.' Although they can belong to the Afro-American and feminist traditions, 'they will first insist on their own name, their own space.' But answering Barbara Smith's claim 'that Zora Neale Hurston, Margaret Walker, Toni Morrison, and Alice Walker use a "specifically black female language",' Deborah McDowell asks, 'is there a monolithic Black female language?

Do Black female high school drop outs, welfare mothers, college graduates and Ph.D.s share a common language? Are there regional variations on this common language?' [47] Particularization is a method of specification; depicting individual voices and the texture of experience rather than generalizing them is a consonant method of presentation.

Particularization specifies the entities studied, contextualization specifies their cultures. In *Sensational Designs*, Jane Tompkins recontextualizes nineteenth-century American novels by asking not what they mean to us but what cultural work they did in their historical situations. Discussing them 'in relation to the religious beliefs, social practices, and economic and political circumstances that produced them', she transforms historical situation from the raw material of texts to the human functions that determine their reception, meaning, and value. Reviewing Hawthorne's literary reputation, Tompkins explains the original circumstances that made his work appear ordinary and the altered ones that 'presented [his] work to its readers in such a way that it possessed the marks of greatness'. [48] Whether a text is good, she argues, 'cannot be settled by invoking . . . examples of literary excellence . . . because these texts already represent one position in the debate they are being called upon to decide. That is, their value, their identity, and their constituent features have been made available for description by the very modes of perception and evaluation that I am challenging' (p. 187). This challenge too is produced by historical situation; as a woman in a male-dominated field, she objects to the narrowness of literary study, absence of women's writings, and disregard of non-imaginative genres. Her point is that there is no neutral position from which we view subjects of study. Our contexts and theirs create what we see of them.

Methods of patterning trace the relations that subsist among the entities studied. Feminist literary critics notice that the same sex/gender ideas reappear in one instance of a medium (a novel), several instances of a medium (novels), or several instances of different media (novels, criticisms, manners, laws). The relation they mark among the ideas is one of structural congruence. The metaphors of erotic domination that, according to Annette Kolodny, male settlers used to describe their relationship to the American continent are the same metaphors that, according to Evelyn Fox Keller, the male founders of modern science used to describe their relationship to nature. The metaphorical congruence suggests, and I expect historical reconstruction will confirm, that the settlers and scientists had similar gender ideologies and stances in their domains of endeavor because they shared the historical situation of late sixteenth- and seventeenth-century England and France.[49] The reasoning that apprehends homologous structures seeks patterns, not causes or classes. But the structures that characterize sex/gender ideas when we analyze them formally and comparatively are static, whereas ideologies change.

Processes, too, can be congruent. In a *tour de force*, Adrienne Rich analyzes compulsory heterosexuality as an institution that secures male dominance.[50] Many people, she notes, assume that heterosexuality is the innate or volitional orientation of most women. Contending that this 'is an enormous assumption to have glided so silently into the foundations of our thoughts' (p. 637), Rich delineates eight ways in which male power compels female heterosexuality. First, men deny women their own sexuality through 'clitoridectomy and infibulation; chastity belts; punishment, including death, for female adultery . . . for lesbian sexuality; psychoanalytic denial of the clitoris. . . .' Second, men force their sexuality on women by 'rape (including marital rape) and wife beating; father-daughter, brother-sister incest; the socialization of women to feel that male sexual "drive" amounts to a right; idealization of heterosexual romance in art, literature, media, advertising, etc.; child marriage; arranged marriage; prostitution; the harem . . .' (pp. 438-9). In these and six other ways, Rich explains, men enforce female heterosexuality. Although the activities differ (performing clitoridectomy on children, idealizing heterosexual romance in novels, pimping) and lead to different immediate ends (denying females their sexuality, persuading them to fall in love, commanding their sexual labor), they and their ends are functionally congruent: they compel the female heterosexuality that maintains a system of male dominance and female submission. The reasoning that identifies these homologous functions patiently seeks dynamic patterns.

Besides congruence, feminist literary critics notice another relation among the entities studied: influence. This is what Gilbert and Gubar's reasoning illuminates when they consider the effects of Milton's patriarchal poetry. Their method, as I explained, is to trace sex/gender ideas circulating from author to text to readers/authors to texts, transformed along the way from patriarchal to dissenting ideology. Discerning congruence and tracing influence are methods suited to analyze the middle ground of a complex system; they treat the entities and the relations that subsist among them. Enlarging these analyses synchronically and diachronically, and weaving in the variables of race, class, affectional preference, and other cultural specificities, feminist literary critics can approximate the sex/gender system that, as Chodorow and Morgan describe it, pervades our existence.[51]

From the systemic quality of our subject as we conceive it, I inferred the reasoning we can employ to specify, pattern, and approximate a system. Another prominent feature of the subject as we conceive it is our agency, our self-reflexive awareness of it, and how we attain that awareness. This feature, too, suggests method. Ruth Bleier, a scientist, 'recognizes the subjective – that is, perceived or constructed – nature of "reality".' What 'distinguishes . . . feminist approaches to knowledge', she observes, 'is the very plurality of our voices that reflect the ever-changing nature of the realities we try to examine and of our perceptions of them.'[52] It is not a technical pluralism that we need to embrace; it is, as lesbian and black feminist critics remind us, our diverse perspectives centered in selves diversified through cultural and personal experience. We come to recognize that agencies and perspectives are centered in our selves, as feminist proverb has it, by grounding ourselves in our experiences, politicizing them, and together constructing a collective reality.

Susan Krieger's *The Mirror Dance*, a study of identity in a mid-western lesbian community, creatively employs these methods. Krieger writes three parts of the book in a conventional first-person manner: she explains her methodology in an introduction, relates it to literary and social science methodologies in an appendix, and briefly describes the community in the first chapter. The body of the text consists of 'the voices, stories, and self-reflections of the different people [she] interviewed'.[53] Here she makes no authorial comments but does select and arrange the interviewees' comments. The result is a 'multiple-person stream of consciousness narrative' whose 'analysis emerges through its ordering: in the way it juxtaposes, compares, and connects the different viewpoints it represents' (pp. 187, xvi). 'Fashioned from multiple viewpoints,' her book affirms the perspectival nature of 'reality' and 'enables an unusually high degree of insight into the totality of a collective experience' (p. 195). It is ordered by a consonant feminist logic: the imposition of 'a pattern of detail in which everything was important' rather than 'a particular angle of vision, line of interpretation, or single theory' (p. 188). And it demands more participation by providing readers with much detail and many viewpoints. It invites them to interpret and decide. Of course, *The Mirror Dance* violates expectations. By 'making a world seem compelling, actual, rich' (p. 180), it frustrates those who are used to abstract models of knowledge that supply them with interpretations and conclusions, but it engages readers, subjects, and investigator in the process of making knowledge.

Counterpoised, then, to the traditional literary subject and methods are the feminist ones: the framing of literature as discrete, objectified entities versus the framing of gender ideologies and culture (including literature) as a dynamic system; the use of methods that abstract and universalize details versus the use of methods that approximate a system; and a normatively imposed awareness versus self-reflexive, collectively attained ones.

An epistemology, I said earlier, consists of assumptions that knowers make about the entities and processes in a domain of study, the relations that obtain among them, and the proper methods for investigating them. Although I alluded to feminist assumptions in the preceding discussion, I shall summarize them here. The entities that populate feminist literary study are sex/gender ideas, people who express them, their effects, their media, and we who study them. Whereas the entities in the traditional domain are assumed to be bounded, abstractable, and often autonomous, those in the feminist domain are assumed to be interactive as a system and demarcated by the decision of inquirers. The methods of traditional literary study include differential, integral, principled, causal, inferential, and analogical thinking; they are employed to classify, interpret, and judge literary works. The methods of feminist literary study include specifying, patterning, and approximating systems that include us; they are employed to discover and change the gendered literary-cultural system. While traditional literary critics as agents fade from the domain of study, leaving their stances like plumes of smoke trailing behind them, feminist literary critics stand forth in a domain of our making, revealing our perspectivity – and theirs.

Feminist epistemology is based on the assumption that we as diverse knowers must insert ourselves and our perspectives into the domain of study and become, self-reflexively, part of the investigation. These perspectives are the requisite of our knowledge. *Perspective* is the effect of relative position and distance; visually it means that the configuration seen varies with the observers' standpoints. Through the circumstances of life, people acquire specific feelings, ideas, and values that situate them relative to *any* subject. Because their situations differ, their perspectives diverge. The circumstances that diversify perspectives are: (1) our affiliations with a sex, race, class, affectional preference, and other cultural circumstances; (2) our personal histories; (3) our technical approaches to inquiry; and (4) our self-reflexivity or awareness of the ways these factors organize existence.

Feminists have shown that we all stand in different relationships to the subjects of science and taste, an assumption I call *perspectivity*, as distinct from objectivity, an allegedly unsituated stance, and uniformity, a normatively imposed one. Unlike these, perspectivity requires us to include people with diverse perspectives, to learn a repertoire of cultural as well as technical perspectives, and to make knowledge collectively. Thus, perspectivity would restructure inquiry by institutionalizing a diversity grounded in cultural, personal, technical, and self-reflexive variables; by using viewpoints as a chief methodology; and by composing manifold knowledge. Reflecting on multiple stances, we need to develop *perspectivism*, a feminist philosophy that counters objectivism, which privileges objects, and subjectivism, which privileges subjects. Perspectivism would bring together, in processes of knowing, the personal and cultural, subjective and objective – replacing dichotomies with a systemic understanding of how and what we see. It would explain how we affiliate culturally, acquire a self-centered perspective, experience the perspectives of others, and deploy multiple perspectives in inquiry. It would show that perspectivity arises from and defines knowers qualified (in both senses of the word) by their experiences, self-reflection, and contingent standpoints.

When we are diverse knowers who insert our agencies and perspectives into literary study, then knowing becomes a collective endeavor grounded in experience, experience gains acceptance as evidence, and knowledge is transformed from an authoritative, freestanding construct to a common, conditional formulation.[54] The criteria for what counts as knowledge change too. 'Truth' no longer functions in the traditional senses of gauging the universality and predictability of knowledge, nor does 'verisimilitude' demand accuracy in representing 'reality'. Instead, equity and epistemic awareness are the standards for self-conscious, other-conscious, relational ways of knowing. Equity pronounces the inadequacy of knowledge that denigrates or excludes the experiences, perspectives, and indeed persons of most of the human race; it prompts us to open the domain of literary study. Epistemic awareness pronounces the inadequacy of critics who avow neutrality and technical virtuosity; it prompts us to enter the domain of literary study and study ourselves. There we place a premium on how much we see not of objects but of ourselves and others as knowers with feelings, ideas, and values.

In league

I have been arguing that feminist literary criticisms share a subject, subject matters, methods of reasoning, and epistemology that differ from those of traditional ones. Now I propose that feminist literary criticisms and the feminist criticisms proceeding throughout the humanities, social sciences, and natural sciences constitute a single inquiry. In league with the developing criticisms of race, class, and affectional preference, they promise a new research tradition.

It is no coincidence that in discussing feminist literary criticisms I cited the ideas of feminists working in other fields. Feminist literary critics, I said, study ideas about sex and gender that people express in literary and critical media. If this sounds suspiciously like what feminist political scientists educe from Lockean politics, what feminist art historians expose in the conventions of nude painting, what feminist psychologists unfold in human development, and what feminist biologists substantiate in objective methodology, it is. The differences among us are mostly medium.

Focusing on ideas about sex/gender, feminists treat literature, political systems, artworks, human development, and scientific methodologies as material somewhat like Lévi-Strauss's *bricolage*, a concept that Edward Wasiolek adapts to literary study. A culture's elaborate rituals of food preparation or burial, Wasiolek explains, do not necessarily indicate a concern with food or burial as such but may simply be 'the matter at hand with which the tribe had to work in building structures to signify other things', such as 'its social, religious, and cultural differentiations'[55] – including those of sex/gender. Just so, the elements of literature can be considered *bricolage*, as can the details of one story or another. In a gendered culture, people express sex/gender ideas in *bricolage*. With elaboration and justification these ideas become a system, an ideology that organizes social existence by specifying the behaviors, duties, powers, and relations of the sexes; their opportunities for education, labor, and pleasure; and their possession of material goods. The object of feminist criticisms is to reveal, not additionally create, the sex/gender ideologies expressed in cultural *bricolage*.

Feminist criticisms in all fields, then, have the same subject matters except the fourth one, the media of expression. Feminist literary critics study the manifestations of sex/gender ideas in literature and criticism. Feminist psychologists treat them in psychic structures and processes. Feminist anthropologists notice them in cultural practices. Feminist political scientists seek them in political systems. Feminist linguists find them in forms and contexts of communication. Feminist historians of science reveal them in subjects, methods, and concepts of research.

Moreover, feminists in all fields perform the tasks that occupy feminist literary critics. First, they gather data on women and sex/gender issues: they discover and read women writers; observe female development; report on female cultural practices; review the status of women in political systems; record female speech; and trace sex/gender in scientific paradigms. Next, they explore a common subject as it is expressed in the particular media they treat: literary and critical works; cognitive and emotional processes; social relations, production, and ritual; models of the individual, family, and state; patterns of gender marking, pejoration, and interruption; evolutionary models and endocrinological research.

Third, they use their data to challenge the organizing concepts of their disciplines for inadequately treating women, neglecting the significance of sex/gender ideologies, and reifying the sex/gender categories that order the daily lives of traditional knowers. Under attack in the disciplines are the literary constructs of canon, history, curriculum, authorship, reading, and scholarship/criticism; the developmental goal of autonomy and the intrapsychic assumption of individualism; the concept that female is to male as nature is to culture; the distinction of public and private and the qualifications for political participation; models of language competence and the notion of a masculine generic; the stance of objectivity, the evolutionary concepts of scarcity and competition, and the dichotomy of physiology and environment. Finally, feminists in all fields criticize traditional methodologies for radical disjunction, objectification, dichot-omization, hierarchical arrangement, faulty universalization, and efface-ment of important qualities.[56]

The feminist criticisms proceeding in these traditional disciplines and in women's studies constitute a single inquiry. The story they are piecing together is how the sex/gender system organizes every aspect of our lives, why, and what we might do to change this unwholesome situation. In an essay aptly titled 'Why has the sex/gender system become visible only now?' Sandra Harding asserts: 'Like racism and classism, the sex/gender system appears to limit and create opportunities within which are constructed the social practices of daily life, the characteristics of social institutions, and all of our patterns of thought. Not only are the "macro" social institutions the way they are in the vast majority of societies because the sex/gender system is interacting with other organic [fundamental] variables to structure them that way, but also the very existence and design of characteristics of daily life to which sex and/or gender seemed irrelevant now appear suffused with sex/gender.'[57] Thus, she concludes, 'what feminist research has been producing during the last decade is the "discovery" of the sex/gender system as an organic [fundamental] social variable which has been functioning in varying intensities and forms throughout most of recorded history' (p. 314). The reason this discovery occurs now, Harding ventures, is that we are in the midst of a paradigm shift. We see the sex/gender system because we belong to a social movement that aims to redistribute power and privilege and because we find that available theories fail to account for the problems that concern us.

Us, as black, lesbian, and working-class feminists remind us, is often appropriated by white, heterosexual, middle-class feminists to generalize their experiences to all women. Women's cultural affiliations in the United States or anywhere else are not the same, and these affiliations, as they intersect sex/gender, create diverse identities, perspectives, and inquiries.

Black feminist perspectives are grounded in experiences of sex and race often unshared, respectively, by black men and white women. Bell Hooks writes in *Ain't I A Woman: Black Women and Feminism* that she can understand 'black female experience and our relationship to society as a whole only by examining both the politics of racism and sexism from a feminist perspective'. Accordingly, she devotes her book to such topics as 'the black woman during slavery, the devaluation of black womanhood, black male sexism, racism within the recent feminist movement, and the black woman's involvement with feminism'.[58] Relating black women's history to black history and feminist history, she emphasizes divergent experiences of race and sex – for instance, rape and compulsory breeding were not rampantly inflicted upon black men nor physical brutality and unceasing labor on white women. However victimized they might be, Hooks points out, both white women and black men have oppressed black women.

'The structures of race and class', Bonnie Thornton Dill remarks, 'generate important economic, ideological, and experiential cleavages among women' which 'lead to differences in perception of self and their place in society'.[59] Education is one such cleavage. Gloria T. Hull and Barbara Smith, editors of *But Some of Us Are Brave: Black Women's Studies*, write that since being brought 'enslaved to this continent, we have been kept separated in every way possible from recognized intellectual work. Our legacy as chattel, as sexual slaves as well as forced laborers, would adequately explain why most Black women are, to this day, far away from the centers of academic power.'[60] The educational deprivations suffered by white women do not include living in a society where their illiteracy was decreed by law and where their access to quality education is still severely curtailed.

The unique experiences and perspectives of black women, along with the racism of a white academy, mandate black feminist inquiry. For example, Dill notes that 'the insistence of radical feminists upon the historical priority, universality, and overriding importance of patriarchy in effect . . . places one's womanhood over and above one's race' (p. 136), a condition of inquiry insupportable by black female experience. Black feminists have established black women's studies to gather data on black women's lives, analyze the braided issues of racism, classism, and sexism, and develop courses. As such, it is one of the new inquiries into race and ethnicity founded by Hispanic, Native American, Third World, and other women.

Until recently heterosexuality and lesbianism were not considered identities, let alone choices.[61] Even now the penalties for departing from heterosexuality are harsh. Lillian Faderman's *Surpassing the Love of Men: Romantic Friendship and Love Between Women from the Renaissance to the Present* documents the long, tortuous history of homophobia, love between women, and the rise of lesbian feminism. In 1975 when the *Purple September* staff encouraged feminists to '*critically assess the normative status of heterosexuality*',[62] the point of view presented in their essay - that women should be free to choose heterosexuality, lesbianism, or bisexuality for themselves - was uncommon. Since that time many feminists have come to believe that lesbianism represents the only viable personal and political alternative.

Lesbian feminists study lesbian lives and works that were censored and still are targets of homophobic 'retribution'. Margaret Cruikshank, the editor of *Lesbian Studies Present and Future*, wonders at having arrived at a time 'when *Matrices: A Lesbian-Feminist Research Letter* lists hundreds of subscribers from several countries; when lesbians of color are publishing numerous books and articles; and when the current edition of

The Lesbian in Literature contains more than seven thousand entries.' Yet 'the concept of "lesbian studies" is still fairly new' and includes both 'grassroots cultural work' and 'the more formally organized *courses* on lesbians which now exist in a few women's studies programs and in women's centers'.[63]

In 1980 when Karen Keener wrote 'Out of the archives and into the academy: opportunities for research and publication in lesbian literature', no taxonomy was on hand except chronology and degree of openness. What distinguishes lesbian literature, she surmises, is not only its subject matter but also its perspectives: 'Like all writers, women writers whose affectional preferences are for women think, feel, and view the world in ways that transcend explicit sexuality. To define our literature in fully human rather than narrowly sexual terms will require describing a lesbian epistemology - an aesthetic sense and a world view that inform the works of lesbian writers' (p. 73). Making the same distinction between subject matter and perspectives, Cruikshank says, 'Usually "lesbian studies" means studies *about* us, but certain books and essays' - for example, Adrienne Rich's *Of Woman Born*, Mary Daly's *Gyn/Ecology*, and Audre Lorde's *Cancer Journals* - 'have so pronounced a lesbian perspective that they can be considered a part of lesbian studies even though they focus on other subjects' (p. x).[64]

A lesbian feminist perspective situates centrally what is marginal to or absent from the heterosexual version of reality: the range of emotional, sexual, and social identifications of women with each other. By denying and abhorring these relations, heterosexual perspectives evince fear and hatred of homosexuality (homophobia), a belief that heterosexuality is superior to homosexuality (heterosexism), and heterocentric vision. In a typical course, Coralyn Fontaine uses three of these concepts to introduce a lesbian feminist perspective: patriarchy, heterosexism, and woman identification.[65] To Marilyn Frye, women's studies likewise appears stubbornly heterosexual: it gives students 'almost entirely heterosexual women's literature, the history of heterosexual women, and analysis of the roles of heterosexual women in work, business, the arts, and heterosexual domestic life'.[66]

While black and lesbian feminists establish inquiries of their own, class feminist critics (like feminist literary critics) are strung between two inquiries - the well-developed marxist analyses of class and the feminist analyses of sex/gender. The resulting dilemmas have been discussed in numerous publications. As Heidi Hartmann notes in her aptly titled essay, 'The unhappy marriage of marxism and feminism: towards a more progressive union', which poses the problem explored in *Women and Revolution*, 'The "marriage" of marxism and feminism has been like the marriage of husband and wife depicted in English common law: marxism and feminism are one, and that one is marxism. Recent attempts to integrate marxism and feminism are unsatisfactory to us as feminists because they subsume the feminist struggle into the "larger" struggle against capital. To continue our simile further, either we need a healthier marriage or we need a divorce.'[67]

Many contributors to this volume favor adapting marxist methods and concepts to feminist issues. Iris Young, for instance, rejects the use of 'dual systems theory', an approach based on the premise that gender relations under patriarchy and economic relations under capitalism are distinct systems that reinforce one another, for a socialist feminism that analyzes gender (pp. 43-69). Emily Hicks doubts the possibility of a rapprochement with marxism, pointing out that 'the relationships between class, race, and sex are what invalidate the universality' of marxist categories. 'Production, reproduction, sexuality, and childrearing differ among classes, racial groups, heterosexuals, and homosexuals' (p. 224). Instead of a feminist analysis of class, she recommends developing an analysis based on nonsynchrony: 'By nonsynchrony I mean the concept that individuals (or groups), in their relation to their economic and political system, do not share similar consciousness of the system or similar needs within it at the same point in time' (p. 221).

The problems of applying marxist concepts to literary representations of race and gender may be seen in Susan Willis's 'Eruptions of funk: historicizing Toni Morrison'. The essay, which examines Morrison's use of funk to disrupt the alienation experienced by her characters during transitional moments in black American history, loses in race and gender analysis what it gains in class analysis. Meanwhile, literatures by and for women of the working classes elude feminist scholars. Often, Paul Lauter reminds us in 'Working-class women's literature: an introduction to study', they exist in oral forms: chronicles, sagas, fictions, poems, ballads, lamentations.[68] Many that appeared in written or printed forms were ephemerae: cheap papers used to wrap pies, stuff shoes, or burn in stoves. Disposable and devalued art, they are seldom preserved in archives, bibliographies, anthologies, and reprints.

Partial in both senses of the word, these criticisms do not now share a common subject, but investigate variously ideas about sex/gender, about race, about class, about affectional preference. As separate inquiries conducted primarily by those who have personal and political stakes in them, they provide us with the matter that is missing from traditional knowledge and with critiques of categorical thinking. At the same time, their integration is necessary for the reconstitution of knowledge. Annette Kolodny makes an eloquent plea in 'The integrity of memory: creating a new literary history of the United States' for wholeness and honesty. Selective exclusion, she argues, has maintained an illusion of unity in traditional histories. But the new literature and scholarship will not be integrated if they are bracketed off under rubrics of 'women writers' and 'minority voices'. Instead gender, race, class, and other cultural differentia must be incorporated through principles of cultural diversity and contextualization which allow us to 'compose a literary history that recovers the integrity of memory'.[69] In league, then, these criticisms promise a new research tradition based on perspectivity – the opening of domains of knowledge and the use of multiple perspectives as the chief methodology in inquiry.

But what are the choices for a traditional literary critic now? Whether he continues to do traditional criticism or enlarges his repertoire is of less consequence, I think, than his response to feminist literary critics. If he fears that the feminist program for knowledge will diminish his opportunities, he may, in league with colleagues, impede the access of feminist scholarship to publication and of feminist scholars to academic institutions. He will not, after all, have to confront the perspectives if he bars the people who have them. Such actions, it is no secret, are taken with distressing frequency against women, feminists, and others who challenge accepted modes. However, if he believes that the feminist program for knowledge will create opportunities for whoever supports it, he might in league with feminists open the domains of knowledge to perspectives and people of every affiliation. The choice, I expect, will not be made by him alone.

Each feminist literary critic has choices too. She can continue to do literary criticism as it has been done but with a veneer of feminist civility. Or she can try to be both a traditional literary critic and a feminist critic, juggling the different subjects, methods, and epistemologies of her two endeavors. Or she can focus on sex/gender ideas in their various literary, critical, and cultural manifestations. But she will, I predict, eventually have to make a choice. Failing to decide on a theoretical system, she will be strung intolerably between fundamentally incompatible inquiries, a traditional one into literature and a feminist one into sex/gender ideas, too consumed by contradiction to advance the work of either. If feminist reconciliation with the dominant male research tradition is improbable and battle wasteful, our focus on sex/gender ideas does not necessarily isolate us in the intellectual universe. We can choose not to confront or dismiss the tradition but to transform it into one of our own making. Speaking for myself, it is by understanding this tradition and the ideologies that order it that I hope, together with others, to reconstitute literary study without the inhumanities that organize it now.

NOTES

I am grateful to Austin M. Wright for a generous initiation into theory and to Michael Hancher, Joan E. Hartman, Annette Kolodny, Susan Léger, James J. Sosnoski, and Mary Trouille for their comments on earlier versions of this essay.

The essay itself is reprinted from *New Literary History* 19 (Autumn 1987) by kind permission.

1   According to scholarly convention, an author uses *we* when he wants to encourage his readers to affiliate with his ideas. I use *we* somewhat differently to denote my affiliation with other feminists on the subjects treated in this essay. I use *I* and *they* to dissent from their views, suggest their originality, or advance my ideas. While feminist readers may join the *we*, non-feminist readers may be jarred by it. The jarring effect is evidence, I think, in favor of my hypothesis that our cultural affiliations and the perspectives they shape predispose us in literary theory and practice.

2   Jehlen 1981: 577.

3   Rosenfelt 1984: 173.

4   DuBois et al. 1985.

5   Pratt 1981: 7; also Kolodny 1975b: 89.

6   Kristeva 1981: 19-20; and Cixous 1981: 45, 49-51. Although French feminists worry about the contamination of all cultural forms, they adapt Lacanian and other theories. Language and silence are also discussed by Jacobus 1981: 207-22; and Gubar 1981: 243-63.

7   For symptoms of divided allegiances, see the remarks of Elaine Showalter on women's and men's literatures, Sue Warrick Doederlein and Patrocinio Schweickart on aesthetic and political interests, and Lawrence Lipking on relative and absolute stances, all in 'Comments on Jehlen's "Archimedes and the paradox of feminist criticism" ', *Signs*, 8, No. 1 (Autumn 1982): 160-76.

8   Accounts of subject matters and methods of reasoning appear in R. S. Crane, 'Introduction', in Crane et al. 1952: 6-8; Richard McKeon, 'The philosophical bases of art and criticism', in ibid.: 463-548; and Wright 1982: 26-8. I am indebted to McKeon for the title of this essay.

9   Laudan 1977: 81; author's italics. Laudan says '*a research tradition is a set of assumptions*' (p. 81). I believe the assumptions structure the domain of knowledge and the research conducted in it.

10 Meyer 1974: 181; hereafter cited in text. Meyer's assumptions are what Stephen Toulmin calls modern ones as distinct from the post-modern ones that scientists interpret and influence the objects they study. Toulmin believes that scientists and humanists employ diverse techniques, modes of analysis, and views of their subject. But when they bring these 'alternative investigative postures' to bear on inquiry, the 'variety of parallel interpretations' they produce 'does not reflect the personal preferences or characteristics' of these individuals, such as 'their personalities, political views, or cultural backgrounds', Toulmin 1982: 102. Keller 1985 is an important critique of modern and post-modern assumptions.

11 This discussion is an abbreviated portion of a work-in-progress, *The Philosophical Bases of Feminist Literary Criticisms* (forthcoming from Oxford University Press). For a fuller account of the stances in scientific and literary inquiry, see Messer-Davidow 1985: 8-24.

12 Showalter 1981: 184-5; and 1977: 12.

13 Karen Keener, 'Out of the archives and into the academy: opportunities for research and publication in lesbian literature', in Hartman and Messer-Davidow 1982: 71-86; hereafter cited in text. Stimpson 1981: 363-79.

14 Walker 1974: 64-70. B. Smith 1977: 25-32. Bethel and Smith 1979: 11-15; B. Smith 1979: 123-7; and Shockley 1979: 133-42. Erlene Stetson, 'Black women in and out of print', in Hartman and Messer-Davidow 1982: 87-90. Margaret Walker, 'On being female, black, and free', in Sternburg 1980: 95-106.

15 For studies, see Christian 1985: chs. 6, 8, 12, and Evans 1984. Some anthologies are *Black-Eyed Susans: Classic Stories By and About Black Women*, ed. Mary Helen Washington (Garden City, N.Y., 1975); *Midnight Birds: Stories of Contemporary Black Women Writers*, ed. Mary Helen Washington (Garden City, N.Y., 1980); *Black Sister: Poetry by Black American Women, 1746-1980*, ed. Erlene Stetson (Bloomington, Ind., 1981); and *Home Girls: A Black Feminist Anthology*, ed. Barbara Smith (New York, 1983). In addition, several novels by black women writers have been reprinted.

16 Robinson 1971: 879; repr. in Robinson 1978, along with other essays on this subject. See also Fetterley 1978: xi, xiii.

17 Garner et al. 1985 contains essays exemplifying this approach. The titles for the three parts of the book - 'Feminists on Freud', 'Rereading patriarchal texts', and 'Women rewriting woman' - focus on women as readers and as writers, the only two subject matters identified in Elaine Showalter's influential essay 'Feminist criticism in the wilderness' (1981).

18 Pratt 1981: 6, 168. See also Ostriker 1982: 68-90.

19 See Harris 1982; Christian 1985: esp. chs. 1, 2, 3, 5, 9, 15, 17; and Christian 1980.

20 Besides Kristeva and Cixous (see n. 6), see Husserl-Kapit 1975: 425-6, 428, 430; and Xavière Gauthier's interview with Julia Kristeva, 'Oscillation du "pouvoir" au "refus"'; Chantal Chawaf, 'La chair linguistique'; and Madeleine Gagnon, 'Corps I', all in Marks and de Courtivron 1980: 165-7, 177-8, 179-80. Some French feminists published in *New French Feminisms* and the journal *Feminist Issues* take audience-centered approaches common to socialist and marxist criticisms. For objections to *l'écriture féminine*, in part on an epistemological basis, see Jones 1981: 246-63; Wenzel 1981: 264-87; and Burke 1981: 288-306.

21 Dorin Schumacher, 'Subjectivities: a theory of the critical process', in Donovan 1975: 1-28; hereafter cited in text. Kolodny 1980: 10-14.

22 That Anthony Burgess objects to Jane Austen's novels because he ' "can gain no pleasure from serious reading . . . that lacks a strong male thrust" ' is one example offered by Ellmann 1968 (p. 23). Critics, she says, treat 'books by women . . . as though they themselves were women, and criticism embarks, at its happiest, upon an intellectual measuring of busts and hips' (p. 29). For feminist versions, see the French feminist works cited in nn. 6, 20, and radical feminist criticisms in the tradition of Daly 1978.

23 For welcome attention to formal conventions, see Rogers 1982: 85-92 (on lyrics); Nussbaum 1984; Woodbridge 1984; and Ferguson 1985: 27-32 (on polemics).

24 Debates about judgment include Pratt 1971: 436-45; Robinson 1971: 879-89; Cheri Register, 'American feminist literary criticism: a bibliographical introduction', in Donovan 1975: 1-28; Kolodny 1975b: 75-92; Morgan 1976: 807-16, hereafter cited in text; Kolodny 1976: 821-32; Donovan 1977: 605-8.

25 Booth 1977: 411; repr. in Booth 1979: 214.

26 Laudan discusses the significance of an ontology in selecting or omitting entities for research (1977: 79-80, 86).

27 MacKinnon 1982: 537; hereafter cited in text.

28 Peggy Kamuf criticizes this sort of literary sex differentiation in 'Writing like a woman', in McConnell-Ginet et al. 1980: 284-99. The best book on the subject is Mary Ellmann's witty *Thinking About Women* (1968).

29 Abel et al. 1983: 4.

30 Deborah S. Rosenfelt, 'The politics of bibliography: women's studies and the literary canon', in Hartman and Messer-Davidow 1982: 11-35; and Lauter 1983: 435-63.

31 Adam Smith, *The Theory of Moral Sentiments*, ed. Raphael and Macfie, 1976 I. 19.

32 Fraya Katz-Stoker, 'The other criticism: feminism vs. formalism', in Cornillon 1973: 316.

33 Kuhn 1963: 48-9.

34 E. D. Hirsch, Jr. discusses conceptions of *literature* in Hirsch 1974: 446-57 and in Hirsch 1976: 130-5. Defensive critics include Cleanth Brooks (1947: 215-18); René Wellek and Austin Warren (1956: 16-19, 73-4, 80, 93, 109, 123-4); and Northrop Frye (1969: 6-7). In a chapter entitled 'The mode of existence of a literary work', Wellek and Warren repudiate the interdependence of literature and other things, of literary study and other studies, and define the work as 'an object of knowledge *sui generis* which has a special ontological status' (p. 156). I believe notions of the radical autonomy, not the particularity, of works are untenable.

35 Representative works are: *Genes and Gender I*, ed. Ethel Tobach and Betty Rosoff (New York, 1978); *Genes and Gender II*, ed. Ruth Hubbard and Marian Lowe (New York, 1979); *Genes and Gender III*, ed. Ethel Tobach and Betty Rosoff (New York, 1980); and *Genes and Gender IV*, ed. Myra Fooden, Susan Gordon, and Betty Hugley (New York, 1983); Lambert 1978: 97-117; Lowe 1978: 118-25; Hubbard et al. 1979; Unger 1979; Vance 1980: 129-43; Baker 1980: 80-96; Shields 1982: 769-97; Longino and Doell 1983: 206-27; Lowe and Hubbard 1983; Bleier 1984; Alper 1985: 7-37.

36 Heilbrun, 1982: 808.

37 Money and Ehrhardt 1972.
38 In other words, gender (cultural categories) is constructed, as feminist research in all fields and especially in anthropology shows. Sex (biological categories) is constructed, as the literature in n. 35 suggests. Sexuality (erotic categories) is constructed; see, e.g., Snitow et al. 1983 and Bleier 'Sexuality, ideology and patriarchy', in Bleier 1984: 162-92.
39 Sedgwick 1985: 1. Poovey 1984. Woodbridge 1984.
40 See, e.g., Bleich 1978; Fish 1980; and McGann 1981: 269-88. Jean Kennard discusses their inadequacies (1981: 69-88).
41 Gilbert and Gubar 1979: 187-8; hereafter cited in text.
42 E.g., Jaggar 1983 analyzes four (liberal, radical, marxist, and socialist) feminist philosophies of human nature comparatively, while Eisenstein 1981 analyzes one (liberal) historically.
43 Kolodny 1975a, and 1984. Newton 1984: 557-75.
44 Olson 1966: 209.
45 Keller 1982: 601; this essay has been reprinted in a different version in Keller 1985.
46 Chodorow 1981: 502.
47 Washington 1981: 10-11. McDowell 1980: 145.
48 Tompkins 1985: 33, hereafter cited in text.
49 In *Reflections on Gender and Science*, Keller (1985) explains the metaphors of erotic domination by aligning early childhood development, cognitive modes, and conceptions of science. She believes that the excessive separation and control experienced by males who acquire gender identity in families where mothers mother structures their stance of objectivity and their conception of science.
50 Rich 1980: 631-60; hereafter cited in text. This essay is widely reprinted.
51 Such analyses are suggested in Elly Bulkin, 'An interchange on feminist criticism: on "Dancing through the minefield",' *Feminist Studies*, 8, no. 3 (Fall 1982), 646-50; Atkinson 1982: 245-7; Avery 1979; McConnell-Ginet 'Linguistics and the feminist challenge', in McConnell-Ginet et al. 1980: 3-25; and Keller 1985: 168-72.
52 Bleier 1982: 726.
53 Krieger 1983: 187; hereafter cited in text.
54 We have few models of collectively made knowledge. For each of the fifteen authors in *Black Women Writers (1950-80): A Critical Evaluation* (Evans 1980) there are a bio/bibliography, two essays by literary critics, and a first-person account by the author herself. The five authors of *Feminist Scholarship: Kindling in the Groves of Academe* (Donovan 1975) wrote the entire book jointly rather than parceling out the sections. Susan Krieger's *The Mirror Dance* (1983) presents both the author and the subjects speaking for themselves.
55 Wasiolek 1982: 632-33.
56 See, e.g., Unger 1983: 9-32; Naomi Scheman, 'Individualism and the objects of psychology', in Harding and Hintikka 1983: 225-44; Sherry B. Ortner 'Is female to male as nature is to culture?', in Rosaldo and Lamphere 1974: 67-87; MacCormack and Strathern 1981; Elizabeth V. Spelman, 'Aristotle and the politicization of the soul', in Harding and Hintikka 1983: 17-30; Okin 1979, esp. 73-96; McConnell-Ginet et al. 1980; Keller 1985; Marian Lowe, 'The dialectics of biology and culture', in Lowe and Hubbard 1983: 39-62; Longino and Doell 1983.

57 Sandra Harding, 'Why has the sex/gender system become visible only now?', in Harding and Hintikka 1983: 312; hereafter cited in text.
58 Hooks 1981: 13. Also see Davis 1981.
59 Dill 1983: 138; hereafter cited in text.
60 Hull et al. 1982: xviii.
61 For two views, see Zimmerman 1984: 663-82 and Krieger 1982: 91-108.
62 The *Purple September* staff, 'The normative status of heterosexuality', in Myron and Bunch 1975: 82; authors' emphasis. Faderman 1981.
63 Cruikshank 1982: ix; hereafter cited in text.
64 See also Zimmerman 1981: 451-75; Daly 1978; Rich 1976; Lorde 1980.
65 Coralyn Fontaine, 'Teaching the psychology of women: a lesbian-feminist perspective', in Cruikshank 1982: 79.
66 Marilyn Frye, 'A lesbian perspective on women's studies', in Cruikshank 1982: 195. See also M. Frye 1983.
67 Heidi Hartmann, 'The unhappy marriage of marxism and feminism: towards a more progressive union', in Sargent 1981: 2; see also Iris Young, 'Beyond the unhappy marriage: a critique of the dual systems theory', ibid.: 43-69, and Emily Hicks, 'Cultural marxism: nonsynchrony and feminist practice', ibid.: 219-37, both hereafter cited in text. For hopeful accounts of the union, see Eisenstein 1979. Eisenstein views marxist analysis as the thesis, radical feminist analysis as the antithesis, and socialist feminist analysis as the synthesis (pp. 5-40).
68 Susan Willis, 'Eruptions of funk: historicizing Toni Morrison', in Gates 1984: 243-83; and Paul Lauter, 'Working-class women's literature: an introduction to study', in Hartman and Messer-Davidow 1982: 109-34, with an extensive bibliography.
69 Kolodny 1985: 300.

REFERENCES

Abel, Elizabeth, Hirsch, Marianne, and Langland, Elizabeth (eds) 1983. *The Voyage In: Fictions of Female Development*. Hanover, NH: University Press of New England.
Alper, Joseph S. 1985. 'Sex differences in brain asymmetry: a critical analysis'. *Feminist Studies* 11, 1 (Spring): 7-37.
Atkinson, Jane Monnig 1982. 'Review essay: anthropology', *Signs* 8, 2 (Winter): 236-58.
Avery, Donna Mae 1979. *Critical Events Shaping Women's Identity: A Handbook for the Helping Professions*. Unpublished monograph. Chicago: Chicago State University.
Baker, Susan 1980. 'Review essay: biological influences on human sex and gender', *Signs* 6, 1 (Autumn): 80-96.
Bethel, Lorraine and Smith, Barbara 1979. 'Introduction', *Conditions Five: The Black Women's Issue*: 11-15.
Bleich, David 1978. *Subjective Criticism*. Baltimore: Johns Hopkins University Press.
Bleier, Ruth 1982. 'Comment on Haraway's "In the Beginning Was the Word": the genesis of biological theory', *Signs* 7, 3 (Spring): 725-7.
Bleier, Ruth 1984. *Science and Gender*. New York: Pergamon Press.
Booth, Wayne 1977. ' "Preserving the Exemplar": or, How not to dig our own graves', *Critical Inquiry* 3, 3 (Spring): 407-23.

Booth, Wayne 1979. *Critical Understanding: The Powers and Limits of Pluralism*. Chicago: University of Chicago Press.

Brooks, Cleanth 1947. *The Well Wrought Urn*. Harvest edn. New York: Harcourt, Brace and World.

Burke, Carolyn 1981. 'Irigaray through the looking glass', *Feminist Studies* 7, 2 (Summer): 288-306.

Chodorow, Nancy 1981. 'Reply', in 'On *The Reproduction of Mothering*: a methodological debate', *Signs* 6, 3 (Spring): 500-14.

Christian, Barbara 1980. *Black Women Novelists: The Development of a Tradition 1892-1976*. Westport, CT: Greenwood Press.

Christian, Barbara 1985. *Black Feminist Criticism: Perspectives on Black Feminist Writers*. New York: Pergamon Press.

Cixous, Hélène 1981. 'Castration or decapitation?', trans. Annette Kuhn, *Signs* 7, 1 (Autumn): 41-55.

Cornillon, Susan Koppelman (ed.) 1973. *Images of Women in Fiction*. Bowling Green: Bowling Green University Popular Press (rev. edn).

Crane, R. S. et al. (eds) 1952. *Critics and Criticism Ancient and Modern*. Chicago: University of Chicago Press.

Cruikshank, Margaret (ed.) 1982. *Lesbian Studies Present and Future*. Old Westbury: Feminist Press.

Daly, Mary 1978. *Gyn/Ecology: The Metaethics of Radical Feminism*. Boston: Beacon Press.

Davis, Angela Y. 1981. *Women, Race and Class*. New York: Random House.

Dill, Bonnie Thornton 1983. 'Race, class, and gender: prospects for an all-inclusive sisterhood', *Feminist Studies* 9, 1 (Spring): 131-50.

Donovan, Josephine (ed.) 1975. *Feminist Literary Criticism: Explorations in Theory*. Lexington: University Press of Kentucky.

Donovan, Josephine 1977. 'Feminism and aesthetics', *Critical Inquiry* 3, 3 (Spring): 605-8.

DuBois, Ellen Carol, Kelly, Gail Paradise, Kennedy, Elizabeth Lapovsky, Korsmeyer, Carolyn W. and Robinson, Lillian S. 1985. *Feminist Scholarship: Kindling in the Groves of Academe*. Urbana: University of Illinois Press.

Eisenstein, Zillah (ed.) 1979. *Capitalist Patriarchy and the Case for Socialist Feminism*. New York: Monthly Review Press.

Eisenstein, Zillah 1981. *The Radical Future of Liberal Feminism*. New York: Longman.

Ellmann, Mary 1968. *Thinking About Women*. New York: Harcourt Brace Jovanovich.

Evans, Mari (ed.) 1980. *Black Women Writers (1950-1980): A Critical Evaluation*. Garden City, NY: Anchor/Doubleday.

Faderman, Lillian 1981. *Surpassing the Love of Men: Romantic Friendship and Love Between Women from the Renaissance to the Present*. New York: William Morrow.

Ferguson, Moira 1985. *First Feminists: British Women Writers 1578-1799*. Bloomington: Indiana University Press.

Fetterley, Judith 1978. *The Resisting Reader: A Feminist Approach to American Fiction*. Bloomington: Indiana University Press.

Fish, Stanley 1980. *Is There a Text In This Class? The Authority of Interpretive Communities*. Cambridge: Harvard University Press.

Frye, Marilyn 1983. *The Politics of Reality: Essays in Feminist Theory*. Trumansburg, NY: Crossing Press.

Frye, Northrop 1969. *Anatomy of Criticism*. New York: Atheneum.

Gardiner, Judith Kegan, Bulkin, Elly, Patterson, Rena Grasso, and Kolodny, Annette 1982. 'An interchange on feminist criticism: on "Dancing through the minefield"', *Feminist Studies* 8, 3 (Fall): 629-75.

Garner, Shirley Nelson, Kahane, Claire, and Sprengnethern, Madelon (eds) 1985. *The (M)other Tongue: Essays in Feminist Psychoanalytic Interpretation*. Ithaca: Cornell University Press.

Gates, Henry Louis Jr (ed.) 1984. *Black Literature and Literary Theory*. New York: Methuen.

Genes and Gender I-IV 1978, 1979, 1980, 1983. Various editors. New York: Gordian Press.

Gilbert, Sandra M., and Gubar, Susan 1979. *The Madwoman in the Attic: The Woman Writer and the Nineteenth-Century Literary Imagination*. New Haven: Yale University Press.

Gubar, Susan 1981. ' "The Blank Page" and the issues of female creativity', *Critical Inquiry* 8, 2 (Winter): 243-63.

Harding, Sandra, and Hintikka, Merrill B. (eds) 1983. *Discovering Reality: Feminist Perspectives on Epistemology, Metaphysics, Methodology, and Philosophy of Science*. Dordrecht: D. Reidel.

Harris, Trudier 1982. *From Mammies to Militants: Domestics in Black American Literature*. Philadelphia: Temple University Press.

Hartman, Joan E. and Messer-Davidow, Ellen (eds) 1982. *Women in Print I: Opportunities for Women's Studies Research in Language and Literature*. New York: Modern Language Association.

Heilbrun, Carolyn 1982. 'A response to *Writing and Sexual Difference*', *Critical Inquiry* 8, 4 (Summer): 805-11.

Hirsch, E. D., Jr 1974. ' "Intrinsic" Criticism', *College English* 36, 4 (December): 446-57.

Hirsch, E. D., Jr 1976. *The Aims of Interpretation*. Chicago: University of Chicago Press.

Hooks, Bell 1981. *Ain't I A Woman: Black Women and Feminism*. Boston: South End Press.

Hubbard, Ruth, Henifin, Mary Sue, and Fried, Barbara (eds) 1979. *Women Look at Biology Looking at Women: A Collection of Feminist Critiques*. Boston: G. K. Hall; Cambridge: Schenkman.

Hull, Gloria T., Scott, Patricia Bell, and Smith, Barbara (eds) 1982. *All the Women Are White, All the Blacks Are Men, But Some of Us are Brave: Black Women's Studies*. Old Westbury: Feminist Press.

Husserl-Kapit, Susan 1975. 'An interview with Marguerite Duras', *Signs* 1, 2 (Winter): 423-34.

Jacobus, Mary 1981. 'The question of language: men of maxims and *The Mill on the Floss*', *Critical Inquiry* 8, 2 (Winter): 207-22.

Jaggar, Alison M. 1983. *Feminist Politics and Human Nature*. Totowa, NJ: Rowman and Allanheld.

Jehlen, Myra 1981. 'Archimedes and the paradox of feminist criticism', *Signs* 6, 4 (Summer): 575-601.

Jones, Ann Rosalind 1981. 'Writing the body: toward an understanding of *l'écriture féminine*', *Feminist Studies*, 7, 2 (Summer): 246-63.

Keener, Karen 1982. 'Out of the archives and into the academy: opportunities for research and publication in lesbian literature', *Women in Print I: Opportunities for Women's Studies Research in Language and Literature*, ed. Joan E. Hartman and Ellen Messer-Davidow. New York: Modern Language Association.

Keller, Evelyn Fox 1982. 'Feminism and science', *Signs* 7, 3 (Spring): 589-602.

Keller, Evelyn Fox 1985. *Reflections on Gender and Science*. New Haven: Yale University Press.

Kennard, Jean 1981. 'Convention coverage or how to read your own life', *New Literary History* 13, 1 (Autumn): 69-88.

Kolodny, Annette 1975a. *The Lay of the Land: Metaphor as Experience and History in American Life and Letters*. Chapel Hill: University of North Carolina Press.

Kolodny, Annette 1975b. 'Some notes on defining a "feminist literary criticism"', *Critical Inquiry* 2, 1 (Autumn): 75-92.

Kolodny, Annette 1976. 'The feminist as literary critic', *Critical Inquiry* 2, 4 (Summer): 821-32.

Kolodny, Annette 1980. 'Dancing through the minefield: some observations on the theory, practice, and politics of a feminist literary criticism', *Feminist Studies* 6, 1 (Spring): 1-25.

Kolodny, Annette 1984. *The Land Before Her: Fantasy and Experience of the American Frontiers, 1630-1860*. Chapel Hill: University of North Carolina Press.

Kolodny, Annette 1985. 'The integrity of memory: creating a new literary history of the United States', *American Literature* 57, 2 (May): 291-307.

Krieger, Susan 1982. 'Lesbian identity and community: recent social science literature', *Signs* 8, 1 (Autumn): 91-108.

Krieger, Susan 1983. *The Mirror Dance: Identity in a Woman's Community*. Philadelphia: Temple University Press.

Kristeva, Julia 1981. 'Women's time', trans. Alice Jardine and Harry Blake, *Signs* 7, 1 (Autumn): 13-35.

Kuhn, Alfred 1963. *The Study of Society: A Unified Approach*. Homewood, IL: Richard D. Irwin and The Dorsey Press.

Lambert, Helen H. 1978. 'Biology and equality: a perspective on sex differences', *Signs* 4, 1 (Autumn): 97-117.

Laudan, Larry 1977. *Progress and Its Problems: Toward a Theory of Scientific Growth*. Berkeley: University of California Press.

Lauter, Paul 1983. 'Race and gender in the shaping of the American literary canon: a case study from the Twenties', *Feminist Studies* 9, 3 (Fall): 435-63.

Longino, Helen, and Doell, Ruth 1983. 'Body, bias, and behavior: a comparative analysis of reasoning in two areas of biological science', *Signs* 9, 2 (Winter): 206-27.

Lorde, Audre 1980. *Cancer Journals*. Argyle, New York: Spinsters' Ink.

Lowe, Marian 1978. 'Sociobiology and sex differences', *Signs* 4, 1 (Autumn): 118-25.

Lowe, Marian and Hubbard, Ruth (eds) 1983. *Woman's Nature: Rationalizations of Inequality*. New York: Pergamon Press.

McConnell-Ginet, Sally, Borker, Ruth, and Furman, Nelly (eds) 1980. *Women and Language in Literature and Society*. New York: Praeger.

MacCormack, Carol P. and Strathern, Marilyn (eds.) 1981. *Nature, Culture and Gender*. Cambridge: Cambridge University Press.

MacKinnon, Catharine A. 1982. 'Feminism, marxism, method, and the state: an agenda for theory', *Signs* 7, 3 (Spring): 515-44.

McDowell, Deborah E. 1980. 'New directions for black feminist criticism', *Black American Literature Forum* 14, 4 (Winter): 153-59.

McGann, Jerome J. 1981. 'The text, the poem, and the problem of historical method', *New Literary History* 12, 2 (Winter): 269-88.

Marks, Elaine and de Courtivron, Isabelle (eds) 1980. *New French Feminisms*. Amherst: University of Massachusetts Press.

Messer-Davidow, Ellen 1985. 'Knowers, knowing, knowledge: feminist theory and education', *Journal of Thought* 20, 3 (Fall): 8-24.

Meyer, Leonard B. 1974. 'Concerning the sciences, the arts - AND the humanities', *Critical Inquiry* 1, 1 (September): 163-217.

Money, John, and Ehrhardt, Anke 1972. *Man and Woman/Boy and Girl*. Baltimore: Johns Hopkins University Press.

Morgan, William W. 1976. 'Feminism and literary study: a reply to Annette Kolodny', *Critical Inquiry* 2, 4 (Summer): 807-16.

Myron, Nancy, and Bunch, Charlotte (eds) 1975. *Lesbianism and the Women's Movement*. Baltimore: Diana Press.

Newton, Esther 1984. 'The mythic mannish lesbian: Radclyffe Hall and the New Woman', *Signs* 9, 4 (Summer): 557-75.

Nussbaum, Felicity A. 1984. *The Brink of All We Hate: English Satires on Women, 1660-1750*. Lexington: University Press of Kentucky.

Okin, Susan Moller 1979. *Women in Western Political Thought*. Princeton: Princeton University Press.

Olson, Elder 1966. 'The dialectical foundations of critical pluralism', *Texas Quarterly* 9, 1 (Spring): 202-30.

Ostriker, Alicia 1982. 'The thieves of language: women poets and revisionist myth-making', *Signs* 8, 1 (Autumn): 68-90.

Poovey, Mary 1984. *The Proper Lady and the Woman Writer: Ideology as Style in the Works of Mary Wollstonecraft, Mary Shelley, and Jane Austen*. Chicago: University of Chicago Press.

Pratt, Annis 1971. 'The new feminist criticism', *College English* 32, 8 (May): 436-45.

Pratt, Annis 1981. *Archetypal Patterns in Women's Fiction*. Bloomington: University of Indiana Press.

Rich, Adrienne 1976. *Of Woman Born: Motherhood as Experience and Institution*. New York: Norton.

Rich, Adrienne 1980. 'Compulsory heterosexuality and lesbian existence', *Signs* 5, 4 (Summer): 631-60.

Robinson, Lillian S. 1971. 'Dwelling in decencies: radical criticism and the feminist perspective', *College English* 32, 8 (May): 879-89.

Robinson, Lillian S. 1978. *Sex, Class and Culture*. Bloomington: Indiana University Press.

Rogers, Katharine M. 1982. *Feminism in Eighteenth-Century England*. Urbana: University of Illinois Press.

Rosaldo, Michelle Zimbalist and Lamphere, Louise (eds) 1974. *Women, Culture and Society*. Stanford: Stanford University Press.

Rosenfelt, Deborah 1984. 'What Women's Studies programs do that mainstreaming can't', *Women's Studies International Forum* 7, 3: 167-75.

Sargent, Lydia (ed.) 1981. *Women and Revolution: A Discussion of the Unhappy Marriage of Marxism and Feminism*. Boston: South End Press.

Sedgwick, Eve Kosofsky 1985. *Between Men: English Literature and Male Homosocial Desire*. New York: Columbia University Press.

Shields, Stephanie A. 1982. 'The variability hypothesis: the history of a biological model of sex differences in intelligence', *Signs* 7, 4 (Summer): 769-97.

Shockley, Ann Allen 1979. 'The black lesbian in American literature: an overview', *Conditions Five: The Black Women's Issue*: 133-42.

Showalter, Elaine. 1977. *A Literature of Their Own*. Princeton: Princeton University Press.

Showalter, Elaine 1981. 'Feminist criticism in the wilderness', *Critical Inquiry* 8, 2 (Winter): 179-205.

Showalter, Elaine, Doederlein, Sue Warrick, Lipking, Lawrence and Schweickart, Patrocinio 1982. 'Comments on Jehlen's "Archimedes and the paradox of feminist criticism"', *Signs* 8, 1 (Autumn): 160-76.

Smith, Adam 1976. *The Theory of Moral Sentiments*. Ed. D. D. Raphael and A. L. Macfie. Vol. I of *The Glasgow Edition of the Works and Correspondence of Adam Smith*. Oxford: Clarendon Press.

Smith, Barbara 1977. 'Toward a black feminist criticism', *Conditions Two*: 25-32.

Smith, Barbara 1979. 'Notes for yet another paper on black feminism, or will the real enemy please stand up', *Conditions Five: The Black Women's Issue*: 123-7.

Smith, Barbara (ed.) 1983. *Home Girls: A Black Feminist Anthology*. New York: Kitchen Table/Women of Color Press.

Snitow, Ann, Stansell, Christine, and Thompson, Sharon (eds) 1983. *Powers of Desire: The Politics of Sexuality*. New York: Monthly Review Press.

Sternburg, Janet (ed.) 1980. *The Writer on Her Work*. New York: W. W. Norton.

Stetson, Erlene (ed.) 1981. *Black Sister: Poetry by Black American Women, 1746-1980*. Bloomington: Indiana University Press.

Stimpson, Catharine R. 1981. 'Zero degree deviancy: the lesbian novel in English', *Critical Inquiry* 8, 2 (Winter): 363-79.

Tompkins, Jane P. 1985. *Sensational Designs: The Cultural Work of American Fiction 1790-1860*. New York: Oxford University Press.

Toulmin, Stephen 1982. 'The construal of reality: criticism in modern and postmodern science', *Critical Inquiry* 9, 1 (September): 93-111.

Unger, Rhoda K. 1979. *Female and Male in Psychological Perspectives*. New York: Harper & Row.

Unger, Rhoda K. 1983. 'Through the Looking Glass: no wonderland yet! (The reciprocal relationship between methodology and models of reality)', *Psychology of Women Quarterly* 8, 1 (Fall): 9-32.

Vance, Carol S. 1980. 'Gender systems, ideology, and sex research: an anthropological analysis', *Feminist Studies* 6, 1 (Spring): 129-43.

Walker, Alice 1974. 'In search of our mother's gardens', *Ms.* (May): 64-70.

Washington, Mary Helen (ed.) 1975. *Black-Eyed Susans: Classic Stories by and About Black Women*. Garden City, NY: Anchor/Doubleday.

Washington, Mary Helen (ed.) 1980. *Midnight Birds: Stories of Contemporary Black Women Writers*. Garden City, NY: Doubleday.

Washington, Mary Helen 1981. 'New lives and new letters: black women writers at the end of the Seventies', *College English* 43, 1 (January): 1-16.

Wasiolek, Edward 1982. 'Wanted: a new contextualism', *Critical Inquiry* 8, 4 (Summer): 623-39.

Wellek, René and Warren, Austin 1956. *Theory of Literature*. 3rd edn, New York: Harcourt, Brace and World.

Wenzel, Hélène Vivienne 1981. 'The text as body/politics: an appreciation of Monique Wittig's writing in context', *Feminist Studies* 7, 2 (Summer): 264-87.

Woodbridge, Linda 1984. *Women and the English Renaissance: Literature and the Nature of Womankind, 1540-1620*. Urbana: University of Illinois Press.

Wright, Austin M. 1982. *The Formal Principle in the Novel*. Ithaca: Cornell University Press.

Zimmerman, Bonnie 1981. 'What has never been: an overview of lesbian feminist literary criticism', *Feminist Studies* 7, 3 (Fall): 451-75.

Zimmerman, Bonnie 1984. 'The politics of transliteration: lesbian personal narratives', *Signs* 9, 4 (Summer): 663-82.

4

Solidarity or Perspectivity?

David R. Shumway

Writing a response to Ellen Messer-Davidow's 'The philosophical bases of feminist literary criticisms' after nine others have already been published is not the easiest of rhetorical situations.[1] There are already *genres* of responses to this essay. Messer-Davidow herself defines two of them in 'Knowing ways', her response to the responses: the personal and the academic (p. 191). I think a more important division is between those commentators who use their space mainly to express agreement with Messer-Davidow (Hubbard, Ling, McKay, Smith, and Tompkins) and those who use it mainly to express their disagreements (Hartman, Goodheart, Graff, and Nelson). We immediately notice several things about this division. First, it is not constructed along pro- vs. anti-feminist lines. In fact, only Goodheart takes what could be called an anti-feminist position. Thus many of the commentators had to choose to emphasize agreement or disagreement since they agreed with Messer-Davidow on some points and not on others. Hartman and Tompkins try to find a middle ground by expressing a substantial amount of both. Secondly, all of the male commentators emphasize disagreement, while only one of the women does, something which may reflect the more developed habits of solidarity among feminist academics. Finally, if we look at the responses themselves, we find that those who agree with Messer-Davidow have the least to say about her essay. Instead of discussing the putative object to which they are responding, they take the occasion to write little essays of their own, making the same move that never fails to draw complaints from audiences listening to commentators at professional meetings. Those who express disagreement, on the other hand, seem to have taken the essay very seriously, to have read it carefully, and to engage the same questions that it engages. So we might ask, by which genre of response is Messer-Davidow better served?

The answer is far from clear. The more interesting responses are among those that agree: Jane Tompkins's 'Me and my shadow' is a brilliant critique of academic discursive practice; Patricia Clark Smith's 'Concerning power, nuclear and otherwise' provides a very effective illustration of the social construction of reality. But what I am saying here is that I think Tompkins and Clark have written pieces that are interesting on their own terms. That they were provoked by Messer-Davidow's essay is high praise for it, but it is not the same as engaging the particular issues that the essay raises. Those who emphasize disagreement do so from quite different angles. Hartman wants to defend the value of literary studies against Messer-Davidow's call for gender studies. Graff argues that what Messer-Davidow calls feminist knowledge and what she calls male-traditional knowledge are in fact two different world hypotheses, contextualism and positivism; he thus wants to separate these theories from gender. Nelson calls attention to Messer-Davidow's dependence on Western metaphysics that have been challenged by continental theorists, most notably the French feminists whom Messer-Davidow quite summarily dismisses. Goodheart attacks Messer-Davidow's conceptual-ization of perspectivism, calling it a 'magical term' that cannot accomplish the things she claims for it. The first three of these commentators express solidarity with feminism. What they criticize is the particular theory and practice of feminism which Messer-Davidow advocates, and thus they engage the issues she has raised.

But let us consider the metaphor I have just used: what does it mean to 'engage an issue'? It does not have anything to do with betrothal, but rather with war. We say that we engage an issue in order to avoid saying that we engage the enemy, since there is in the academic world a presumption of solidarity among scholars in a discipline. Normally in academia, such solidarity is not said to be based on shared politics. On the contrary, differences in political opinions are expected, but members of a discipline are said to share a devotion to the discovery of the truth. Such solidarity is based on objectivity, however, and it is incompatible with the assumption of perspectivity.

Of course, this solidarity is only presumed. The character of academic disciplines tends to make all of us seek to individualize ourselves, to differentiate ourselves appropriately from others. The most appropriate way, as Tompkins so ably illustrates, is to find a mistake in the other's reasoning. In so doing, one not only differentiates oneself, one also gains a hierarchical distinction over the other. Of the commentators in *New*

Literary History, only Goodheart plays this game unambiguously, but all of the others who emphasize disagreement, as well as Tompkins (who in effect has her cake and eats it too), participate in it, whatever their motives. But those who express agreement also establish their differences from the author whose work they are discussing by writing about something different. Like these responses, my response will also participate in the game of distinction, since any difference within a disciplinary regime is measured or ranked. I could, of course, choose to ignore my differences with Messer-Davidow, and just express the solidarity I have both with feminism and with the project of remaking knowledge. But to do so would be to ignore weaknesses in Messer-Davidow's argument that are disabling to the projects we share. The kinds of questions that Messer-Davidow seeks to answer in 'The philosophical bases of feminist literary criticisms' are important enough to deserve debate. And because Messer-Davidow and I begin in solidarity, our disagreement can be productive in spite of our complicity in disciplinary structures.

It seems necessary at this point to indicate that feminism is of vital importance, and not only because it is a social movement which demands equity for a majority of the world's population, as if that were not enough. Writers such as Graff might argue, however, that this makes feminism really a kind of parochial intellectual position which should be broadened to include the demand for equity and contextualism for all. But feminism is not just another version either of Enlightenment politics or contextualist philosophy, but a radically new conception of human and social relations. Thus feminism is not merely an aspect of cultural studies, but one of its structuring principles. For example, feminism provides a model for a new way to organize cultural studies through its strong sense of the collective. What Annette Kolodny proposed for feminism, 'a communal frame of mind which encourages debate and dialogue among individuals . . . who are, first and foremost, committed to the validity of the shared effort',[2] I have argued could become the basis for a counter-disciplinary practice throughout cultural studies.[3] Secondly, feminism is important as a model of a new kind of politics, perhaps even a post-politics, although that construction may seem to suggest that we have already reached an era when we can abandon politics, and this is emphatically *not* what I mean. What I do mean is that feminism has done what Foucault said political theory has not done: it has cut off the head of the king; it no longer regards power as something that can be gained by the capture of sovereignty.[4] Feminism seeks a more massive change in human relations than marxist theory has usually proposed, but it knows that it cannot bring about such change merely by capturing the state. Feminists were conducting the kind of 'revolutionary action' Foucault proposed for many years before he proposed it, something Foucault could have used to his advantage if he had taken feminism seriously.

Now the foregoing suggests an answer to Gerald Graff's question about why we should call the study of the formation of knowledge which Messer-Davidow proposes 'feminist'. The project has been profoundly influenced by feminist theories and methods, and it must continue to be or it will fail. The concern Messer-Davidow shows with the historical formation of bodies of knowledge – the project Foucault calls genealogy –is in turn vital for feminism, and this project represents for me a second area of solidarity with her. And like her, I am not content merely to describe the current formation of knowledge; I want to change it. The change that she proposes is that feminist literary criticism regard its object not as literature but as our ideas about gender. My own agenda is not identical, but in one sense it is compatible. Since I argue that the humanities need to become cultural studies, I believe that major cultural constructions such as gender – but also race and class – ought to be our objects of attention. Our projects do have different foci, to be sure, and this suggests a second answer to Graff. He, I think, has misread Messer-Davidow when he says she 'equates' historicizing, self-reflexive theory and practice with feminism. Contextualism and self-reflexivity are for her typical of feminism and necessary for the feminist project she wants to establish, but they are not sufficient for feminism. Her central project, as I under-stand it, is to establish a field of study with gender as its object. Such a project would, at least as she has described it, exclude much that is contextual and self-reflexive in literary and cultural studies. Messer-Davidow would probably argue that feminism by definition must privilege gender. This might at first seem justifiable, at least on strategic grounds, until it is recognized that such a strategy will marginalize issues of race and class.

But the problems with Messer-Davidow's essay go beyond the new conception of feminist criticism she proposes. Another is the way she tells the history of Western knowledge and literary studies in particular. Her history explains 'traditional' or 'male' or 'objectivist' knowledge as emerging from something like an epistemological mistake, one which, it is implied, derives from the larger cultural construction, maleness. This dominant form of knowledge is contrasted with an emergent form she labels 'feminist' or 'perspectivist'. The radical difference of feminist knowledge is announced early on in the essay when she notes that some feminist critics 'continue to borrow, either purposefully or unwittingly, from traditional schools – archetypal, marxist, structuralist, psycho-analytic, semiotic, deconstructive, and hermeneutic, to name a few'. The first point that needs to be made about this is that most 'traditional' literary scholars – whom I would take to be either philologists or New Critics – would not find any of these 'schools' to be traditional. In fact, as Timothy Reiss argues in chapter 1 of this volume, feminism is older than many of the 'traditional' schools Messer-Davidow names here. I take it, then, that 'traditional' is used as a synonym for 'male', a form of thinking she suggests later is characterized by 'differential, integral, principled, causal, inferential, and analogical' reasoning (p. 70). The 'traditional construal of reality' is 'another male construction', and hence, 'insofar as methods uncritically introduce into our work aspects of male-created reality, they subvert our task of transforming it' (p. 71). So traditional schools of literary criticism carry with them forms of reasoning and a construction of reality that is male.

It is clear that a particular dominant construction will tend to 'subvert' emergent constructions that challenge it. Thus Messer-Davidow's point at one level must be accepted. The problem, however, is that the way she defines the male-created reality is at once too narrow and too broad. The list of logical operations is too narrow, in the sense that the dominant reality cannot be said to be founded on these forms of reasoning. The dominant reality is not 'founded' at all. It is rather an imposition that develops *ad hoc* out of the interests of those in power. The logical operations listed are more accurately described as tools, to recall a term from Audre Lorde's claim that 'it is impossible to destroy the master's house with the master's tools.'[5] But as Amy Ling asks, why? If the master has a crowbar or a wrecking ball it will work on his house just as well as on any other. Logical tools help maintain hegemony, but to call them 'male' tools or weapons is to fail to recognize that they can also dismantle it. There is no reason why logical operations cannot be tools of feminism, but, more importantly, feminists have little choice. These logical operations may be male-created, but their creation is at this point irrelevant, for they are now imbedded in the very structure of our language. Though women and men do use this language differently, the difference is minuscule compared to the broad cultural differences between, say, South Asian languages, such as Burmese or Javan, and European languages, such as English or French.

The pervasiveness of logical operations such as inference, integration, and analogy is attested to, if by nothing else, by Messer-Davidow's own use of them. Her essay, as many of the commentators note, is characterized by reasoning and language typical of dominant academic discourse. Her very project, to provide 'philosophical bases' for feminist criticisms, participates both in philosophy, which claims itself to be the master discourse of Western culture, and in foundationalism, since she seeks explicitly to provide the bases of feminist criticisms. I do not point out these contradictions to show that Messer-Davidow's logic is flawed, but rather to show that she uses the only kind of reasoning available to her – indeed to all of us. Of course, Messer-Davidow does not even attempt to create an alternative to logocentrism, but even those who do seek such alternatives – Derrida, Cixous, Kristeva – are aware of the fact that they mostly fail.

On the other hand, Messer-Davidow's characterization of male-created reality is too broad in the sense that if reality is entirely a male construction, then there is no hope of change, for there can be no outside. Under this conception, there is nothing capable of subversion. We do not need to search for feminism's origins to assert that it has emerged in the midst of the construction of the reality it opposes. If this reality is treated as a totality – and much of Messer-Davidow's language seems to suggest this in spite of her perspectivist theory – then feminism can only be understood as a part of it, and thus as not different. But while this totalizing position is implicit in Messer-Davidow's claims about 'male reality', it is clearly not the position she wants to hold. That position seems to assume a condition of multiple totalities or 'perspectives' which groups within a culture collectively share. At first glance, Messer-Davidow's perspectives seem not, like phenomenology's, those of an individual consciousness or consciousnesses, but rather more like what Richard Rorty and others who call themselves neo-pragmatists have called community solidarity.

In 'Solidarity or objectivity?', Rorty says that 'there are two principle ways in which reflective human beings try, by placing their lives in a larger context, to give sense to those lives.'[6] One of these ways is to tell a story of contribution to a particular community, which may be an actual historical one in which the tellers live or may be a mythical one populated with heroes and heroines of history and fiction. The other way is to describe themselves as standing in immediate relation to some non-human reality. The first of these ways exemplifies a desire for solidarity and the second, the desire for objectivity. Objectivity treats Truth as desirable for its own sake, and it conceives of truth as corresponding to reality. Those who want to ground solidarity in objectivity must construct an epistemology which consists of procedures of justification that will guarantee the naturalness or universality of beliefs. On this view, 'the various procedures which are thought of as providing rational justification by one culture may or may not really *be* rational.' Epistemology is thus a project spawned by a desire to escape the limitations of one's community. Those who privilege solidarity, on the other hand, do not need an epistemology, since truth is simply 'what it is good for *us* to believe'. On this view, objectivity is still desirable, but only to establish as much intersubjective agreement as possible, 'to extend the reference of "us" as far as we can' (p. 5).

So far, Rorty's distinction between solidarity and objectivity seems good for us to believe. But where it gets him, and us if we are willing to follow him, is not so good. In the last sentence quoted above, the 'us' seems to be infinitely variable. Thus one could presumably belong to numerous different communities, each of which one might at different moments be trying to extend. Later, however, it turns out that all of us who are members of Rorty's audience belong to a single community, that of the liberal intellectuals. Those of us who seek solidarity with the revolutionary aspirations of say, Third World peoples, are simply out of luck. As Western liberal intellectuals, none of us can really take seriously their critique of our culture. Our ethnocentricity prohibits our adopting their ethnocentricity (pp. 12–13).

Now the relevance of Rorty's article to Messer-Davidow's should I think be clear, even though their critique of Western thought is hardly identical. While both Rorty and Messer-Davidow criticize Western thought for attempting to distance knowledge or belief from those who know or believe, Messer-Davidow is unwilling to give up epistemology. This is not the 'mistake' that Tompkins calls to our attention, Messer-Davidow's conflation of epistemology with the practice of a research tradition. Rather Messer-Davidow's project is to provide an epistemology, a ground for that naturalness or universality of beliefs within what she calls a perspective or what Rorty would call a community. But these two terms don't quite match. A perspective is always a view of something. Messer-Davidow's language betrays her assumption that there remains a reality apart from any single perspective at which we are all looking from different angles. Her solution to the weakness of what she defines as the present male way of thinking is to find another angle, the feminist. Notice that the opposition here is strained: male knowledge is contrasted not with female knowledge, but feminist knowledge. One form of knowledge is a function of gender; the other is a function of a theory. There is thus a confusion in Messer-Davidow's article about how perspectives are constituted. Sometimes, when she speaks of male knowledge, or 'cultural affiliations of sex, race, class, affectional preference and other circumstances' it seems as though perspectives are places where circumstances trap one. If one were, as I am, a white, male, professional-managerial, heterosexual, untenured, etc. person this would lock one into a white, male, professional-managerial, heterosexual, untenured, etc. perspective on the world which one would be powerless to change, although certain events could presumably change this perspective: gaining tenure, a sex-change, or a loss of professional status and income, for example. This position I take to be identical to Rorty's when he claims that we cannot escape our liberal, intellectual community, although he defines his determining affiliations differently. On the other hand, Messer-Davidow's project for doing away with the gender system would seem to imply the possibility of leaving one perspective for another without leaving one's actual cultural/historical place. Indeed, much of Messer-Davidow's argument is designed to demonstrate that characteristics of men and women are not biologically determined but culturally constructed and therefore susceptible to change. In this view, perspectives seem to be functions of the construction of knowledge itself. But notice that now the grounds have been shifted from solidarity with one's group to some conception of epistemology.

The question that Rorty's argument raises about this latter position is what grounds could be used to decide what conception of knowledge we need. Those grounds would have to be 'objective' in the sense that they would appeal to people outside of the perspectival group which is proposing them. This position is crucial for feminism as a post-political project which seeks not merely to replace the king with a queen, but to change the behavior of men and women towards each other in all areas of human life. But this question could also be raised about Rorty's own model. How can 'we' extend the range of agreement with 'our' beliefs unless 'we' can show in terms of other beliefs why 'ours' are better to believe? This requires that some common *ground* be established between the different communities. In this light, we can see why the appeal to objectivity is so powerful; what we cannot see is how to do without it.

Perspectivism offers no solution to this problem. It can explain why people believe different things, but not why they should believe even some of the same things. It thus ultimately leads one to the isolation that so troubles Husserl's phenomenological perspectivism. That this is no mere 'logical conclusion' is demonstrated by the fact that autobiography figures so heavily in the responses to Messer-Davidow's essay. Strangely, however, Messer-Davidow repeatedly asserts that perspectivism is somehow conducive to collectivity. In fact, perspectivism of a sort is characteristic of, *pace* Messer-Davidow, traditional humanistic scholarship in literature and other fields. Humanism has long claimed its distinction from science on the grounds that both the objects with which it deals and the perspectives with which they are dealt are unique. A humanist does not believe that his interpretation can be duplicated by any trained observer in spite of the fact that he may claim to use objectively available evidence from the work he is interpreting. The result of this ideology has been the fracturing of knowledge in the humanities into a myriad of competing, irreconcilable interpretations. While Messer-Davidow spends much energy attacking 'the research tradition' in literary studies, the analysis of the humanities I have just proposed would suggest that there is no research tradition in literary studies in the sense that there is one in biology or physics. There are doubtless a group of practices that have been carried on under the name of literary studies, but they lack precisely the collective character of work described by Kuhn or Toulmin in the research traditions of the natural sciences.[7]

In our essay 'Critical protocols', James Sosnoski and I argue that this traditional perspectivism of the humanities needs to be replaced by a collectivism, in which those studying culture would seek to agree to agree, rather than to agree to disagree. This model neither assumes nor mandates agreement; rather, it assumes disagreement and treats agreement as a goal. For example, we advocate the formation of research groups around common political positions, but we assume that a range of disagreement would remain in such groups, and in fact be vital to their functioning.[8] The model of knowledge our argument assumes differs from both Messer-Davidow's and Rorty's. It replaces the ocular metaphor of Messer-Davidow and much of Western thought with a metaphor of social organization. Our position holds that knowledge is not a function of what we see, but who we side with. Thus solidarity here is a behavior we can to some extent choose to engage in. The claim is not that we are in any simple sense 'free' to do so, but that our habits and our beliefs will tend to direct us to choose solidarity or reject it. As intellectuals trained in a bourgeois culture, solidarity is not an easy habit to acquire. In the United States especially, collective political action of the sort fostered by British materialist feminists is anathema because of the lack of a living socialist tradition in our politics. We learn to believe in the ideology of individualism and we are constantly individuated by disciplinary strategies and techniques. But self-reflexivity makes us aware of these beliefs and habits, and, while it does not guarantee our ability to change them, it does give us the possibility of changing them. Whether we try to do so or not is an issue of both belief and of power.

This brings me to what I regard as the most significant weakness of Messer-Davidow's essay, its failure to conceptualize the formation of knowledge in terms of power. Messer-Davidow writes as if the current, historically arbitrary construction of gender served no one's interests; that it is merely the result of an epistemological mistake. The absence of a critique of patriarchal power in her essay leads her to emphasize the need for reconstruction of knowledge to the exclusion of the reconstruction of power relations. Here I think the absence of reference by Messer-Davidow to British feminism, with its strong marxist influence, becomes significant.[8] Her theory repeats the error of which Marx accused Hegel, making the material world a function of our ideas rather than the other way round. We need to stand Messer-Davidow on her feet by asserting that knowledge is structured as it is because it serves the current sexual/economic/racial/cultural division of power and wealth. The goal of feminism, then, whether in the academy or out, is the dismantling of this hierarchy. The critique of knowledge is an important part of this effort, because it can show how what we call truth serves to maintain that hierarchy. But to make feminism simply the study of our ideas of sex and gender would be to create yet another enterprise thoroughly in keeping with the anthropological humanism that has structured our discourse since Kant. Feminism can pose and fulfil more radical possibilities than Messer-Davidow envisions.

NOTES

1   Messer-Davidow's essay, responses by Joan E. Hartman, Cary Nelson, Ruth Hubbard, Gerald Graff, Patricia Clark Smith, Amy Ling, Nellie McKay, Jane Thompkins, Eugene Goodheart, and Messer-Davidow's reply were published as 'A discussion: the

philosophical bases of feminist literary criticisms', a special section of *New Literary History*, 19 (Fall 1987). A revised version of Tompkins's essay appears in this volume, pp. 121-39.

2   Kolodny 1975: 91.
3   See Shumway and Sosnoski, n.d.
4   I owe this insight to Linda Singer.
5   Lorde's remark (from Lorde 1981) is paraphrased by McKay in 'A discussion' (p. 162).
6   Rorty 1985: 3.
7   Kuhn's account (1970) defines an academic discipline as a community which shares a paradigm. Toulmin defines a discipline as a 'communal tradition of procedures and techniques for dealing with practical theoretical problems' (1972: 142).
8   Sosnoski further develops this argument in 'A mindless man-driven theory machine: intellectuality, sexuality, and the institution of criticism', in *Feminism and Institutions: Dialogues on Feminist Theory*, ed. Linda Kauffman (Oxford: Basil Blackwell, 1989).
9   See Barrett 1980.

REFERENCES

'A discussion: the philosophical bases of feminist literary criticisms', a special section of *New Literary History*, 19 (Fall 1987): 63-194.

Barrett, Michèle 1980. *Women's Oppression Today: Problems in Marxist Feminist Analysis*. London: Verso.

Foucault, Michel 1980. *Power/Knowledge: Selected Interviews and Other Writings 1972-1977*. Ed. Colin Gordon. Trans. Gordon et al. New York: Pantheon.

Kolodny, Annette 1975. 'Some notes on defining a feminist literary criticism', *Critical Inquiry* 2 (Autumn): 75-92.

Kuhn, T. S. 1970. *The Structure of Scientific Revolutions*. 2nd edn. Chicago: University of Chicago Press.

Lorde, Audre 1981. 'The master's tools will never dismantle the master's house', in *This Bridge Called My Back: Writings by Radical Women of Color*, ed. Cherrie Moraga and Gloria Anzaldua. Watertown, Mass.: Persephone Press.

Rorty, Richard 1985. 'Solidarity or objectivity', in *Post-Analytic Philosophy*. Ed. John Rajchman and Cornel West. New York: Columbia University Press: 3-19.

Shumway, David R. and Sosnoski, James J. n.d. 'Critical protocols', distributed in *The GRIP Report*, Vol. 2. Available from the GRIP Project, Dept of English, Carnegie Mellon University.

Sosnoski, James 1989. 'A mindless man-driven theory machine: intellectuality, sexuality and the institution of criticism', in *Feminism and Institutions: Dialogues on Feminist Theory*, ed. Linda Kauffman. Oxford: Basil Blackwell.

Toulmin, Stephen 1972. *Human Understanding: The Collective Use and Evolution of Concepts*. Princeton: Princeton University Press.

Part II

The Body Writing/Writing the Body

These essays remind us that, in the words of Adrienne Rich, 'every mind resides in a body'. They focus on the gendered body in the act of writing, and on the function of individual identity and experience in critical theory. Some of the essayists reject theory altogether, arguing that it has elided the differences of gender, race, and class. Others explain how critical theory has helped to illuminate those differences by historicizing and politicizing the body. They all examine the relation of the individual to the collective, and relate theories of subjectivity to the social construction of gender. These essays move from a re-evaluation of the importance of individual experience to an analysis of feminism's relation to other emancipatory struggles.

If Reiss describes Wollstonecraft as being bound up, constricted and constructed by an all-pervasive Enlightenment discourse, in 'Me and my shadow', Jane Tompkins rebels against the constrictions of academic discourse, which is a legacy of the Enlightenment. Tompkins sees Ellen Messer-Davidow as being confined by the very discourse she claims to challenge. What's so great, Tompkins asks, about the discourse of Western rationalism, which systematically erases the body of the female speaking subject? An epistemology which excludes emotions from the process of attaining knowledge radically undercuts women's epistemic authority. Tompkins seeks to break out of that epistemological straitjacket by laying bare the devices of formal expository prose and by shattering the dichotomy between her public persona and her private, shadow self.

In 'Citing the subject', Gerald M. MacLean maintains that Tompkins's argument reinscribes bourgeois feminism and bourgeois individualism - the very idealist and essentializing strains which so many theorists have tried to dismantle, particularly those who combine materialist-feminism with deconstructive practice. MacLean's own subversive strategy is to experiment with writing in an associational, epistolary mode (the paradigmatic mode of the female voice), a mode which is also confessional. He seeks to unite this mode with a cogent theoretical analysis of the contributions materialist-feminism and deconstruction have made to all of his public and private selves.

Joseph Allen Boone, in 'Me(n) in feminism: who(se) is the sex that writes?' similarly experiments with the personal voice. He speculates about the possibility of the male feminist voice finding its body; maleness, he reminds us, is not merely a metaphor for patriarchy, as the marginality of gay men reveals. He speaks as a male feminist critic who seldom hears male voices which represent his own position, but who nevertheless sometimes finds himself excluded from feminist inquiry. He enumerates the kinds of inquiries male feminists are making, and suggests directions for future research.

In 'Men against patriarchy', Toril Moi considers the complexity of men's relations to feminism and feminist theory, and notes how frequently American critics confine their discussions of feminism to academia. By limiting his discussion to the narrow sphere of literary studies, Boone reveals his preoccupations with the hierarchy and prestige of the academy, and overlooks the fact that academic feminism is part of a larger political movement.

5
Me and My Shadow

Jane Tompkins

I wrote this essay in answer to Ellen Messer-Davidow's 'The philosophical bases of feminist literary criticisms' which appeared in the Fall 1987 issue of *New Literary History* along with several replies, including a shorter version of this one. As if it weren't distraction enough that my essay depends on someone else's, I want, before you've even read it, to defend it from an accusation. Believing that my reply, which turns its back on theory, constituted a return to the 'rhetoric of presence', to an 'earlier, naive, untheoretical feminism', someone, whom I'll call the unfriendly reader, complained that I was making the 'old patriarchal gesture of representation' whose effect had been to marginalize women, thus 'reinforcing the very stereotypes women and minorities have fought so hard to overcome'. I want to reply to this objection because I think it is mistaken and because it reproduces exactly the way I used to feel about feminist criticism when it first appeared in the late 1960s.

I wanted nothing to do with it. It was embarrassing to see women, with whom one was necessarily identified, insisting in print on the differences between men's and women's experience, focusing obsessively on women authors, women characters, women's issues. How pathetic, I thought, to have to call attention to yourself in that way. And in such bad taste. It was the worst kind of special pleading, an admission of weakness so blatant it made me ashamed. What I felt then, and what I think my unfriendly reader feels now, is a version of what women who are new to feminism often feel: that if we don't call attention to ourselves *as* women, but just shut up about it and do our work, no one will notice the difference and everything will be OK.

Women who adopt this line are, understandably, afraid. Afraid of being confused with the weaker sex, the sex that goes around whining and talking about itself in an unseemly way, that can't or won't do what the big boys do ('tough it out') and so won't ever be allowed to play in the big boys' games. I am sympathetic with this position. Not long ago, as organizer of an MLA session entitled 'Professional politics: women and the institution', I urged a large roomful of women to 'get theory' because I thought that doing theory would admit us to the big leagues and enable us at the same time to argue a feminist case in the most unimpeachable terms – those that men had supplied. I busily took my own advice, which was good as far as it went. But I now see that there has been a price for this, at least there has been for me; it is the subject of my reply to Ellen. I now tend to think that theory itself, at least as it is usually practiced, may be one of the patriarchal gestures women *and* men ought to avoid.

There are two voices inside me answering, answering to, Ellen's essay. One is the voice of a critic who wants to correct a mistake in the essay's view of epistemology. The other is the voice of a person who wants to write about her feelings (I have wanted to do this for a long time but have felt too embarrassed). This person feels it is wrong to criticize the essay philosophically, and even beside the point: because a critique of the kind the critic has in mind only insulates academic discourse further from the issues that make feminism matter. That make *her* matter. The critic, meanwhile, believes such feelings, and the attitudes that inform them, are soft-minded, self-indulgent, and unprofessional.

These beings exist separately but not apart. One writes for professional journals, the other in diaries, late at night. One uses words like 'context' and 'intelligibility', likes to win arguments, see her name in print, and give graduate students hardheaded advice. The other has hardly ever been heard from. She had a short story published once in a university literary magazine, but her works exist chiefly in notebooks and manila folders labelled 'Journal' and 'Private'. This person talks on the telephone a lot to her friends, has seen psychiatrists, likes cappuccino, worries about the state of her soul. Her father is ill right now, and one of her friends recently committed suicide.

The dichotomy drawn here is false – and not false. I mean in reality there's no split. It's the same person who feels and who discourses about epistemology. The problem is that you can't talk about your private life in the course of doing your professional work. You have to pretend that epistemology, or whatever you're writing about, has nothing to do with your life, that it's more exalted, more important, because it (supposedly) *transcends* the merely personal. Well, I'm tired of the conventions that keep discussions of epistemology, or James Joyce, segregated from meditations on what is happening outside my window or inside my heart. The public-private dichotomy, which is to say, the public-private *hierarchy*, is a founding condition of female oppression. I say to hell with it. The reason I feel embarrassed at my own attempts to speak personally in a professional context is that I have been conditioned to feel that way. That's all there is to it.

I think people are scared to talk about themselves, that they haven't got the guts to do it. I think readers want to know about each other. Sometimes, when a writer introduces some personal bit of story into an essay, I can hardly contain my pleasure. I love writers who write about their own experience. I feel I'm being nourished by them, that I'm being allowed to enter into a personal relationship with them. That I can match my own experience up with theirs, feel cousin to them, and say, yes, that's how it is.

> When he casts his leaves forth upon the wind [said Hawthorne], the author addresses, not the many who will fling aside his volume, or never take it up, but the few who will understand him. . . . As if the printed book, thrown at large on the wide world, were certain to find out the divided segment of the writer's own nature, and complete his circle of existence by bringing him into communion with it. . . . And so as thoughts are frozen and utterance, benumbed unless the speaker stand in some true relation with this audience – it may be pardonable to imagine that a friend, a kind and apprehensive, though not the closest friend, is listening to our talk. (Nathaniel Hawthorne, 'The Custom-House', *The Scarlet Letter*, pp. 5-6)

Hawthorne's sensitivity to the relationship that writing implies is rare in academic prose, even when the subject would seem to make awareness of the reader inevitable. Alison Jaggar gave a lecture recently that crystallized the problem. Western epistemology, she argued, is shaped by the belief that emotion should be excluded from the process of attaining knowledge. Because women in our culture are not simply encouraged but *required* to be the bearers of emotion, which men are culturally conditioned to repress, an epistemology which excludes emotions from the process of attaining knowledge radically undercuts women's epistemic authority. The idea that the conventions defining legitimate sources of knowledge overlapped with the conventions defining appropriate gender behavior (male) came to me as a blinding insight. I saw that I had been socialized from birth to feel and act in ways that automatically excluded me from participating in the culture's most valued activities. No wonder I felt so uncomfortable in the postures academic prose forced me to assume; it was like wearing men's jeans.

Ellen Messer-Davidow's essay participates – as Jaggar's lecture and my précis of it did – in the conventions of Western rationalism. It adopts the impersonal, technical vocabulary of the epistemic ideology it seeks to dislocate. The political problem posed by my need to reply to the essay is this: to adhere to the conventions is to uphold a male standard of rationality that militates against women's being recognized as culturally legitimate sources of knowledge. To break with the convention is to risk not being heard at all.

This is how I would reply to Ellen's essay if I were to do it in the professionally sanctioned way.

The essay provides feminist critics with an overarching framework for thinking about what they do, both in relation to mainstream criticism and in relation to feminist work in other fields. It allows the reader to see women's studies as a whole, furnishing useful categories for organizing a confusing and miscellaneous array of materials. It also provides excellent summaries of a wide variety of books and essays that readers might not otherwise encounter. The enterprise is carried out without pointed attacks on other theorists, without creating a cumbersome new vocabulary, without exhibitionistic displays of intellect or esoteric learning. Its practical aim – to define a field within which debate can take place – is fulfilled by *New Literary History*'s decision to publish it, and to do so in a format which includes replies.

(Very nice, Jane. You sound so reasonable and generous. But, as anybody can tell, this is just the obligatory pat on the back before the stab in the entrails).

The difficulty with the essay from a philosophical, as opposed to a practical, point of view is that the theory it offers as a basis for future work stems from a confused notion of what an epistemology is. The author says: 'An epistemology . . . consists of assumptions that knowers make about the entities and processes in a domain of study, the relations that obtain among them, and the proper methods for investigating them' (p. 87). I want to quarrel with this definition. Epistemology, strictly speaking, is a *theory* about the origins and nature of knowledge. As such, it is a set of ideas explicitly held and consciously elaborated, and thus belongs to the practice of a sub-category of philosophy called epistemology. The fact that there is a branch of philosophy given over to the study of what knowledge is and how it is acquired is important, because it means that such theories are generated not in relation to this or that 'domain of study' but in relation to one another: that is, within the context of already existing epistemological theories. They are rarely based upon a study of the practices of investigators within a particular field.

An epistemology does not consist of 'assumptions that knowers make' in a particular field; it is a theory about how knowledge is acquired which makes sense, chiefly, in relation to other such theories. What Messer-Davidow offers as the 'epistemology' of traditional literary critics is not *their* epistemology, if in fact they have one, but her description of what she assumes their assumptions are, a description which may or may not be correct. Moreover, if literary critics should indeed elaborate a theory of how they got their beliefs, that theory would have no privileged position in relation to their actual assumptions. It would simply be another theory. This distinction – between actual assumptions and an observer's description of them (even when one is observing one's own practice) – is crucial because it points to an all-important fact about the relation of epistemology to what really gets done in a given domain of study, namely this: that epistemology, a theory about how one gets one's knowledge, in no way determines the particular knowledge that one has.

This fact is important because Messer-Davidow assumes that if we change our epistemology, our practice as critics will change, too. Specifically, she wants us to give up the subject–object theory, in which 'knowledge is an abstract representation of objective existence,' for a theory which says that what counts as knowledge is a function of situation and perspective. She believes that it follows from this latter theory that knowledge will become more equitable, more self-aware, and more humane.

I disagree. Knowing that my knowledge is perspectival, language-based, culturally constructed, or what have you, does not change in the slightest the things I believe to be true. All that it changes is what I think about how we get knowledge. The insight that my ideas are all products of the situation I occupy in the world applies to all of my ideas equally (including the idea that knowledge is culturally based); and to all of everybody else's ideas as well. So where does this get us? Right back to where we were before, mainly. I still believe what I believe and, if you differ with me, think that you are wrong. If I want to change your mind I still have to persuade you that I am right by using evidence, reasons, chains of inference, citations of authority, analogies, illustrations, and so on. Believing that what I believe comes from my being in a particular cultural framework does not change my relation to my beliefs. I still believe them just as much as if I thought they came from God, or the laws of nature, or my autonomous self.

Here endeth the epistle.

But while I think Ellen is wrong in thinking that a change of epistemology can mean a change in the kinds of things we think, I am in sympathy with the ends she has in view. This sympathy prompts me to say that my professionally correct reply is not on target. Because the target, the goal, rather, is not to be fighting over these questions, trying to beat the other person down. (What the goal is, it is harder to say.) Intellectual debate, if it were in the right spirit, would be wonderful. But I don't know how to be in the right spirit, exactly, can't make points without sounding rather superior and smug. Most of all, I don't know how to enter the debate without leaving everything else behind – the birds outside my window, my grief over Janice, just myself as a person sitting here in stockinged feet, a little bit chilly because the windows are open, and thinking about going to the bathroom. But not going yet.

I find that when I try to write in my 'other' voice, I am immediately critical of it. It wobbles, vacillates back and forth, is neither this nor that. The voice in which I write about epistemology is familiar, I know how it ought to sound. This voice, though, I hardly know. I don't even know if it has anything to say. But if I never write in it, it never will. So I have to try. (That is why, you see, this doesn't sound too good. It isn't a practiced performance, it hasn't got a surface. I'm asking you to bear with me while I try, hoping that this, what I write, will express something you yourself have felt or will help you find a part of yourself that you would like to express.)

The thing I want to say is that I've been hiding a part of myself for a long time. I've known it was there but I couldn't listen because there was no place for this person in literary criticism. The criticism I would like to write would always take off from personal experience. Would always be in some way a chronicle of my hours and days. Would speak in a voice which can talk about everything, would reach out to a reader like me and touch me where I want to be touched. Susan Griffin's voice in 'The way of all ideology'. I want to speak in what Ursula LeGuin, at the Bryn Mawr College commencement in 1986, called the 'mother tongue'. This is LeGuin speaking:

> The dialect of the father tongue that you and I learned best in college . . . only lectures . . . Many believe this dialect – the expository and particularly scientific discourse – is the *highest* form of language, the true language, of which all other uses of words are primitive vestiges . . . And it is indeed a High Language . . . Newton's *Principia* was written in it in Latin . . . and Kant wrote German in it, and Marx, Darwin, Freud, Boas, Foucault, all the great scientists and social thinkers wrote it. It is the language of thought that seeks objectivity.
> . . . The essential gesture of the father tongue is not reasoning, but distancing – making a gap, a space, between the subject or self and the object or other. . . . Everywhere now everybody speaks [this] language in laboratories and government buildings and headquarters and offices of business . . . The father tongue is spoken from above. It goes one way. No answer is expected, or heard.
> . . . The mother tongue, spoken or written, expects an answer. It is conversation, a word the root of which means 'turning together.' The mother tongue is language not as mere communication, but as relation, relationship. It connects . . . Its power is not in dividing but in binding . . . We all know it by heart. John have you got your umbrella I think it's going to rain. Can you come play with me? If I told you once I told you a hundred times. . . . O what am I going to do? . . . Pass the soy sauce please. Oh, shit . . . You look like what the cat dragged in . . . . (pp. 3-4)

Much of what I'm saying elaborates or circles around these quotes from LeGuin. I find that having released myself from the duty to say things I'm not interested in, in a language I resist, I feel free to entertain other people's voices. Quoting them becomes a pleasure of appreciation rather than the obligatory giving of credit, because when I write in a voice that is not struggling to be heard through the screen of a forced language, I no longer feel that it is not I who am speaking, and so, there is more room for what others have said.

One sentence in Ellen's essay stuck out for me the first time I read it and the second and the third: 'In time we can build a synchronous account of

our subject matters as we glissade among them and turn upon ourselves.'
(p. 79)

What attracted me to the sentence was the 'glissade'. Fluidity,
flexibility, versatility, mobility. Moving from one thing to another
without embarrassment. It is a tenet of feminist rhetoric that the personal
is political, but who in the academy acts on this where language is
concerned? We all speak the father tongue, which is impersonal, while
decrying the fathers' ideas. All of what I have written so far is in a kind of
watered-down expository prose. Not much imagery. No description of
concrete things. Only that one word, 'glissade'.

> Like black swallows swooping and gliding
> in a flurry of entangled loops and curves . . .

Two lines of a poem I memorized in high school are what the word
'glissade' called to mind. Turning upon ourselves. Turning, weaving,
bending, unbending, moving in loops and curves.

I don't believe we can ever turn upon ourselves in the sense Ellen
intends. You can't get behind the thing that casts the shadow. *You* cast
the shadow. As soon as you turn, the shadow falls in another place. Is still
your shadow. You have not got 'behind' yourself. That is why self-
consciousness is not the way to make ourselves better than we are.

Just me and my shadow, walkin' down the avenue.

It is a beautiful day here in North Carolina. The first day that is both
cool and sunny all summer. After a terrible summer, first drought, then
heat-wave, then torrential rain, trees down, flooding. Now, finally,
beautiful weather. A tree outside my window just brushed by red, with
one fully red leaf. (This is what I want you to see. A person sitting in
stockinged feet looking out of her window – a floor to ceiling rectangle
filled with green, with one red leaf. The season poised, sunny and chill,
ready to rush down the incline into autumn. But perfect, and still. Not
going yet.)

My response to this essay is not a response to something Ellen Messer-
Davidow has written; it is a response to something within myself. As I re-
read the opening pages I feel myself being squeezed into a straitjacket; I
wriggle, I will not go in. As I read the list 'subject matters, methods of
reasoning, and epistemology', the words will not go down. They belong
to a debate whose susurrus hardly reaches my ears.

The liberation Ellen promises from the straitjacket of a subject-object epistemology is one I experienced some time ago. Mine didn't take the form she outlines, but it was close enough. I discovered, or thought I discovered, that the post-structuralist way of understanding language and knowledge enabled me to say what I wanted about the world. It enabled me to do this because it pointed out that the world I knew was a construct of ways of thinking about it, and as such, had no privileged claim on the truth. Truth in fact would always be just such a construction, and so, one could offer another, competing, description and so help to change the world that was.

The catch was that anything I might say or imagine was itself the product of an already existing discourse. Not something 'I' had made up but a way of constructing things I had absorbed from the intellectual surround. Post-structuralism's proposition about the constructed nature of things held good, but that did not mean that the world could be changed by an act of will. For, as we are looking at this or that phenomenon and re-seeing it, re-thinking it, the rest of the world, that part of it from which we do the seeing, is still there, in place, real, irrefragable as a whole, and making visible what we see, though changed by it, too.

This little lecture pretends to something I no longer want to claim. The pretense is in the tone and level of the language, not in what it says about post-structuralism. The claim being made by the language is analogous to what Barthes calls the 'reality effect' of historical writing, whose real message is not that this or that happened but that reality exists. So the claim of this language I've been using (and am using right now) lies in its implicit deification of the speaker. Let's call it the 'authority effect'. I cannot describe the pretense except to talk about what it ignores: the human frailty of the speaker, his body, his emotions, his history; the moment of intercourse with the reader - acknowledgment of the other person's presence, feelings, needs. This 'authoritative' language speaks as though the other person weren't there. Or perhaps more accurately, it doesn't bother to imagine who, as Hawthorne said, is listening to our talk.

How can we speak personally to one another and yet not be self-centered? How can we be part of the great world and yet remain loyal to ourselves?

It seems to me that I am trying to write out of my experience without acknowledging any discontinuity between this and the subject matter of the profession I work in. And at the same time find that I no longer want to write about that subject matter, as it appears in Ellen's essay. I am, on the one hand, demanding a connection between literary theory and my own life, and asserting, on the other, that there is no connection.

But here is a connection. I learned what epistemology I know from my husband. I think of it as more his game than mine. It's a game I enjoy playing but which I no longer need or want to play. I want to declare my independence of it, of him. (Part of what is going on here has to do with a need I have to make sure I'm not being absorbed in someone else's personality.) What I am breaking away from is both my conformity to the conventions of a male professional practice and my intellectual dependence on my husband. How can I talk about such things in public? How can I *not*.

Looking for something to read this morning, I took three books down from my literary theory shelf, in order to prove a point. The first book was Félix Guattari's *Molecular Revolution*. I find it difficult to read, and therefore have read very little of it, but according to a student who is a disciple of Deleuze and Guattari, 'molecular revolution' has to do with getting away from ideology and enacting revolution within daily life. It is specific, not programmed – that is, it does not have a 'method', nor 'steps', and is neither psychoanalytic nor marxist, although its discourse seems shaped by those discourses, antithetically. From this kind of revolution, said I to myself, disingenuously, one would expect some recognition of the personal. A revolution that started with daily life would have to begin, or at least would have sometimes to reside, at home. So I open at a section entitled 'Towards a new vocabulary', looking for something in the mother tongue, and this is what I find:

> The distinction I am proposing between machine and structure is based solely on the way we use the words; we may consider that we are merely dealing with a 'written device' of the kind one has to invent for dealing with a mathematical problem, or with an axiom that may have to be reconsidered at a particular stage of development, or again with the kind of machine we shall be talking about here.
>
> I want therefore to make it clear that I am putting into parentheses the fact that, in reality, a machine is inseparable from its structural articulations and conversely, that each contingent structure is dominated (and this is what I want to demonstrate) by a system of machines, or at the very least by one logic machine. (p. 111)

At this point, I start to skip, reading only the first sentence of each paragraph.

'We may say of structure that it positions its elements . . .'
'The agent of action, whose definition here does not extend beyond this principle of reciprocal determination . . .'
'The machine, on the other hand remains essentially remote . . .'
'The history of technology is dated . . .'
'Yesterday's machine, today's and tomorrow's, are not related in their structural determinations . . .'

I find this language incredibly alienating. In fact, the paragraph after the one I stopped at begins: 'The individual's relation to the machine has been described by sociologists following Friedmann as one of fundamental alienation.' I will return to this essay some day and read it. I sense that it will have something interesting to say. But the effort is too great now. What strikes me now is the incredibly distancing effect of this language. It is totally abstract and impersonal. Though the author uses the first person ('The distinction I am proposing', 'I want therefore to make it clear'), it quickly became clear to me that he had no interest whatsoever in the personal, or in concrete situations as I understand them – a specific person, at a specific machine, somewhere in time and space, with something on his/her mind, real noises, smells, aches and pains. He has no interest in his own experience of machines, or in explaining why he is writing about them, what they mean to him personally. I take down the next book: *Poetry and Repression* by Harold Bloom.

This book should contain some reference to the self, to the author's self, to ourselves, to how people feel, to how the author feels, since its subject is psychological: repression. I open the book at page 1 and read:

Jacques Derrida asks a central question in his essay on 'Freud and the Scene of Writing': 'What is a text, and what must the psyche be if it can be represented by a text?' My narrow concern with poetry prompts the contrary question: 'What is a psyche, and what must a text be if it can be represented by a psyche?' Both Derrida's question and my own require exploration of three terms: 'psyche,' 'text,' 'represented.'
'Psyche' is ultimately from the Indo-European root . . . (p. 1)

– and I stop reading.

The subject of poetry and repression will involve the asking and answering of questions about 'a text' - a generalized, non-particular object that has been the subject of endless discussion for the past twenty years, - and about an equally disembodied 'psyche' in relation to the thing called 'a text' - not, to my mind, or rather in view of my desires, a very promising relation in which to consider it. Answering these questions, moreover, will 'require' (on whose part, I wonder?) the 'exploration' of 'three terms'. Before we get to the things themselves - psyches, texts - we shall have to spend a lot of time looking at them *as words*. With the beginning of the next paragraph, we get down to the etymology of 'psyche'. With my agenda, I get off the bus here.

But first I look through the book. Bloom is arguing against canonical readings (of some very canonical poems) and for readings that are not exactly personal, but in which the drama of a self is constantly being played out on a cosmic stage - lots of references to God, kingdom, Paradise, the fall, the eternal - a biblical stage on which, apparently, only men are players (God, Freud, Christ, Nietzsche, and the poets). It is a drama that, although I can see how gripping Bloom can make it, will pall for me because it isn't *my* drama.

Book number three, Michel Foucault's *History of Sexuality*, is more promising. Section One is entitled 'We "other Victorians"'. So Foucault is acknowledging his and our implication in the object of the study. This book will in some way be about 'ourselves', which is what I want. It begins:

> For a long time, the story goes, we supported a Victorian regime,
> and we continue to be dominated by it even today. Thus the image
> of the imperial prude is emblazoned on our restrained, mute, and
> hypocritical sexuality. (p. 3)

Who, exactly, are 'we'? Foucault is using the convention in which the author establishes common ground with his reader by using the first person plural - a presumptuous, though usually successful, move. Presumptuous because it presumes that we are really like him, and successful because, especially when an author is famous, and even when he isn't, 'our' instinct (I criticize the practice and engage in it too) is to want to cooperate, to be included in the circle the author is drawing so cosily around 'us'. It is chummy, this 'we'. It feels good, for a little while, until it starts to feel coercive, until 'we' are subscribing to things that 'I' don't believe.

There is no specific reference to the author's self, no attempt to specify himself. It continues:

At the beginning of the seventeenth century . . .

I know now where we are going. We are going to history. 'At the beginning of the seventeenth century a certain frankness was still common, it would seem.' Generalizations about the past, though pleasantly qualified ('a certain frankness', 'it would seem'), are nevertheless disappointingly magisterial. Things continue in a generalizing vein – 'It was a time of direct gestures, shameless discourse, and open transgressions.' It's not so much that I don't believe him as that I am uncomfortable with the level or the mode of discourse. It is everything that, I thought, Foucault was trying to get away from, in *The Archaeology of Knowledge*. The primacy of the subject as the point of view from which history could be written, the bland assumption of authority, the taking over of time, of substance, of event, the imperialism of description from a unified perspective. Even though the subject matter interests me – sex, hypocrisy, whether or not our view of Victorianism and of ourselves in relation to it is correct – I am not eager to read on. The point of view is discouraging. It will march along giving orders, barking out commands. I'm not willing to go along for the march, not even on Foucault's say-so (I am, or have been, an extravagant admirer of his).

So I turn to 'my' books. To the women's section of my shelves. I take down, unerringly, an anthology called *The Powers of Desire* edited by Christine Stansell, Ann Snitow, and Sharon Thompson. I turn, almost as unerringly, to an essay by Jessica Benjamin entitled 'Master and slave: the fantasy of erotic domination', and begin to read:

> This essay is concerned with the violence of erotic domination. It is about the strange union of rationality and violence that is made in the secret heart of our culture and sometimes enacted in the body. This union has inspired some of the holiest imagery of religious transcendence and now comes to light at the porno newsstands, where women are regularly depicted in the bonds of love. But the slave of love is not always a woman, not always a heterosexual; the fantasy of erotic domination permeates all sexual imagery in our culture. (p. 281)

I am completely hooked, I am going to read this essay from beginning to end and proceed to do so. It gets better, much better, as it goes along. In fact, it gets so good, I find myself putting it down and straying from it because the subject is *so* close to home, and therefore so threatening, that I need relief from it, little breathers, before I can go on. I underline vigorously and often. Think of people I should give it to to read (my husband, this colleague, that colleague).

But wait a minute. There is no personal reference here. The author deals, like Foucault, in generalities. In even bigger ones than his: hers aren't limited to the seventeenth century or the Victorian era. She generalizes about religion, rationality, violence. Why am I not turned off by this as I was in Foucault's case? Why don't I reject this as a grand drama in the style of Bloom? Why don't I bridle at the abstractions as I did when reading Guattari? Well?

The answer is, I see the abstractions as concrete and the issues as personal. They are already personal for me without being personal*ized* because they concern things I've been thinking about for some time, struggling with, trying to figure out for myself. I don't need the author to identify her own involvement, I don't need her to concretize, because these things are already personal and concrete for me. The erotic is already eroticized.

Probably, when Guattari picks up an article whose first sentence has the words 'machine', 'structure', and 'determination', he cathects it immediately. Great stuff. Juicy, terrific. The same would go for Bloom on encountering multiple references to Nietzsche, representation, God the father, and the Sublime. But isn't erotic domination, as a subject, surer to arouse strong feeling than systems of machines or the psyche that can be represented as a text? Clearly, the answer depends on the readership. The people at the convenience store where I stop to get gas and buy milk would find all these passages equally baffling. Though they *might* have uneasy stirrings when they read Jessica Benjamin. 'Erotic domination', especially when coupled with 'porno newsstands', does call some feelings into play almost no matter who you are in this culture.

But I will concede the point. What is personal is completely a function of what is perceived as personal. And what is perceived as personal by men, or rather, what is gripping, significant, 'juicy', is different from what is felt to be that way by women. For what we are really talking about is not the personal as such, what we are talking about is what is important, answers one's needs, strikes one as immediately *interesting*. For women, the personal is such a category.

In literary criticism, we have moved from the New Criticism, which was anti-personal and declared the personal off-limits at every turn - the intentional fallacy, the affective fallacy - to structuralism, which does away with the self altogether - at least as something unique and important to consider - to deconstruction, which subsumes everything in language and makes the self non-self-consistent, ungraspable, a floating signifier, and finally to new historicism which re-institutes the discourse of the object - 'In the seventeenth century' - with occasional side glances at how the author's 'situatedness' affects his writing.

The female subject *par excellence*, which is her self and her experiences, has once more been elided by literary criticism.

The question is, why did this happen? One might have imagined a different outcome. The 1960s paves the way for a new personalism in literary discourse by opening literary discussion up to politics, to psychology, to the 'reader', to the effects of style. What happened to deflect criticism into the impersonal labyrinths of 'language', 'discourse', 'system', 'network', and now, with Guattari, 'machine'?

I met Ellen Messer-Davidow last summer at the School of Criticism and Theory where she was the undoubted leader of the women who were there. She organized them, led them (I might as well say us, since, although I was on the faculty as a visiting lecturer, she led me, too). At the end of the summer we put on a symposium, a kind of teach-in on feminist criticism and theory, of which none was being offered that summer. I thought it really worked. Some people, eager to advertise their intellectual superiority, murmured disappointment at the 'level' of discussion (code for, 'my mind is finer and more rigorous than yours'). One person who spoke out at the closing session said he felt bulldozed: a more honest and useful response. The point is that Ellen's leadership affected the experience of everyone at the School that summer. What she offered was not an intellectual performance calculated to draw attention to the quality of her mind, but a sustained effort of practical courage that changed the situation we were in. I think that the kind of thing Ellen did should be included in our concept of criticism: analysis that is not an end in itself but pressure brought to bear on a situation.

Now it's time to talk about something that's central to everything I've been saying so far, although it doesn't *show*, as we used to say about the slips we used to wear. If I had to bet on it I would say that Ellen Messer-Davidow was motivated last summer, and probably in her essay, by anger (forgive me, Ellen, if I am wrong) anger at her, our, exclusion from what was being studied at the School, our exclusion from the discourse of 'Western man'. I interpret her behavior this way because anger is what fuels my engagement with feminist issues; an absolute fury that has never even been tapped, relatively speaking. It's time to talk about this now, because it's so central, at least for me. I hate men for the way they treat women, and pretending that women aren't there is one of the ways I hate most.

Last night I saw a movie called *Gunfight at the OK Corral*, starring Burt Lancaster and Kirk Douglas. The movie is patently about the love-relationship between the characters these men play – Wyatt Earp and Doc Holliday. The women in the movie are merely pawns that serve in various ways to reflect the characters of the men, and to advance the story of their relationship to one another. There is a particularly humiliating part, played by Jo Van Fleet, the part of Doc Holliday's mistress – Kate Fisher – whom he treats abominably (everybody in the movie acknowledges this, it's not just me saying so). This woman is degraded over and over again. She is a whore, she is a drunkard, she is a clinging woman, she betrays the life of Wyatt Earp in order to get Doc Holliday back, she is *no longer young*, (perhaps this is her chief sin). And her words are always in vain, they are chaff, less than nothing, another sign of her degradation.

Now Doc Holliday is a similarly degraded character. He used to be a dentist and is now a gambler, who lives to get other people's money away from them; he is a drunk, and he abuses the woman who loves him. But his weaknesses, in the perspective of the movie, are glamorous. He is irresistible, charming, seductive, handsome, witty, commanding; it's no wonder Wyatt Earp falls for him, who wouldn't? The degradation doesn't stick to Kirk Douglas; it is all absorbed by his female counterpart, the 'slut', Jo Van Fleet. We are embarrassed every time she appears on the screen, because every time, she is humiliated further.

What enrages me is the way women are used as extensions of men, mirrors of men, devices for showing men off, devices for helping men get what they want. They are never there in their own right, or rarely. The world of the Western contains no women.

Sometimes I think *the world* contains no women.

Why am I so angry?

My anger is partly the result of having been an only child who caved in to authority very early on. As a result I've built up a huge storehouse of hatred and resentment against people in authority over me (mostly male). Hatred and resentment and attraction.

Why should poor men be made the object of this old pent-up anger? (Old anger is the best anger, the meanest, the truest, the most intense. Old anger is pure because it's been dislocated from its source for so long, has had the chance to ferment, to feed on itself for so many years, so that it is nothing but anger. All cause, all relation to the outside world, long since sloughed off, withered away. The rage I feel inside me now is the distillation of forty-six years. It has had a long time to simmer, to harden, to become adamantine, a black slab that glows in the dark.)

Are all feminists fueled by such rage? Is the molten lava of millenia of hatred boiling below the surface of every essay, every book, every syllabus, every newsletter, every little magazine? I imagine that I can open the front of my stomach like a door, reach in, and pluck from memory the rooted sorrow, pull it out, root and branch. But where, or rather, who, would I be then? I am attached to this rage. It is a source of identity for me. It is a motivator, an explainer, a justifier, a no-need-to-say-more greeter at the door. If I were to eradicate this anger somehow, what would I do? Volunteer work all day long?

A therapist once suggested to me that I blamed on sexism a lot of stuff that really had to do with my own childhood. Her view was basically the one articulated in Alice Miller's *The Drama of the Gifted Child*, in which the good child has been made to develop a false self by parents who cathect the child narcissistically. My therapist meant that if I worked out some of my problems – as she understood them, on a psychological level – my feminist rage would subside.

Maybe it would, but that wouldn't touch the issue of female oppression. Here is what Miller says about this:

> Political action can be fed by the unconscious anger of children who have been . . . misused, imprisoned, exploited, cramped, and drilled. . . . If, however, disillusionment and the resultant mourning can be lived through . . . , then social and political disengagement do not usually follow, but the patient's actions are freed from the compulsion to repeat. (p. 101)

According to Miller's theory, the critical voice inside me, the voice I noticed butting in, belittling, doubting, being wise, is 'the contemptuous introject'. The introjection of authorities who manipulated me, without necessarily meaning to. I think that if you can come to terms with your 'contemptuous introjects', learn to forgive and understand them, your anger will go away.

But if you're not angry, can you still act? Will you still care enough to write the letters, make the phone calls, attend the meetings? You need to find another center within yourself from which to act. A center of outgoing, outflowing, giving feelings. Love instead of anger. I'm embarrassed to say words like these because I've been taught they are mushy and sentimental and smack of cheap popular psychology. I've been taught to look down on people who read M. Scott Peck and Leo Buscaglia and Harold Kushner, because they're people who haven't very much education, and because they're mostly women. Or if not women, then people who take responsibility for learning how to deal with their feelings, who take responsibility for marriages that are going bad, for children who are in trouble, for friends who need help, for themselves. The disdain for popular psychology and for words like 'love' and 'giving' is part of the police action that academic intellectuals wage ceaselessly against feeling, against women, against what is personal. The ridiculing of the 'touchy-feely', of the 'Mickey Mouse', of the sentimental (often associated with teaching that takes students' concerns into account), belongs to the tradition Alison Jaggar rightly characterized as founding knowledge in the denial of emotion. It is looking down on women, with whom feelings are associated, and on the activities with which women are identified: mother, nurse, teacher, social worker, volunteer.

So for a while I can't talk about epistemology. I can't deal with the philosophical bases of feminist literary criticisms. I can't strap myself psychically into an apparatus that will produce the right gestures when I begin to move. I have to deal with the trashing of emotion, and with my anger against it.

This one time I've taken off the straitjacket, and it feels so good.

NOTES

Parts of this essay are reprinted from *New Literary History* 19 (Autumn 1987), by kind permission.

REFERENCES

Benjamin, Jessica 1983. 'Master and slave: the fantasy of erotic domination', in *The Powers of Desire: The Politics of Sexuality*, ed. Ann Snitow, Christine Stansell, and Sharon Thompson. New York: Monthly Review Press: 280-9.

Bloom, Harold 1976. *Poetry and Repression: Revision from Blake to Stevens*. New Haven, Conn.: Yale University Press.

Foucault, Michel 1980. *The History of Sexuality, Volume I: An Introduction*. Trans. Robert Hurley. New York: Vintage Books. Copyright 1978 by Random House, Inc. [Originally published in French as *La Volonté de Savoir*, Paris: Editions Gallimard, 1976.]

Griffin, Susan 1982. 'The way of all ideology', in *Made from the Earth: an Anthology of Writings*. New York: Harper and Row: 161-82.

Guattari, Félix 1984. *Molecular Revolution: Psychiatry and Politics*. Trans. Rosemary Sheed, intro. David Cooper. New York: Penguin Books. [First published as *Psychanalyse et transversalité* (1972), and *La Révolution moléculaire* (1977).]

Hawthorne, Nathaniel 1960-1. *The Scarlet Letter and Other Tales of the Puritans*. Ed. with an intro. and notes by Harry Levin. Boston, Mass.: Houghton Mifflin Co.

LeGuin, Ursula 1986. 'The mother tongue', *Bryn Mawr Alumnae Bulletin* (Summer): 3-4.

Miller, Alice 1983. *The Drama of the Gifted Child*. New York: Basic Books.

6

Citing the Subject

Gerald M. MacLean

Detroit, 24 September 1987

Dear Jane,

Between December and February I wrote you a series of letters. They were never mailed. The first one wasn't even a letter. It didn't know what it was. It only knew it wasn't an entry in a reading journal. Perhaps the others aren't letters either, really. After all, they have footnotes. But they were written with you in mind and each of them began 'Dear Jane', just like this one. We've never met. What impertinence! But I feel the need to be liked and I didn't want you to dislike me because of what I was thinking about saying in response to your essay. So when I saw that you had written 'when a writer introduces some personal bit of story into an essay, I can hardly contain my pleasure', I decided to write about myself, to use personal experience as a fitting means of response. The epistolary form came later. Only now, having thought about what you say of someone else, that 'unfriendly' reader, I find myself thinking again about what I was doing, covering my criticisms of your essay by using an informal style, and insinuating my will by doing what you asked, by seeking to give you pleasure. What impertinence! But not really. How can 'I' pleasure 'you'? Isn't that just what's at issue here, the problematics of presence? I have written *about* myself only in the way Pope uses 'about' in *The Dunciad* to describe how scholars 'describe a thing till all men doubt it, / And write about it, goddess, and about it' (IV. 251-2). That's the challenge of theory, that maybe there's no 'it' to get to. You admire a sentence of Ellen Messer-Davidow's - 'In time we can build a synchronous account of our subject-matters as we glissade among them and turn upon ourselves' - but admit that you 'don't believe we can ever turn upon ourselves in the sense Ellen intends'. I agree, though for different reasons. What worries me about the final clause in Messer-Davidow's sentence is how that inward turn effects a climactic reinscription of the self that is capable of self-knowledge. From here, I think, we start to disagree. I am not sure about your subsequent objection, the way you posit a '*You*' casting the shadow. We've met this figure, this '*You*', before. It has a familiar history that you astutely describe as the desire 'to make ourselves better than we are'. This commitment to self-improvement substitutes for a commitment to more radical transformations in a social order that exploits people because of their race, class, or gender. Self-improvement is what we have come to expect from phallic narratives, for improving stories about heroic individuals invariably ignore material oppression and collective action. The last thing that Christian in *The Pilgrim's Progress* does after achieving salvation is to expel Ignorance, to 'bind him hand and foot, and have him away'. But it is at just this moment in Bunyan's tale of self-improvement that the writer awakes to 'behold, it was a dream.'[1] Even Bunyan finally marks the problem of the self-knowing subject.[2]

Los Angeles, 23 December 1986

This is not a journal.

These will not be journal entries.

America: I was once told that showing an interest in an author's life and personality was a peculiarly American activity that had very little to do with the 'practical criticism' in which I was being trained. At Cambridge in the early 1970s,[3] there was, it is true, the rather marginal figure of George Watson holding out for biographical criticism.[4] But the more general challenge to formalism, I recall, came from the moralists and historicists who moved outside the text: to read Milton you must understand the Civil Wars.

Freud: As an Englishman in graduate school in America during the late 1970s, I was taught by Irvin Ehrenpreis to recognize how this 'American' concern for the author's life was partly a result of the place Freud occupied in American intellectual life, though a Freud transplanted into a Puritan culture that, having already begun with the Bible, *Paradise Lost*, and *The Pilgrim's Progress*, was predisposed to regard literary texts as keys to self-improvement.

Feminism: It seems odd, then, that as we approach the end of the 1980s, I find myself having to shift my conceptual grid once again, for Jane Tompkins's essay is a polemic for the return of the personality of the writer (her own, and the artist's). I needn't shift gears to 'accommodate' feminism, since that would not be simply Whiggish, but would also misrepresent the challenge with which, in the figure of the politicized personality, feminism challenges literary criticism. For feminism does not supply the most recent move in the manifest destiny of progress so much as it provides the possibility of the ultimate critique of progress.

As a white, heterosexual, first-world male writing about feminism, I write from a double displacement. But this displacement can only be a productive site of struggle rather than solipsism, since the feminist strategy of personalizing the political is itself double, providing a voice for what was once situated outside while denying not the voice but the objectivity of the insider, the 'typical' male position. If I begin by problematizing Tompkins's recuperation of authorial presence, I do so in order to situate what I have to say at the limits determined by my own socio-sexual position, and by my own historical circumstances, 'directly found, given and transmitted from the past',[5] as Marx would have it.[6] What, I believe, Tompkins has in mind is not so much the return of the 'person' behind the newly enfranchised 'voice' of the 'woman' – though she might well be read this way – but the displacement of the authority of the text by the supplement of the writer.[7]

Detroit, 7 January 1987

Dear Jane,

This is not, then, a journal. This is a response to your response to Ellen Messer-Davidow's essay 'The philosophical bases of feminist literary criticisms'. That final plural, 'criticisms', is crucial since the essay directly addresses the *historical* institutionalization of knowledge. Your argument for the return of the authorial body, on the other hand, is an exploration of the psychoanalytical self inhabiting the *persona* of a professional intellectual. Where Messer-Davidow seeks to displace the voice of a history written by and for men, you do battle with the ghosts of more specifically introjected fathers: Hawthorne, Joyce, Freud, Bloom, Fish. Where Messer-Davidow raises the problematics of feminist literary criticisms as an *epistemological* concern for the first time – 'my aim is to suggest a way of reconstituting knowledge that evolves from feminist perspectives' (p. 64)[8] – she reveals a space which you close off in order to generate a personal response. Your concern for a more precise definition of 'epistemology' seems to me to derive its substance from a metaphysics of presence that, being explicitly personal, is consequently political, though with what Messer-Davidow might call an 'inflection' towards psychologism. I am interested in the political limits and implications of your call for the return of the person.

Detroit, 10 January 1987

Dear Jane,

I am horrified to notice that I haven't written to thank you for kindly sending me, by express, a copy of Messer-Davidow's essay early last December. Thank you.

I have just finished reading it for the second time and am concerned with your observation that Messer-Davidow employs, not unselfconsciously, the codes of the dominant tradition of philosophical discourse, a tradition which – from the opening of her essay – she is eager to center against the plurality of feminist responses in order to displace it as both troublesome and unnecessary to feminists. The problem here, it seems to me, becomes most apparent in the ending of the essay which relies for its political edge upon the ideology of free choice. But hasn't her analytical frame already begun to prove unstable, long before the essay's end? Can't we see it breaking out into assertive positivism by the end of the opening summary when, significantly, she takes on the category of 'formalism' and writes: 'gender traits do not *rightfully* characterize literary forms and language' and 'our *ontology* specifies that people and literary works exist as distinct orders' (p. 69; my emphases)? Her aim, to mark how feminist critics 'who borrow . . . traditional subject-matters necessarily encounter intractable problems' seems as shrewd as the insight which soon follows, that the institutionalization of knowledge has led to a situation in which 'the objects of evaluation and the standards are built into the subject-matters' of literary texts.[9] Nevertheless, I am not sure that 'intractability' is so much a condition of the 'problems' as it is a symptom of an insufficiently theorized humanism, a condition of her own philosophical stance which – as you observe – depends too fully upon the need to engage the dominant masculist discourse in its own terms.

Messer-Davidow misses how the 'troubles' encountered by feminist literary critics who borrow from the subject-matters and methods of the 'research tradition' recrystallize in less intractable ways when the feminist enterprize engages deconstructive marxism. This is an important point since it is upon the basis of her analysis of these troubles that Messer-Davidow offers her solution, which does not make the problems disappear. Her self-critical deployment of an objective method becomes assertive positivism when she encounters an ideology of presence:

formalism. Instead of problematizing the ontology which specifies the alterity of 'people and literary works', she offers up the pluralism of that democratic 'smorgasbord' of 'traditional schools - archetypal, marxist, structuralist, psychoanalytic, semiotic, deconstructive, and hermeneutic, to name a few' (p. 63). Yet it seems to me that the only respect in which we can use these terms to constitute a 'tradition' is that they occupy space within the theoretical discourses of those male-dominated institutions which, in our times, produce those discourses; but, that said, are not the discontinuities more compelling? more politically nuanced? more likely to signal sites where those institutions are most fragile and susceptible to strategic interventions by feminists? It is surely an especially depoliticized feminism that can coordinate archetypal criticism with deconstruction - the one lovingly struggling to recover and reproduce the conditions and forces that forge the tradition at hand, while the other laughingly waves away those constructs as airy nothings, the fantasies and delusions of centuries of masculist fears and anxieties? In my view, deconstructive marxism offers a better strategy for addressing this problematic, for I know of no marxism[10] that, in seeking to demystify the ontological status of the circuits of capital, is not specifically committed to the overthrow of the current institutional control of the means of knowledge production. Despite Messer-Davidow's acknowledgment of the pressures of sexual preference and race on feminist criticism, she barely addresses the urgent claims of Third World women whose oppression under First World imperialism has been historically instituted by capital exchange.

Significantly, both of you ignore the work of Gayatri Spivak, which offers the most forceful critique of the philosophical bases of feminist criticisms. I wish I had with me a copy of her article on 'Revolutions that as yet have no model'. As I understand it, the argument that in order to change the conditions of women's oppression we must change the logic of capital, need not entail subsuming 'the feminist struggle into the "larger" struggle against capital', as Heidi Hartmann puts it, but rather involves situating the terms 'feminism' and 'marxism' (or 'women's oppression' and 'oppression under the logic of capital') *deconstructively*, privileging neither term but seeking rather to make possible their mutual, though discontinuous, articulation.[11] More specifically, the problem Messer-Davidow cannot avoid is the impossibility of reinscribing sex/gender into literary history, analysis, or theory without necessarily engaging questions of class. Her own use of the term 'criticisms', her not infrequent recognition of the deconstructive critique of presence, and her occasional inclusion of the term 'class', reveal the basic liberal pluralism which underlies her enterprise. That is what undermines its political edge, since the 'troubles' of which she writes are those of a 'feminism' seeking to integrate the production of 'women' with the traditional production of literary knowledge.[12] 'We have moved', you write, 'from the New Criticism . . . to structuralism . . . to deconstruction . . . and finally to new historicism . . .'. There it is, the history of criticism in progress form (why does only the first stage get capitals?). What really astonishes me about your defeatist narrative is how it reinscribes the phallic narrative of progress for the sake of a reactionary, anti-feminist argument that is, in any case, true only to the extent that it ignores important work by feminist critics. I too am worried by what passes for 'new historicism' since, as Louis Montrose points out, this term has commonly managed to displace or disable the political commitments of 'cultural materialism'.[13] But your denial of theoretical work by women in order to regret a 'new personalism' that never came about is, arguably, a worse instance of 'pretending . . . women aren't there' than the masculist text you rightly expose (though what could a feminist critic expect from 'the world of the Western', if not the homoerotics of male bonding?). If you 'sometimes . . . think *the world* contains no women', maybe that's because you choose not to see them.

What is at issue here is not only the immediate practical problem of women achieving power within existing cultural institutions, but also the equally immediate and practical problem of refabricating those institutions. 'The literary system', Messer-Davidow writes, 'has not yet admitted the entities and processes that most concern feminist literary critics – our own human ones.' Beyond questions of women in the professions, the problem only becomes fully visible once we articulate sex/gender with race-class, not to indicate a simple homology between the political struggles of 'women' with those of racial or social 'minorities', but to maintain a necessary stance towards the 'problem' as an *overdetermination*. Blake and Marx agreed that the condition of the free development of each is the condition of the free development of all. Admitting the human entities and processes into the social systems and institutions which generate, establish and reproduce the fantasies of late capitalism simply cannot take place without effecting radical change in those systems and institutions.

If this is at all like your agenda, I agree. Where I am not so sure is where you stamp your feet and refuse to change what you believe simply because of a change in the ways you understand yourself to have come to believe that way.[14] When you eventually come to read Deleuze and Guattari, for example, they might help you advance your argument against oedipalizing patriarchal structures. I was struck by the way your expectations turn their 'molecular revolution' into a trope from *The Pilgrim's Progress* – 'a revolution that started with daily life would have to begin . . . at home', which is just where Christian begins his journey.[15] But the passage you quote from Guattari begins with the problem of the mechanization of the subject under advanced capitalism; how much closer to home can one get today? Isn't that the ironic edge of 'the kind of machine we shall be talking about here?' And Foucault's 'we' that you object to is surely a strategic 'we' that seeks to implicate us in the prudery, as well as the discourse of sexuality, that imperialism necessitates. It is a political strategy that you are, of course, free to deny the way you do. But I do hope you might consider how, in the year of celebrating the American Constitution, we are a people who are free to terrorize women outside abortion clinics while allowing our government to pour arms into Central America. I don't find Foucault's 'we' chummy or cosy because I am pretty sure what it does is force us into the recognition that just this sort of connection might be crucial to the project of general liberation from that old story of the male will to power.

Detroit, 4 February 1987

Dear Jane,

My response is now three weeks behind schedule, yet my desk remains covered with notes reminding me of things not to be left out. Since last writing, I have been back to Los Angeles to visit my wife who still lives and works there: but you understand the strains of being married to someone in the same professional field. Most of our books stay in the house we rent in West Hollywood, so, like you, I looked around my favorite bookshelf and found some things that I want to write to you about. I came upon Alice Jardine's piece challenging men to 'talk their bodies', and shall try to address it.[16] And I also found the Spivak essay. The final paragraph is the one I wanted since it addresses this problem about speaking personally without being self-centered:

> even in the most superficial and minimal analysis, one of the most striking characteristics of any version of advanced capitalism is the fragmentation and decentralization of the individual's putative politi-

cal and economic control over her own life. One of the peculiar and paradoxical by-products of this system is to generate a conviction of individual centrality among most members of the intellectual, bourgeois, as well as managerial classes . . . accompanied by either a dispirited anguish against 'their' power, or a spirited faith in 'our' proliferation, with assorted permutations and combinations, of course. The official philosophy of this group is an individualism more or less disguised as pluralism. The generalizable result: lack of any conceivable interest in a collective practice toward social justice.[17]

I think that the itinerary of your response, from those 'two voices answering' to feeling good at having removed the straitjacket, offers a richly nuanced account of this 'conviction'. Since you indicate that professional pressures cause you to hide part of yourself, maybe the way you think, feel and live personally *and* professionally needs to change.

You write: 'it's the same person who feels and who discourses . . . . The problem is that you can't talk about your private life in the course of doing your professional work.' I'm not sure that's true; I'm not sure you can avoid it even writing academic prose. But hasn't the task of those of us involved with intellectual production, as Foucault suggested, become predominantly a matter of talking, not only our talk among ourselves but also the talk of people like those employed in clerical and service positions by the institutions that also employ us? And in any case, doesn't professional discourse include teaching? Maybe instead of just passing on 'hardheaded advice' to your students you could talk to them, professionally, about your interest in the erotics of domination and violence.[18] I am curious about your reasons for mentioning the 'people at the convenience store'. Is it work or class/race or both that marks them as at once other from you and yet the same in their lack of interest in abstract analyses like those of Guattari and Foucault? Diane Turner's report of sexual harassment in the work place offers an amazing insight into working-class consciousness: reading it, I wonder about the woman who could write *this* while working as a cleaner.[19]

What worries me most is your final move, what you do with your anger at a male-dominated culture that subordinates and erases women and their lives. Isn't Alice Miller betraying you by upholding the doctrine of individual uniqueness, a doctrine that centers the self within a personal experience that only has meaning in relation to the formation of that subjectivity? Isn't this one of the more compelling forms of masculist hegemony, this privatization of the personal? Don't we find here that anti-feminist edge to much conventional psychoanalysis which treats women's suffering and oppression as (reversible) products of personal responsibility and choice rather than as necessary conditions of a political arena in which surplus-value must be extracted from 'women'?

Are you sure that the anger you feel is a problem only of 'coming to terms with', 'learning to forgive and understand' those 'contemptuous introjects' so that 'your anger will go away?' And what if it does? why should you wish it to go, *that* way? Isn't the point of recognizing the conditions of this personal anger to politicize it? Beginning with an analysis of the socio-political formations of the family which produced those introjects in the first place? Isn't there more than a likely chance that the desire to treat graduate students as the objects of your hard-headed advice signals a reaction-formation defined by parental/professional pressures that need to be subverted rather than reproduced? Feeling good because one has learned to come to terms with daddy's will simply doesn't take us very far, but to theorize it might lead us to understand and thereby disable the erotics of domination.

So here I am, doing what I was trained to do, telling 'women' what to do, how to think and behave. And I am doing it in that body-less 'objective' language. This is not what feminism wants from men; though I do think there is a familiar and pernicious habit of mind in Alice Miller's attempt to depoliticize women's anger to which I am entitled to object. And I also think that understanding how we come to knowledge can radically alter our relation to what we can believe. On the epistemological question, I find Adrienne Rich both illuminating and persuasive:

> we should [not] be training women students to 'think like men.'
> Men in general think badly: in disjuncture from their personal lives,
> claiming objectivity where the most irrational passions seethe,
> losing, as Virginia Woolf observed, their senses in the pursuit of
> professionalism. It is not easy to think like a woman in a man's
> world, in the world of the professions; yet the capacity to do that is a
> strength which we can try to help our students develop. To think
> like a woman in a man's world means thinking critically, refusing to
> accept the givens, making connections between facts and ideas
> which men have left unconnected. It means remembering that every
> mind resides in a body; remaining accountable to the female bodies

in which we live; constantly retesting given hypotheses against lived experience. It means a constant critique of language, for as Wittgenstein (no feminist) observed, 'The limits of my language are the limits of my world.'[20]

The collective emphases here seem right; they connect with what I think I am trying to do in my professional practice. There are difficulties in my trying to teach women students from a 'feminist' stance. I don't think anyone has begun to examine fully the range of erotic interactions that go on between students and teachers. In class I flirt, consciously and consistently. But I play for laughs and flirt with the men too. I talk about sex a good deal, distinguish it from sexuality and gender, demonstrate how lifeless the canonical works we must read would be without this discourse of sex, and introduce marginal texts which problematize sexual relationships. Teaching in North America, my privileged (English) accent helps a great deal: I can parrot Monty Python voices. My body helps too: over six feet long and skinny, limp-wristed but capable of dashing gestures. Being a man, with this voice and this body, it is easy to play between the farcical and serious modes. Yet like all teachers, I can never fully know just what effect(s) I have.

A student in my freshman class wrote, in a journal response to Stephen Heath's *The Sexual Fix* which we had been discussing: 'Apparently from what Heath conveys, we still center around the worship a dominance of the phallus.' So the problem is 'power' after all. Do we simply correct the grammar? or do we praise the will to use 'center' reflexively thus? or ask about the metaphoric problems of centering 'around?' And how do we know, in these instances, about meaning and intention? The same male student – who continued with a vague comment about the Dionysian cults of ancient Greece – had opened the same journal entry with a self-parodic discussion of orgasm as something that men 'gave' to women. How do we adjudicate these questions of personal experience and knowledge, of literacy and intention? I wrote the sentence on the board, fed the class the line about 'a phallus is a symbol of power, while a penis is only a piece of meat' to the (predictable) laughs, and then outlined the implications of the word-choice – 'we', 'still', 'center', 'dominance' – and the syntax, by drawing a phallus on the board and labelling it the transcendental signifier. We agreed that *up* is always good/true/beautiful while *down* is always evil/false/ugly. I then read Steve's lines about how he took pleasure from 'giving' his girlfriend an orgasm; and we all laughed at the fantasy of

he-with-the-phallus-who-gives. We all agreed that men have some strange
ideas. Prompted by Gail, a twenty-five-year-old divorced mother who
suggested that Heath identified the problem of voyeurism, of men looking
for sex by looking at women, only to fall into the trap himself, several of
the other women agreed that they had noticed this too. We couldn't
connect this insight about men, enjoyment and sight with phallic
organization – though maybe we will later in the term when we read
Rosalind Coward's *Female Desire* – but went on to laugh at the voyeurism
implicit in my asking them to write 'personally' in their journals.

I need to be liked, perhaps because I was brought up by a single parent
after my father left when I was three. Living with Mother while she
struggled to maintain a set of inappropriate values, I quickly learned the
compromise of passive obedience, of internalizing and censoring my own
desires into a trouble-free conformity. I was much alone: perhaps the
origins of my addiction to reading. We lived on the dole in a depressed city
in the south of England where a benevolent educational authority stepped
in and promoted my educatability. Mother's conviction that she was too
good to work – which both legitimated and problematized living on
payments from a welfare system that classified her as 'unemployed' –
were, presumably, confirmed by the family task: make sure the boy does
well. At the age of nine I was tracked for the grammar school to which I
went two years later. Here, in an advanced-placement class, I was
interviewed by the headmaster when I was thirteen about my university
options since to complete state curricula it would be necessary for me to
specialize the subsequent year. I already knew the answer. It had been
discussed at home. Among family at Christmas, it had been the one topic
on which my opinion had been solicited by relatives I had only ever met at
such annual gatherings. I hated school. Of course. It was easy to do what
they wanted, but that made doing it tedious and irritating. I fidgeted.
Being tall and gangly, I simply couldn't sit still. For years stern voices
broke off amidst discussion of Virgil's grammar or some subtler problem
facing the papacy in Avignon to announce that I was to 'Stop fidgeting!'

When I went to college Mother's dole stopped. The minimal social
security payments to which she was now entitled were fixed to cover only
rent: she would have to find gainful employment for the rest. Mother's
moral principles fell apart under the weekly investigations at the
Employment Exchange. She took a job in an old people's home, a suitably
genteel establishment. Combined with voluntary work – assisting at a
weekly luncheon club for ambulatory old-age pensioners living in the

hideous high-rise apartments that typify the housing policies of post-war England – caring for the terminally bed-ridden old ladies gave Mother a new 'center', one that provided a not-inglorious uniform, social status and a minimal material base apart from family or the social services. There was, I recall, talk of her being nominated for civic office as a magistrate – but she had to decline since the position was honorific and therefore unpaid.

Mother died ten years after putting her back out at work, shifting one of her ladies during a blanket bath. Out of work and into the collapse of the public health system, Mother carried her fragile body, scarred by thirty years of cigarette smoking and the strains of solitude. The back injury wouldn't respond to treatment; a hysterectomy uncovered what might have been cancer. Dispirited, intermittently furious – 'I could have made something of my life!' – and self-pitying, Mother continued to decay. The family were dispersed and generally independent in the typical *petit bourgeois* sort of way. Mother lived alone. When obliged to take to a wheelchair at the age of sixty-two, she gave up, committed herself to the local psychiatric hospital and died of a stroke ten days later in November 1983.

I was teaching in Ontario, my first post-doctoral appointment. Donna and I had begun our first year of professional separation in September: how could she turn down the offer of a job at Princeton? I had just arrived back in Kingston from driving her to the Syracuse airport when an uncle in Toronto phoned with the news of Mother's death.

Two years later I told all this to a psychiatrist in Ann Arbor as the occasion for my being there to see him. I had just read Alice Miller's book about 'gifted' children and felt what all readers are encouraged to feel, that I hadn't grieved properly. The previous year Donna had resigned from Princeton for a terminal appointment at Michigan that coincided with my move to Detroit. That winter, during a period of gloom which reading Miller led me to associate with guilt over Mother's death, I had hit Donna during an argument over nothing that important. This must not happen again. The analyst wanted a contract of two hours a week for a minimum of four years. As part of my commitment to analysis, I was to pay for all sessions, even those I knew I couldn't attend. He told me I had unresolved problems with my mother, which was of course no more than I had told him on arrival. I didn't sign up. I couldn't afford the percentage my insurance wouldn't pay. And after the diagnostic sessions I no longer felt that problems with Mother had very much to do with the specific problem of my violence. I was already aware of an important body of work being done on male violence, but began to notice how this knowledge is typically constituted as a science of the other. When I learned just how common 'domestic' violence is, I recall being both horrified and amazed since my own experience had seemed so unusual. While living the contradiction that what I did may be 'normal' but not therefore legitimate (or even very much like the paradigms offered), I remain convinced that institutional privileges and pressures, a whole lifetime of them yet to be encountered, still bear more directly than my 'earliest affective experience with [my] mother'.[21] I am still surprised, when talking about this, to find how many men and women have personal experience of violence. The knowledge that my act was really not so unusual is no comfort. Rather it has made me angry at the way we all put up with so much that is intolerable. In terms of scholarship, for example, there is the way historians continue to ignore the struggles and achievements of women, the problem at which I began directing my research.[22] I wonder, Jane, what more you might have to say on the problems of your husband's 'influence'. I was sad you left this topic of marriage/professional pressures in symptomatic silence.

I am trying to demonstrate how thinking about how I knew changed what I thought. Doesn't Miller partly generate the narcissism from which she assumes we all suffer by describing a 'drama' of the 'gifted' with which her readers are bound to identify? Aren't her politics suspect? Why recuperate Freud's seduction theory the way she does? For myself, why should I want to account for my violence by discovering links with Mother's death? Miller writes: 'If we were to tell a patient that in other societies his perversion would not be a problem, that it is a problem here sheerly because it is our society that is sick and produces constrictions and constraints, this would certainly be partially true, but it would be of little help to him. He would feel, rather, that, as an individual, with his own individual history, he was being passed over and misunderstood; for this interpretation makes too little of his own very real tragedy' (p. 99). That is just what theory has led me not to believe, that the importance of my own tragic history has meaning only for me in the recesses of my perversions. What I think matters is how mine is a typical history that will (tragically) be repeated, in various forms, so long as we continue to believe that it is primarily the subject and not the structure that needs help, needs to be changed. If I suggest that for those of us in the 'intellectual, bourgeois . . . managerial classes' which Spivak describes, the erotics of domination entails the articulation of personal, professional and political forces in order to facilitate the extraction of surplus-value in the form of our need for psychiatric 'benefits', I do so because it makes better sense of my experience. And that experience is one that includes a 'wife' who says 'no', who does not respond to my temper-tantrums the way Mother did, whose intellectual sophistication often awes me, and who has taught me that the personal is always political even when it seems most private.

So that's why I am not so sure that we should identify 'theory itself' as 'one of the patriarchal gestures women *and* men ought to avoid', even though I am aware how theory has often been implicated in male sexism.[23] In 'Men in feminism', Alice Jardine suggests that one thing men need to do is learn how to talk their bodies. She provides a list of topics some of which I have tried to address. I have spoken of my mother, death, madness, paranoia, and desire. And I have added violence since it surely underwrites the operations of erotics and domination; in my case, I continue to believe, at the point of a socio-professional breakdown requiring a change in my attitude towards the profession and a change in the way I work. Rather than paying for analytical introspection in which some self-revealing 'I' might learn to play out my memories in order to reaffirm my sense of centrality in my 'own very real tragedy', as Miller would have me do, I have realigned how I think about my work and my relation to the profession, not through a single act of will but through a constant collective negotiation. This is not, exactly, a rejection of psychoanalysis; forms of psychoanalysis and therapy differ, and not all are as complacently silent on the socio-political structuring of the subject or the political redirection of feminist anger. But the *dominant* profile of psychiatric and psychoanalytical practices under late capitalism remains too often complicit with the notion of a therapeutic individualism, the recuperation of a subject whose anger must be made deeply and specifically personal and then made 'to go away'. Together with the enormous financial investment that therapy represents, with or without medical insurance, this depoliticizing tendency marks the purely psychoanalytical path to personal rehabilitation as suspect for a feminist practice. This is not, then, a complete rejection of psychoanalysis, but an attempt at repositioning the subject of analysis. So to those feminist scholars who have shared social, professional and always already political insights with me, who have taught me where to direct my anger - to Carol Barash, Laura Brown, Claire Crabtree, Julia Emberley, Moira Ferguson, Elaine Hobby, Linda Kauffman, Tania Modleski, Felicity Nussbaum, Tilottama

Rajan, Hilary Schor, Gayatri Spivak, Rachel Weil, Marilyn Williamson, and Winnie Woodhull – I confidently insist that I know violence need not be the only inevitable result of anger.

NOTES

1 The closing words of the first part of John Bunyan's *The Pilgrim's Progress* (1678), ed. Sharrock (1965: 205).

2 For a recent, important example of the American tradition of reading literary texts as vehicles for self-improvement, see the chapter on *Uncle Tom's Cabin* in Tompkins 1985: 122-46.

3 See Colin MacCabe, 'Class of '68: Elements of an intellectual autobiography 1967-81', in MacCabe 1985; pp. 1-32 for a general critique of 'Cambridge English' during this time. See also entries by Muriel Bradbrook and Raymond Williams in *My Cambridge*, ed. Ronald Hayman (London: Robson, 1977), pp. 38-52, pp. 53-70, and Mulhern 1979.

4 Watson's 'Everyman' editions of Dryden's *Of Dramatic Poesy and Other Essays*, 2 vols (London: Dent, 1962), and Coleridge's *Biographia Literaria* (London: Dent, 1965) were standard though unofficial critical texts for those 'reading English' at this time.

5 *The Eighteenth Brumaire of Louis Bonaparte* (1852), repr. in *The Marx-Engels Reader*, ed. Tucker, 2nd edn 1978: 595.

6 The problem here might be called the 'Tootsie-syndrome' by which men are needed to tell women how to live, act and think. The best challenge comes from the gay perspective which theorizes the question of sexual preference beyond the allure of libertarian free-choiceism, as the displacement of a politics of difference by a politics of identity.

7 See Derrida, trans. Spivak, 1974; repr. 1980: 141-64.

8 It is not surprising that Messer-Davidow's concern for a political epistemology ignores the extensive work done in this field by marxist literary theorists. The development of a materialist epistemology is central to the marxist commitment to the social constitution of consciousness. For a politically hostile history of these debates within marxist literary theory, see Fokkema and Ibsch 1978, repr. 1986: 81-135. But see also Volosinov 1973, repr. 1986, which challenges Saussurean linguistics by means of elaborating a materialist epistemology.

9 This echoes I. A. Richards's discovery that, stripped of their author and title, 'great' poems were no more likely to stimulate positive student readings than minor works.

10 On 'small "m" marxism' see Swindells 1984: 56-70, following Coward 1983.

11 On the antagonism between marxism and feminism, see Hartmann 1981: 2, see also Rowbotham 1973; repr. 1981; Barrett 1980; Weir and Wilson 1984: 74-103, and Barrett's response (Barrett 1985: 143-7).

12 In 'Scattered speculations on the question of value' (1985b: 73-93), Spivak links the problem of 'subjectivity' with 'textuality' by arguing that 'if the subject has a

'materialist' predication, the question of value necessarily receives a textualized answer' (p. 74).

13 Montrose 1986: 5-12. Compare Dollimore 'Shakespeare, cultural materialism and the New Historicism', in Dollimore and Sinfield 1985: esp. 3.

14 For literary theory, the problem is that this belief in the irreversible 'self' - a symptomatic ideal of bourgeois individualism - fails to meet the post-structuralist denial of the subject position. As Spivak writes in 'Feminism and critical theory' (1985a: 121): 'the discourse of the literary text is part of a general configuration of textuality, a placing forth of the solution as the unavailability of a unified solution to a unified or homogeneous, generating or receiving, consciousness.' See also Benton's introduction to Althusser's concept of 'interpellation,' which posits the social constitution of 'the subject and its subjection' in Benton 1984: esp. 173-99; the phrase is from p. 197. Compare Macdonell 1986: 36-42, and Althusser's own formulation in 'Ideology and ideological state apparatuses', in Althusser 1971: 127-86.

15 Jacques Derrida links this habit of reading according to prior expectation with the journey of the unitary self in a lyrical passage of *The Post Card: From Socrates to Freud and Beyond* (1987): 'Because I still like him, I can foresee the impatience of the *bad* reader: this is the way I name or accuse the fearful reader, the reader in a hurry to be determined, decided upon deciding (in order to annul, in other words to bring back to oneself, one has to wish to know in advance what to expect, one wishes to expect what has happened, one wishes to expect (oneself)). Now, it is bad, and I know no other definition of the bad, it is bad to predestine one's reading, it is always bad to foretell. It is bad, reader, no longer to like retracing one's steps' (p. 4).

16 Alice Jardine, 1984: 23-30; repr. in *Men In Feminism*, ed. Alice Jardine and Paul Smith (London: Methuen, 1987), pp. 54-61.

17 Spivak 1980: 48.

18 Besides the many excellent pieces on politicizing the classroom, see David Herreshoff's essay on the class discontinuities between students at Wayne State and the University of Michigan during the late 1960s (1984: 38-45).

19 For those of us who work in universities and suffer from the illusions of centrality vis-à-vis intellectual production, Turner's piece offers an excellent reminder of how intellectual and textual production takes place in industry; 1986: 106-16.

20 Rich 1978, repr. in *Gendered Subjects: The Dynamics of Feminist Teaching*, ed. Margo Culley and Catherine Portuges (London: Routledge and Kegan Paul, 1985), p. 28.

21 Miller 1981: 99.

22 The recovery of the lives, works and achievements of early English feminists has recently produced some important corrective studies, such as Ferguson 1985, Rogers 1982, Nussbaum 1984, and Prior 1985. On how the considerable social and political achievements of women in England during the Civil Wars of the seventeenth century were culturally suppressed at the Restoration, see the introduction to my edition of Poullain de la Barre's *The Woman As Good As The Man* (1988). On the silencing of proletarian women poets by traditional literary history, see Landry 1987.

23 See Modleski 1984: 12-13.

156 *Gerald M. MacLean*

REFERENCES

Althusser, Louis 1971. 'Ideology and ideological state apparatuses', in *Lenin and Philosophy and Other Essays*, trans. Ben Brewster. London: Monthly Review.

Barrett, Michèle 1980. *Women's Oppression Today: Problems in Marxist Feminist Analysis*. London: Verso.

Barrett, Michèle 1985. 'Weir and Wilson on feminist politics', *New Left Review*, 150: 143-7.

Benton, Ted 1984. *The Rise and Fall of Structural Marxism*. New York: St. Martins.

Bradbrook, Muriel 1977. *My Cambridge*. Ed. Ronald Hayman. London: Robson.

Bunyan, John 1965. *Pilgrim's Progress* (1678). Ed. Roger Sharrock. Harmondsworth: Penguin.

Coward, Rosalind 1983. *Patriarchal Precedents: Sexuality and Social Relations*. London: Routledge and Kegan Paul.

Derrida, Jacques 1976. *Of Grammatology*. Trans. Gayatri Chakravorty Spivak. Baltimore: Johns Hopkins University Press.

Derrida, Jacques 1987. *The Post Card: From Socrates to Freud and Beyond*. Trans. Alan Bass. Chicago: University of Chicago Press.

Dollimore, Jonathan 1985. 'Shakespeare, cultural materialism and the New Historicism', in *Political Shakespeare: New Essays in Cultural Materialism*, ed. Jonathan Dollimore and Alan Sinfield. Manchester: Manchester University Press.

Ferguson, Moira 1985. *First Feminists: British Women Writers 1578-1799*. Bloomington: Indiana University Press.

Fokkema, Douwe and Ibsch, Elrud 1978. *Theories of Literature in the Twentieth Century*. Repr. New York: St. Martin's.

Hartmann, Heidi 1981. 'The unhappy marriage of marxism and feminism: towards a more progressive union', in *Women and Revolution*, ed. Lydia Sargent. Boston: South End Press.

Herreshoff, David 1984. 'Teaching Mark Twain in the 1960s, 1970s, and 1980s', *The Monthly Review* (June): 38-45.

Jardine, Alice 1984. 'Men in feminism: odor di uomo or compagnons de route?', *Critical Exchange*, 18: 23-30. Repr. in *Men In Feminism*, ed. Alice Jardine and Paul Smith, London: Methuen 1987.

Landry, Donna 1987. 'The resignation of Mary Collier: some problems in feminist literary history', in *The New Eighteenth Century: Theory, Politics, English Literature*, ed. Felicity Nussbaum and Laura Brown. London: Methuen.

MacCabe, Colin 1985. *Tracking the Signifier. Theoretical Essays: Film, Linguistics, Literature*. Minneapolis: University of Minnesota Press.

Macdonnel, Diane 1986. *Theories of Discourse: An Introduction*. Oxford: Blackwell.

Marx, Karl 1978. *The Marx-Engels Reader*. Ed. Robert Tucker. 2nd edn, New York: Norton.

Miller, Alice 1981. *The Drama of the Gifted Child*. Trans. Ruth Ward. New York: Basic Books.

Modleski, Tania 1984. *Loving With A Vengeance: Mass-Produced Fantasies For Women*. London: Methuen.

Montrose, Louis 1986. 'Renaissance literary studies and the subject of history', *English Literary Renaissance*, 16: 5-12.

Mulhern, Francis 1979. *The Moment of 'Scrutiny'*. London: New Left Books.

Nussbaum, Felicity 1984. *The Brink of All We Hate: Social Satires on Women 1660-1750*. Lexington: University of Kentucky Press.

Poullain de la Barre, Francois 1988. *The Woman As Good As The Man*. Ed. Gerald M. MacLean. Detroit: Wayne State University Press.

Prior, Mary (ed.) 1985. *Women in English Society 1500-1800*. London: Methuen.

Rich, Adrienne 1985. 'Taking women students seriously'. Repr. in *Gendered Subjects: The Dynamics of Feminist Teaching*, ed. Margo Culley and Catherine Portuges, London: Routledge and Kegan Paul.

Rogers, Katharine 1982. *Feminism in Eighteenth-Century England*. Urbana: University of Illinois Press.

Rowbotham, Sheila 1973. *Woman's Consciousness, Man's World*. Repr. Harmondsworth: Penguin, 1981.

Spivak, Gayatri Chakravorty 1980. 'Revolutions that as yet have no model: Derrida's *Limited Inc.*', *Diacritics* 10: 29-49.

Spivak, Gayatri Chakravorty 1985a. 'Feminism and critical theory', in *For Alma Mater: Theory and Practice in Feminist Scholarship*, ed. Paula A. Treichler, Cheris Kramarae and Beth Stafford. Urbana: University of Illinois Press.

Spivak, Gayatri Chakravorty 1985b. 'Scattered speculations on the question of value', *Diacritics*, 14: 73-93.

Swindells, Julia 1984. 'Falling short with Marx: some glimpses of 19th century sexual ideology', in *Literature/Teaching/Politics*, 4: 56-70.

Tompkins, Jane 1985. *Sensational Designs: The Cultural Work of American Fiction, 1790-1860*. New York: Oxford University Press.

Turner, Diane 1986. 'The wages of virtue', *New Left Review*, 159: 106-16.

Volosinov, V. N. 1973. [Bakhtin, Mikhail] *Marxism and the Philosophy of Language*. Trans. 1973; repr. L. Matejka and I. R. Titunik. Repr. Cambridge: Harvard University Press 1986.

Watson, George (ed.) 1962. *John Dryden: Of Dramatic Poesy and Other Essays*. 2 vols. London: Dent.

Watson, George (ed.) 1965. *S. T. Coleridge: Biographia Literaria*. London: Dent.

Weir, Angela and Wilson, Elizabeth 1984. 'The British Women's Movement', *New Left Review*, 148: 74-103.

Williams, Raymond 1977. *My Cambridge*. Ed. Ronald Hayman. London: Robson.

7

Of Me(n) and Feminism: Who(se) is the Sex that Writes?

Joseph Allen Boone

The lead essay in *Men in Feminism* opens with an eye-catching assertion, one that is as provocative as it is literally and figuratively *arresting*. 'Men's relation to feminism', Stephen Heath writes, 'is an impossible one. This is not said sadly nor angrily . . . but politically.'[1] Heath's claim to dispassionate objectivity and political correctness notwithstanding, the contents of this volume soon make it very clear that a great many of his colleagues are indeed angry and/or sad when it comes to the politics and claims of men's relation to feminism: these essays fairly bristle with the antagonistic emotions conjured forth by the subject matter announced in the controversial title of the volume – an antagonism fueled by the very wording of that title, in which the loaded preposition 'in' is made to bear the weight of a rather questionable relation between men and feminism. But that relation, according to Heath, is also supposedly 'an impossible one', and it is telling to note how Heath's formulation has set the tone for, as well as defined the limits of and boundaries to, nearly all the discussion that follows: one critic after the other in *Men in Feminism*, whatever his or her personal reading of the issue, nonetheless accedes to the *theoretical impossibility* of men ever being 'in' feminism *except* as an act of penetration, violence, coercion, or appropriation. Further speculation is thus arrested at the very point of transgression (the title's suspect 'in'); in place of connection, in the place of connection (that pivot between 'men'/'feminism'), anger and resentment break loose.

I'd like to suggest, however, that 'being *in*' isn't the only relation possible between men/feminism, and hence I'll take the present opportunity to redirect our attention to the *possibilities* (rather than impossibilities) inherent in the potential conjunction of men *and* feminism. For if we can find our way out of Heath's incapacitating metaphor of arrest, we may also find a way out of an equally incapacitating anger over the issue of inclusion/exclusion. This is not to ignore the very real political ramifications of questions of being 'in' or 'out', nor is it, I hope, to overlook the dangers of speaking for such 'possibility' in a phallocentric world where power is still overwhelmingly male-identified; rather it is an attempt to chart a path whereby these points of contention, these potential limits, do not automatically bar our thinking through the issue of men and feminism. At the same time, I'd also like to suggest that *theorizing* the topic, as Heath and company often eloquently do, while it is obviously essential, also risks becoming essentializing; the issues suffusing the topic of men and feminism should not come to be perceived merely as a set of grammatical relations ('in' or 'for' or 'against'), at the expense of the simultaneously lived and practiced dimensions of that relation.

Thus, I'd like to risk personalizing the issue in the pages that follow, rather than leaving it an exclusively theoretical one. And one way of doing this, as the first half of my title (perhaps too playfully) suggests, will be to coax forth a bit of the 'me', the personal pronoun hidden in the word 'men', the biologically determined category to which that pronoun also belongs – that individual 'me' in this case being the voice of a man who for years now has found in feminism a theory, praxis, and way of life that has become synonymous with his, my, sense of identity. In exposing the latent multiplicity and difference in the word 'me(n)', we can perhaps open up a space within the discourse of feminism where a male feminist voice *can* have something to say beyond impossibilities and apologies and unresolved ire. Indeed, if the male feminist can discover a position *from which* to speak that neither elides the importance of feminism to his work nor ignores the specificity of his gender, his voice may also find that it no longer exists as an abstraction – the case leveled against several of the male contributors to *Men in Feminism* – but that it in fact inhabits a body: its own sexual/textual body. In this regard, the really crucial question for feminists – male and female alike – is how to formulate terms for presenting the issue of 'men and feminism' so as not to limit its possibilities, overdetermine its body, from the onset.

My analysis will begin with precisely this danger. For at least in the field of literary criticism, it strikes me that the most important *public* discussions of the topic-to-date have been cast, however consciously or unconsciously, in terms of a two-dimensional oppositionality that has negatively structured our very perception of the issue, both as a theory and as a reality. In order to investigate the ways in which the debate surrounding men and feminism has been articulated, along with the premises underlying those articulations, I have chosen to focus on five random moments through which the topic has at once been made visible and indeed become politicized *as an issue* over the past few years: (1) Elaine Showalter's publication of 'Critical cross-dressing' in 1983, the first prominent summary of the 'male feminist' phenomenon; (2) the controversial double panel 'Men in Feminism I & II' presented at the 1984 MLA Convention; (3) another MLA panel, on 'Male feminist voices', in which I participated in 1986; (4) the publication, last year, of *Men in Feminism*, which stems from the panel of the same name; and, finally, (5) the conceptualization of this very volume on gender and theory (originally subtitled 'dialogues between the sexes'). There is nothing absolute or binding about these stages, I hasten to emphasize, for they consist of events to which I have had very personal and indeed subjective relations – be it as friend, outsider, spectator, or contributor. But that is part of my point, for it has been in the very intimacies and awkwardnesses of my position in relation to each of these events that I have recurrently experienced the aforesaid gap between the 'me' and 'men' in 'me(n)'. And, as the following section will now detail, it has been my experience of this discontinuity that has in turn inspired me to question the discursive formations whereby the concept of men and feminism, transformed into a territorial battlefield, has attained its currently 'impossible' status.

Narratives of impossibility

Although feminism has always remained acutely aware of its relation to men, the reverse situation hasn't necessarily been true. One of the great insights of Elaine Showalter's simultaneously witty and serious 'Critical cross-dressing: male feminists and the woman of the year' was to pinpoint the formation of one such moment of reversal. For, by tapping into two seemingly unrelated cultural events to show the same masculine anxiety operating in both, Showalter proposed a link between an unexpected, and unexpectedly popular, phenomenon in several early 1980s films – the rise of the female impersonator or male heroine – and an equally unexpected phenomenon in academic circles – the avowal, by several prominent male literary critics, of their 'conversion' to feminist literary theory.[2] In planning her essay as a review article for *Raritan*, Showalter had on hand a number of seemingly disparate texts from which to extract this unlikely thread: Susan Dworkin's *Making Tootsie*,

Jonathan Culler's *On Deconstruction*, Terry Eagleton's *The Rape of Clarissa* and *Literary Theory*; Terry Castle's *Clarissa's Ciphers*; Nina Auerbach's *Woman and the Demon*. In particular, the pseudo-feminism embodied in the film *Tootsie* (where Dorothy Michaels's *female* 'power', after all is said and done, is only a *man's* masquerade) provided Showalter with a fascinating analogue for analyzing as instances of 'critical cross-dressing' the recently donned garb of feminist theory apparent in Culler and Eagleton's books. Within this framework, Showalter argues that the irony of Culler's attempt to bring feminism positively to bear on deconstruction lies in his reluctance to foreground the relation of his own gender to such an endeavor; much as he advocates deconstruction's incorporation of feminist methods as a positive gain, he himself remains the untainted deconstructor, the removed and authorizing interpreter or 'analyst of feminist critical work' (p. 126) who has (safely) positioned himself *outside* the feminist readings that he is, in actuality, often producing. Eagleton's claim to find an ally for his marxist agenda in feminism emerges as a more pernicious masquerade than Culler's: in fact, Showalter argues, Eagleton assumes the rhetoric of feminist criticism in order to compete with, dominate over, and ultimately recuperate it for his own aggrandizement. Rather than a 'revolutionary' coupling of the two *-isms*, his reading of *Clarissa* might be said to recapitulate a traditionally figured marriage, with the marxist 'groom' ultimately silencing his feminist 'bride' by speaking over-loudly for and on behalf of her.[3]

Through such provocative and perceptive readings, then, Showalter's review gives expression to the very understandable fear of the appropriation or 'raid' (p. 129) of feminist criticism by male critics eager to cash in on its early successes. But Showalter's focus, from its very beginning, also unconsciously problematizes the issue she is investigating, namely by making what she calls the 'first wave of male feminist criticism' (p. 131) appear synonymous with what is in fact a highly select and specialized group of well-known critics – Wayne Booth, Robert Scholes, Culler, and Eagleton are the male critics the article actually names. All four are very powerful men in the academy already identified with specific schools of criticism other than feminist criticism, and with strong pre-existing allegiances that therefore almost inevitably overdetermine and modify their professions of feminist sympathy. By not raising the possibility that the most empathetic, least appropriative feminist critical practice might be happening *elsewhere* – away from public view, by precisely those men who lack the academic power, rank, or numerous publications of

Showalter's 'cross-dressers' – 'Critical cross-dressing' therefore creates the illusion of a discursive field in which 'male feminism' can only be perceived in terms of a struggle for power among superpowers (Showalter versus Eagleton, say), and hence as potentially antagonistic, intrusive, or threatening to those who have fought for years to legitimize feminism within the academy. There is a catch here, of course, for the problem is *not* Showalter's ignorance (or dismissal) of an 'other side' to male feminism (on the contrary: as those who know her can attest, she has been one of the most generous and openly receptive supporters of young male scholars engaged in feminist research.) The catch is in the simple fact that 'Critical cross-dressing' was designated, from its beginnings, as a review article of books published in 1982–3; and the trends that Showalter finds in that published work, augmented by her perception of the suspect 'feminism' of films like *Tootsie*, are indeed congruent with her conclusions. The irony is that the terms that her overview evolved out of its highly specific context – that of the book review – quickly became for many other interested and concerned feminists *the* terms for examining the whole issue of men and feminism as 'men in feminism'.

In speaking of the contexts that shape a text's reception, however, I feel I owe my readers an explanation of the contexts shaping my own reception of this article. As I forewarned in my introductory remarks, each of the stages I will be tracing has its very personal dimension, and 'Critical cross-dressing' is no exception. In this case, the context was provided by Harvard's Center for Literary Studies, which in the autumn of 1984 created its Feminist Literary Theory Seminar – a Harvard 'first'. And the topic of discussion for the first meeting, as one of my colleagues, Marjorie Garber, informed me, was to be Showalter's article. My initial excitement was brought to a halt, however, when Marge apologetically added that, against her own recommendation, men were specifically not invited to this meeting; some of the founding members felt that the topic was too sensitive, that the women in the seminar needed to reach a group consensus before opening its doors to men. 'But I'll pirate you my copy of the essay,' Marge said with a complicitous wink, 'under the circumstances, I'd love to hear your reactions!' On the one hand, I can't say that I didn't find it somewhat ironic that women from as far away as Dartmouth and Wesleyan could come to my institution to discuss 'male feminism', while I – one of the only nominally practicing 'male feminists' I knew of on campus at that time – couldn't. But, on the other hand, I'd been in the field too long to dismiss lightly the claims of separatism at specific historical junctures, and so I tried to convince myself not to make too much out of this one incident. *Nonetheless*, as might well be imagined, the immediate result was that I read the Showalter article with extra special care, determined to discover my difference from the 'male feminists' of the article's title - I didn't want to be assimilated to men who, metaphorically speaking, had usurped my presence in the seminar room! It is little wonder, then, that 'Critical cross-dressing' came to mark a significant plateau in my perception of 'male feminism' as a more problematic issue than I'd previously experienced it; it marked (or marked out, one might say) my position as a feminist at Harvard in a new light.

These reflections are intimately connected to the second event that I have chosen to examine as a significant moment in the politicization of the concept of male feminism: the volatile double panel, organized under the title 'Men in feminism: men and feminist theory', that took place at the 1984 MLA Convention in Washington, D.C. For, once again, it was a personal exchange - again involving my institutional relation to Harvard, and Harvard's nascent relation to Women's Studies - that first brought this particular event to my attention. The setting for this exchange was a dinner held on 13 December 1984 for one of the English Department's candidates for a Women's Studies position - exactly one week, incidentally, after the *second* meeting of the Feminist Literary Theory Seminar, to which men as well as women had been invited. Seated at a long table at a Cambridge restaurant named 'Autre Chose', Alice Jardine and I literally found ourselves 'les autres', shunted to the far end of the table so that the senior faculty members in attendance could grill the candidate from its center, as it were. It turned out to be a fortuitous exclusion from the dominant discourse, however, since it brought Alice and myself - we'd arrived at Harvard the same year - into dialogue for the first time. And in our getting to know each other, Alice mentioned the problems she was having coming up with a satisfactory response paper for an MLA panel she was on, a panel on men and feminism (I didn't pick up on the 'in' at that point): she didn't find the two papers (Heath's and Smith's) she'd received very helpful, didn't want to sound dictatorial or better-than-thou about what they, or other men interested in feminism, should be saying, but didn't want to let these guys entirely off the hook for being so persistently abstract either. Even now I can remember wondering why *these* men were the ones speaking to the subject if they were so bad, but at the time I decided to wait till the Convention and judge for myself.

For, despite Alice's ambivalence (with which I could empathize, given her position as respondent), the intention of the panel from my position (as one of its subjects) seemed entirely credible and even potentially admirable - namely, to give voice to the growing perception among men and women alike that the increased participation of men in feminist discourse added a new and problematical dimension to the history of feminist criticism. But the very constitution of the panel, as I was to discover two weeks later, posed the enunciation of the problem in an equally problematic way. Male panelists - not Showalter's now (in)famous 'cross-dressers' but, as Jardine stressed, 'those men who are *really trying* . . . our allies' (p. 56; emphasis added) - were invited by the panel's organizer, Paul Smith, to *theorize* about their relation to feminism for the first session, whereupon, in the second meeting, the women respondents took the men to task for theorizing rather than practicing what they preached. Among the men, two of the panelists, Paul Smith and Stephen Heath, fairly explicitly set themselves up as outsiders wishing to be 'in' to feminism, while the third, Andrew Ross, sidestepped any direct consideration of his role as a male feminist by offering a specific case-analysis of sexual difference.[4] Besides Alice, the second panel consisted of Judith Mayne, Elizabeth Weed, and Peggy Kamuf, and the collective tone that emerged from their responses was one of a general weariness at having, once again, to be the ones to say, in Alice's paraphrase, ' "That's not quite it . . . you're not there yet" ' (p. 54); from all four there also emerged the shared suspicion that to the extent that men were 'there' in feminism at all, it was, again in Alice's words, 'to speak about "something else" - some "larger issue" ' (p. 55).[5]

But while much of the criticism of male appropriations of feminist theory for 'larger' ends, as in Showalter's essay, was clearly on target, *the very format* of the two panels (men as a unified body visually and temporally set against women as a unified body; men speculating about 'entering' the ranks of feminist women; the latter reprimanding the former for their bad behavior, 'rather tired' [p. 88] imitations of feminist theory, and 'all too familiar' [p. 72] arguments 'which do not take us very far' [p. 71]), disturbingly seemed to reproduce the two-sided oppositionality against which the feminist concept of difference ideally sets itself: potential dialogue had become confrontation between two 'sides' aligned by gender, sides whose interaction was thereby doomed to reinforce stereotypes of both sexes (men blunder in, women scold). In the process the question of differences within and between the men's perspectives, much less the women's, was set aside. One didn't have to read far between the lines, for example, to discern Smith's disagreements with Heath, and vice versa; in many ways Ross and Mayne's methodology, or Heath and Kamuf's style, shared perhaps more in common than Ross did with Heath, or Mayne with Kamuf; furthermore, gender differences notwithstanding, Jardine's down-to-earth approach was the *only* one to offer a pragmatic outline of what a male feminist praxis might include. In a word, the demarcations along the lines of gender valorized by the panels' format hardly provided the final word on the complexity of viewpoints being expressed.

Sitting in the audience, eager to see an issue so close to home being treated seriously yet frustrated by its very airing, I experienced a series of contradictory reactions. First of all, throughout the men's talks, I kept thinking how they were not speaking for me, for the 'me' in 'men', or, for that matter, for my male friends; in particular, Heath and Smith's excessively abstract attempts to intellectualize their relation to feminism seemed a detour for setting that relation into practice – for all their words and wordplays, for all their confessional techniques, their texts seemed void of any body, any immediate presence: I couldn't touch them, they didn't touch me. During the question period that followed and intermittently throughout the second panel, moreover, I found myself siding with the women's anger against those hypothesized male entrepreneurs jumping on the 'feminist theory bandwagon' (p. 57) now that most of the groundwork had been done; the intrusiveness of such critics happened at my expense too, I found myself thinking, I had 'been there' years before the arrival of these belated converts, with their too-easy criticisms and how-to mandates. And yet a third impression simultaneously set in: for, as the female critiques accelerated, I began to feel a belated sympathy for the actual men (rather than the hypothesized appropriators) who had participated in the morning's session. They, after all, by virtue of their age and lack of professional status alone, were far from being the 'born-again' Bandwagoners or 'Divide and Conquerors' (p. 56) under censure, and yet the format which they had either helped organize or agreed to participate in was setting them up in a no-win situation, it struck me, a no-win situation that in the long run simply enacted a reversal on an all-too-familiar female dilemma: be vulnerable, expose your uncertainties, then listen without recourse to response as your offerings are picked apart. It was now, it appeared, the man's turn to suffer and be silent. And yet it was *not* even that simple or symmetrical a reversal, the more I thought about it; for the very format of the panel had also channeled the *earned* authority of these women to criticize the arguments of these three men into a depressingly traditional 'feminine' role: their authority all of a sudden *appearing* merely that of the proverbially castrating mother scolding her wayward sons, their authority voicing itself only secondarily or reactively, in response to men's words.[6] Nor was my discomfort at the outcome of the session entirely gender-bound; a female colleague with whom I'd attended the second session expressed a similar estrangement from these women who were - supposedly - also speaking for her. As I left the panel, I kept trying to imagine where my voice fitted in the spectrum I had just witnessed, and, more pointedly, which of the two panels I would have chosen to participate in, had I had the choice: in either case, in my case, in the case of feminist scholarship at large, *whose* is the sex, finally, that speaks?

I had my chance to appear on the other side of the audience two years later, when I was asked by Laura Claridge and Elizabeth Langland to moderate an MLA panel they were arranging on 'Male feminist voices within a patriarchal language' - the focus this time around being on the 'sympathetic' male writer, rather than the male critic, attempting to write in a non-phallic mode. At the time I couldn't imagine a more ideal situation. Laura and Elizabeth were seeking a moderator in name so that they could at once organize the panel and present papers on it, and thus I would get a free trip to the MLA with a minimal amount of work - merely introducing the session and the speakers. Moreover, the panel's prospectus struck me very much as a step in the right direction. It suggested that we locate the male voice as a third or odd term in a gendered discourse that consists of (at least) man, woman, and the dominant cultural ideology that we call patriarchy: that is, maleness needn't be assumed to be coeval with patriarchy, with woman symmetrically positioned on the other side of the proposition. But the very *construction* of the panel - as I found when I read the selected papers - tended to blur this important move and reinstate a male-female opposition. Part of the problem was, simply, the plain old element of chance that enters into the arrangement of any panel. For it so happened, first, that all the chosen panelists were women (although both men and women applied), and second, that all their papers, while excellent, nonetheless focused on *men writing about women* - only indirectly, if at all, on men writing about their own sexuality and desire. Which again set up a situation in which it was rather easy, *too* easy, to criticize the male writer for attempting to speak on behalf of women, rather than on behalf of his own anxieties as a man incapacitated by language and patriarchal law; whether the subject was Shelley on feminine ideality, Emerson on Margaret Fuller, Forster on the Schlegel sisters, or Hardy on Tess, sympathy was shown to transform itself into a form of appropriation as the authorial voice inevitably became entangled with the patriarchal rhetoric against which it was ostensibly rebelling.[7]

But such critiques, however applicable to these authors, couldn't begin to answer a number of other questions that such a panel *might* have opened up. What difference, for instance, might the perspective of a man on the panel have made? Had any panelists – male *or* female – examined a male author's exploration of his own sexuality, might a more 'authentic' male – as opposed to phallocentric and appropriative – desire been located? What of the male writer writing from a gay or otherwise marginalized perspective of race or class? (Forster, the one homosexual author under consideration, was only examined, tellingly, in regard to his views on women, not on how his difference from a heterosexual male norm might have influenced those views.) And even when the male writer focuses on the 'feminine', might there be alternatives beyond 'appropriation' – instances, however rare, when he has let femaleness transform, redefine, his textual erotics, allowed himself *to be read through* femininity and femaleness, rather than become the authorizer speaking on behalf of it?

Having unconsciously precluded an exploration of these differences – the modalities of position that would have indeed rendered man as a third or odd term for analysis in the investigation of gendered discourses – the panel's very constitution had in fact reconstituted 'man' as a homogeneous entity, the 'fall-guy' for a one-sided rather than really radical deconstruction. Moreover, as the one man on stage, I found the question of positionality all the more immediate. There I was, by the virtue of having been listed in the program as the panel's moderator and having introduced its speakers, in the perceived position of having selected this panel, endorsed its version of 'male feminism', and authorized four women to speak to the subject (a doublebind: not only for potentially offending some women by seeming to assume a 'male' right to authorize their voices, but equally for offending some men by seeming to cede their story, their voices, to women). And yet there I was, just the same, the one male among four women on stage and the one person who *wasn't* speaking, whose participation was peripheral to the main event in a discussion, ironically enough, of male feminist voices.

Beyond panels often lie essay collections-in-the-making, which has proved to be the case for both the panels I've mentioned: we now have Jardine and Smith's *Men in Feminism*, and Claridge and Langland's *Escaping Patriarchy: Male Writing and Feminist Inquiry* is forthcoming. Thus the fourth stage in this account of the emerging public discourse on men and feminism centers on the way these anthologies contribute to what can or cannot be said about men's participation in feminist criticism. As my introductory remarks have no doubt already indicated, I'm not very happy with *Men in Feminism* as a totality; the collection almost unwittingly seems, like a self-generating machine, to recapitulate the problems inherent in the panel from which it originated. Telling in this regard is the semi-apologetic tone of the brief Introduction that the co-editors, Jardine and Smith, have written to the volume. For while they seem to agree in feeling the 'question of "men in feminism" [to be] a relatively unpromising one' (p. vii), they make no effort to restate the issue to make it less 'unpromising' or less problematic, either for themselves or for their potential readership. Another warning sign emerges a few lines later, when they announce that 'it became clear almost immediately . . . that most (though, finally, not all) of our contributors would be straight, white academics', which they admit to be one of the book's limits (p. viii). Just why or how the latter fact 'became clear almost immediately' gave me pause when I first read it. *Who*, I wondered, had they sought out as potential contributors? For what seems 'unpromising' or limited here is not so much the topic itself as any *framing* of the question (symbolized in the deliberate retention of the controversial title, 'men *in* feminism') that would make 'it clear almost immediately' that most of its male contributors would more likely than not be men 'in(to)' feminism in the most troublesome sense of the word.

As if in confirmation of this suspicion, who are some of the men that the table of contents reveals to be numbered among the path-breaking thinkers on the subject? Of seven added contributors, Jacques Derrida, Robert Scholes, Denis Donoghue (in small print), and Terry Eagleton (in a reply to Showalter) – critics whose relation to feminism has never been, to risk understatement, unproblematic. Is this the best one could do, I wondered (instantly creating in my mind lists of other, often lesser-known male critics who actually *do* feminist work, assume the feminist label, don't just talk in and around the subject)?[8] In opting for visibility and name-recognition over proven commitment to the cause, indeed, the editors' inclusion of such men as these reproduced the problem that I've already noted in relation to Showalter's essay: the price of spotlighting 'famous' names as the representatives of a movement which inevitably forms elsewhere than in the dominant discourse is to risk precluding what can be said differently, other than in the language of the 'straight, white academic'. Given this set-up, there's a certain uncanny poetic justice in the fact that, by the time one reads the last essay in the collection, Jardine's 'bandwagon' has been transformed by Rosi Braidotti into a veritable 'bulldozer': 'Blinded by what *they* have learned to recognize as "theory," *they* bulldoze their way through feminism . . . *They* are walking all over us . . . *"They"* are the best male friends we [women]'ve got, and *"they"* are not really what we had hoped for' (pp. 234-5; emphasis added). Braidotti's very rhetoric of repetition has transformed 'men' into an army of indistinguishable, unnamed 'they's'; in the process any idea of 'me(n)' has vanished altogether.

The problem of choosing one's contributors - an editorial problem not unrelated, of course, to the exigencies of the marketplace - takes on a different slant when one turns to the *female* critics not originally on the panel but included in *Men in Feminism*. While Nancy Miller, Naomi Schor, Jane Gallop, and Elaine Showalter, to cite four names, are, like Derrida and company, not exactly 'unknowns' in the academy either, their experience and demonstrable expertise in feminist studies make them logical candidates to speak on or to the subject of male feminism. What I find somewhat problematic in the selection of these added female contributors, then, has less to do with the question of their visibility and more to do with the way that, as a group, their essays construct - or avoid - the subject of 'male feminism' itself.[9] For example, Naomi Schor's article, 'Dreaming dissymmetry: Barthes, Foucault, and sexual difference', strikes me as superb, one of the best individual essays in the entire collection; but, nonetheless, by virtue of its rather exclusive focus on Barthes and Foucault, it has the effect of shifting the discussion from 'male feminism' to yet more examples of - if we stretch our imagination - 'men in(to) feminism'. Instead of Showalter's Anglo-American cross-dressers, this time round we get an elite class of French, post-structuralist, male intellectuals whose fascination with castrati and hermaphrodites (no longer simply a question of men-parading-as-women, but of men-women) becomes the basis for theories of sexual discourse that ultimately enforce dreams of sexual 'in-difference', in Schor's apt phrase, of a lost paradise of blissful indeterminacy that transcends sexual specificity. But in so attempting to move *beyond* difference, both critics, as Schor shows, *also* in effect refuse feminism's claim of female difference. This move leads

Schor to generalize that 'no feminist theoretician *who is not also a woman* has ever fully espoused the claims to a feminine specificity. . . . Even the most enlightened among the male feminists condone claims to female specificity *only* as a temporary tactical necessity' (p. 109). While Schor's reading of Barthes's and Foucault's displacement of sexual difference is right on target (though it might acknowledge more fully how their *own* historical specificity as gay men of a particular generation contributes to their over-idealization of a certain kind of polymorphous 'in-difference'), the larger conclusion that Schor draws depends on what is in fact a *highly selective* focus. Indeed, because of this focus, the trajectory of Schor's argument unconsciously repeats the *clinamen*, or 'shift away from' (p. 103), of which she accuses Barthes and Foucault – a shift or swerve in argument whereby two men with only an implicit relation to feminism are transformed into universal exemplars of 'even the most enlightened . . . male feminists', who have all unfortunately got it wrong.

Another of the collection's highlights is Nancy Miller's unpacking of the male anger hidden behind platitudes of universal judgment in Denis Donoghue's vitrolic attack in the *New Republic* on Gilbert and Gubar's *Norton Anthology of Literature by Women*.[10] But Miller's 'Man on feminism', in the long run, gives us just what her title announces: *a man*, one man unfortunately speaking for too many men, holding forth *on* feminism, certainly *not* speaking on behalf of the male feminist. Insightful as its analysis of this anti-feminist man is, Miller's essay doesn't, in the long run, contribute very much to the subject of a male feminist practice. However, I would like to suggest that the specific terms of the case she makes against Donoghue *do* turn out to be highly relevant to the hidden imperatives shaping this collection's presentation of that subject. For, in revealing the way in which Donoghue's gripe with feminism actually disguises his battle with post-structuralist theory 'over ownership of [literary] discourse' (p. 141) – that is, a struggle between the Big Daddies of Humanism and Deconstruction, in which feminist criticism serves as the pretext, the agency of mediation – Miller's argument startled me into an awareness of the degree to which many of the contributors to *Men in Feminism* use the subject 'male feminism' in much the same way, as *their* pretext to wage other critical wars. In the process, ironically, 'male feminism' comes to occupy in structural terms the traditional position of women in patriarchy – the ultimately expendable item of exchange that merely gets the conversation going. No wonder my vague discomfort, then, with several of these selections. For it is not that any of them are 'bad', but that they often have other, hidden, or not-so-hidden, agendas. Thus, for example, when Jane Gallop uses the occasion of her essay to unmask the sexism of Jean Baudrillard's theories of seduction, it turns out that her real interest is in addressing the relation of French theory to feminism (the idea of men and feminism, or even anti-feminism, has entirely dropped out of the picture by the last paragraph). Likewise, Robert Scholes's 'Reading like a man' actually serves more as an occasion to attack Culler's deconstructive practice (in reading 'as a woman') than as any kind of exploration of the subject announced in his title (broached only in his concluding sentence). And the palpable antagonism of Rosi Braidotti's confrontational opening ('Somewhere along the line I am viscerally opposed to the whole idea . . . the feminist space is not [men's] and not for them to see' [p. 233]) eventually reveals itself as a reaction against the post-structuralist 'death of the subject' (p. 237) that she sees threatening feminism's search for female subjectivity.[11] (The latter, incidentally, is exactly the grounds of contention in the dialogue between Jane Tompkins and Gerald M. MacLean in the present volume.) In the end, it is no surprise that *Men in Feminism* becomes a territorial battlefield, reproducing the discursive thrusts of its title, when the very issues at stake have been so clouded, disguised, or otherwise silenced.

Still, the collection does move beyond the panel, in directions that should be acknowledged as well. While the numbers of male-female contributors are kept in equal ratio, the effect is less divisive, since the added selections are not necessarily grouped by gender; something like a true dialogue emerges from this heterogeneous mixture, a quality abetted by the fact that the reader has the option of creating a reading order of his or her own choice out of the entries offered. And some of the added male contributors do have something different to say: 'well known' as he is, Richard Ohmann's prominence does not stand in the way of his reflective frank comments on his involvement in women's studies at Wesleyan; Cary Nelson's thoughtful piece forms the singular example of a man who forthrightly identifies himself as a feminist critic and takes responsibility for that identification; Craig Owens provides 'the' gay perspective, usefully illustrating the homophobia that can creep into feminist discourse.[12] And, in addition, the invitations to the original panelists to respond to their own contributions (which both Heath and Ross do) keep the inquiry from becoming close-ended. Although I haven't seen the final result, the Claridge-Langland volume also promises to move beyond its panel format in exciting directions; several male contributors, none easily assimilable to the other, are being included, and at least some will be talking about men's experience.

But the danger is always there of reinstating those potentially blinding symmetries that a feminist understanding of difference should instead encourage us all as feminists to unravel, to move beyond. Thus, as a kind of coda to this part of my essay, I'd like to speculate on the form – and formulation – of this present collection, *Gender and Theory*. One of the editor's explicit agendas, as I have understood it, has been to give voice to less well-known critics. Although her collection was already in the works before *Men in Feminism* appeared, once it was published she sought to redress its imbalances; the format of essay-plus-response was self-consciously conceived as a means of making an ongoing dialogue part of that redressing (as opposed to cross-dressing) process. Yet, curiously, what did I find when I looked back at the wording of the letter I received inviting me to contribute? Inevitably: 'the collection is arranged so that *male essayists* are responded to by *feminist theorists*, and vice versa, and presently includes the following . . .' (emphasis added). 'Male essayists' versus 'feminist theorists'; once again, two sides of a divide, and I'm not sure where I belong. For note, the wording does *not* stipulate '*female* feminist theorists', although that is the obvious, albeit perhaps unintentional implication, since all of 'the following' – take a look back at the table of contents – *are* male-female pairs. So I will choose, for my peace of mind, to take advantage of this slight opening in phraseology, and to consider myself not one of the 'male essayists' but include myself among the 'feminist theorists' – and if that gesture complicates the problem of identification for *my* respondent, it may also create for (her? him?) a field of imaginative play that will continue to liberate our current discourses on and around the subject of 'men and feminism'. For, when it comes to feminist criticism, especially in a collection originally subtitled 'dialogues between the sexes', I again repeat, only half facetiously, whose *is* the sex that writes?

Possible narratives

In the following section, I should like to pick up on various hints strewn throughout the prior commentary that, if stitched together, might help shift the direction that the issue of men and feminism has hitherto followed and, in the process, redirect our attention to various areas from which male feminist criticism might logically *emerge* rather than sink in (Heathian) impossibility. The following, of course, is only a partial list:

1   One such directive is for concerned women to stop considering the words of highly visible male theorists as *the* gospel on men's potential to theorize their relation to feminist theory and practice. This is not to say that, for instance, Derrida's wish to 'write as a woman' or Culler's prescriptions for 'reading as a woman reading as a woman reading . . .' might not be helpful; but it is to suggest that as long as their perspectives are part of a 'larger agenda', such pronouncements will be of limited use, particularly to men concerned with theorizing the construction of male identity.

2   Second, we need to account for an important generational factor if we are to begin to measure with more discrimination the multiplicities of men's relations to feminism. For, as Andrew Ross rightly points out in his 'response' essay in *Men in Feminism*, there are now 'men [in academia] young enough for feminism to have been a primary component of their intellectual formation' (p. 86). This was certainly so in my case – having written an undergraduate honors thesis on three American women writers under the supervision of a sympathetic male adviser, I proceeded in graduate school to study under four feminist-minded professors (three women and one man), meeting virtually no resistance to my incorporation of feminist theory into my dissertation project. The emergence of a whole generation of young men educated in feminism, of course, does not in itself allay the problem of recuperation or appropriation, but it does, I would argue, create a scenario qualitatively *different* from the 'Bandwagoning' or 'Divide and Conquer' theories of male feminism offered by Jardine and others. Such theories generally are more applicable to older male critics with, as Ross puts it, a significant 'pre-feminist' past, who thus tend to respond to feminism as either an alluring 'other' or an overwhelming threat, or both at once. Moreover, if the 'facticity' (Ross, p. 86) of feminist-educated young men makes a difference, so too, potentially, does its corollary: the fact that there are now young women in academia – including the students I've taught – whose education in feminism has at least partially been shaped, for better or worse, by men with scholarly interests in gender. Again, this is not to say that this new situation does not pose its own dangers, but simply to recognize a reality, one that *may* shift the way in which future generations of women regard

men 'doing' feminism as something less than the problem it now seems to be.

3   A third, related point that has emerged from what I've had to say thus far concerns the danger of lumping all 'men' together as a uniform category. What I hope we've begun to learn in this regard is that all feminists, male and female alike, need to be particularly attentive to those marginalized male voices whose interests may intersect with, or move along paths that are congruent to, but not the same as those already marked out by feminist interests to date. If men are to take to heart Jardine's warning against the 'suppression of the diversity and disagreement within the [feminist] movement itself' (p. 57), women and men alike need to keep the same principle in mind when judging the possibilities of a male feminist critical activity, its own potential for diversities, divergence, and disagreement. This recognition is exactly what Stephen Heath elides when he resigns himself to the fact that men's attempts at a 'male writing' can only reproduce itself, turn out more of the 'same'. Tellingly, he leaves unexplored a parenthetical qualification that he inserts at this very moment: '(unless perhaps [such writing emerges] in and from areas of gay men's experience)' (p. 25).

For the fact is, at this historical juncture, that a good percentage – though certainly not all – of the men in the academy who are feminism's most supportive and least belligerent 'allies' *are* gay. Somehow this fact and its implications seem to get lost in most of the preceding discussions of male feminism. From Stephen Heath's to Rosi Braidotti's essays, a lot of the generalizations made about men's desire to become a part of feminism *take for granted* the 'heterosexual' basis of that desire – the predominant imagery of penetration, indeed, is but one clue to the preponderance of these assumptions. In contrast, a recognition of the presence and influence of gay men working in and around feminism has the potential of rewriting feminist fears about 'men *in* feminism' as a strictly heterosexual gesture of appropriation. On the other hand, Jane Gallop, while fielding questions after a talk on Roland Barthes at Harvard a few years ago, suggested that she found gay male feminists even more threatening than heterosexual male feminists, precisely because she feared their ability to form a feminist critical economy entirely independent of women. Such seems to me an unreasonable fear, one whose homophobic basis is not unrelated to the tendency, noted above, to assume that the only desire propelling men toward feminism is 'heterosexual' – and it is a fear which the inaugural conference of the newly formed Center for

Lesbian and Gay Studies at Yale, held over two days in October 1987, went far to dispel. What impressed me most about this landmark event, the first of its kind, was the extent to which 'gay studies' as an intellectual event was able to *begin* at a highly sophisticated, theoretical level precisely *because of* the informing influence of feminism; what one saw demonstrated throughout was a convergence of feminist method and gay studies – epitomized in the conference's presiding intellectual 'presence', Eve Sedgwick – in the service of creating a discipline and an agenda that claims to be neither superior to nor the same as feminism, but rather in an ever-present relation of contiguity with the originating politics of feminism.

Hence, in acknowledging the possible plurality of male feminist voices, gay or otherwise defined, we must also acknowledge the fact that their work on gender and sexuality may take directions that might not be of *immediate* interest or relevance to *some* female feminists, directions which may indeed veer from the 'domain' of ideas conventionally associated with women's studies; as the Yale Conference indicated, such 'use' of feminist discourse need not be an appropriation, recuperating the latter into old systems, but rather a legitimate *extension* of feminist philosophy whereby pre-existing systems themselves are transformed, recuperated into a discourse that remains feminist at its core. I can make my point no better than by 'borrowing' Nancy Miller's words in order to so 'extend' them: 'feminist criticism is not about more of the same. It is about the imagination of difference that does not break down into two agendas, but [that] opens onto a complicated map of contiguities' (pp. 141-2). So, too, in the potential mappings of male desire in the academy, whether the topic ultimately crops up under the 'heading' of male feminism, men's studies, gender studies, masculine subjectivity, male sexuality, gay studies, men and the family, or other titles.

As with any political theory, there is always, of course, the very real danger of feminism being used irresponsibly by men, particularly when it leaves its established domains. Thus, I'd like to close with a few observations, garnered from my own subjective experiences, that other men interested in practicing feminist criticism might like to consider.

1   My first impulse is simply to encourage men to *identify with* feminism, taking on without fuss the label of 'feminist' if that is indeed your interest and true to the work you're producing. If you *are* offering

feminist interpretations, then go ahead (to paraphrase Showalter's advice) and read 'as a feminist' and not a 'female impersonator': acknowledge both the centrality of feminism and your gender to your practice. [13]

2   Second, men participating in feminism should make their own oppressive structures (ideological, social, psychological) *present* for critique, rather than hiding them under a veil of abstract musing. Part of this process, for example, is simply to remember the multiple ways in which the 'me' in 'me(n)' - whose cause I've been advocating all along - is nonetheless gendered male, *does* belong, after all, to the biological and social group 'men'. This is an identification for which, at some point, all of us feminist men must take responsibility. For, as Cary Nelson puts it in his essay in *Men in Feminism*, feminist theory by definition 'throws discourse into a material domain' in which 'we [men] are humanly present in our work and responsible for its social and personal consequences' (p. 162). What, for example, happens when we academic 'me(n)' must take part in specifically male spheres of action or power? To what degree do we choose to disguise, or not, our commitments to feminism? How do we sometimes take advantage of our born status as 'men' to negotiate the treacherous process of establishing a professional identity and continuing to exist within the limitations of our specific institutional circumstances? Whenever such circumstances tempt us to 'pass' as 'men' rather than 'me(n)', what do we do with, where do we leave, our female allies?

3   Third, the male feminist critic needs to be willing to forge a definition of himself as a man that makes room for the acknowledgement of a difference and a sexuality that is truly heterogeneous. The pontifications about Female Sexuality or The Feminine among certain self-appointed 'male feminists' that have rightly disturbed so many women are much less likely to be present in the critic who allows himself to be defined by the plurality of his sexuality.

4   Which means, really, to quote Jardine quoting Hélène Cixous, *that men still have everything to say about their sexuality*; and this is one of the logical, crucial, and hopefully inevitable directions in which a male feminism must develop. For instance, what do the texts we men read and produce and teach have to say - or avoid saying - about the relation of son to father, man to his own masculinity, to his physical body, to his homoeroticism, to desire and its multiple effects on his and others' pleasures? In this regard, I find Jardine's entire list of 'appropriate' areas of exploration for the would-be male feminist right to the point. My only

caveat is that many of these have already been put into practice by the male critics that I know: instead of endlessly speculating about the 'feminine' or the enigma of 'Woman', they, we, are learning 'to speak *as* . . . body-coded male[s]' (p. 60) precisely in order to re-imagine man. Which is inevitably to change the shape of patriarchy and its discourses as well.

5   Such acts, hence, are not only theoretical but also political, which ties in with a final observation I'd like, tentatively, to raise. As women in the feminist movement have done so successfully for two decades, I think of how eventful it would be if more feminist-minded men also began to experience the positive value of collectivity, of establishing their own networks of relationship, seeking each other out in communal rather than homosocial patterns of bonding. This is not to suggest we should begin forming exclusive men's clubs (that would indeed only be to produce more of the same), but to remind ourselves that women should not be our only resource for certain kinds of support and nurture. I would like to think that such a phenomenon – men *really* trusting men – would signal a cataclysmic change in the structures of our contemporary society, dealing the traditional notion of the Old Boys' Network a blow from which it might hopefully never recover.

But, my friend Patsy Yaeger, reading this essay, said musingly: here is the one point in your paper where I begin to feel uncomfortable and need to be convinced by something more: how can you trust groups of men not to repeat the old order, or not to erase women altogether in forming their cosy communities? I hesitate, too: I want to assure Patsy that the 'me(n)' for whom I've been speaking are different, not in-different to such dangers. Then I think back to my hypothesis, following my reading of Nancy Miller's essay, of the way in which our current discourses on male feminism have already constituted such men as the odd element, the expendable item of exchange, in current critical debates; and, to the degree that truly feminist-minded men also occupy the position of outsider in the homosocial transactions that make up patriarchy, perhaps, just perhaps, the linking together of their, our, individualities could establish a counter-network of exchange necessarily subversive of traditional masculine networks of power. A community *with* phalluses, rather than the community *as* Phallus – as someone put it in a discussion of this essay – need only threaten the existing patriarchal order, not women individually or feminism as a movement.

So I tell myself, telling Patsy, but I don't know: this may be *my* dream of utopia (as opposed to Barthes's, or Foucault's), marking in fact an 'impossible' limit beyond which male feminism cannot go – and yet, even so, that limit of possibility is one that I'd like, for now, for me, for men, to keep in view.

NOTES

1 Heath, 'Male feminism', in Jardine and Smith 1987: 1. All further references to this collection appear in the text.

2 Showalter, 'Critical cross-dressing: male feminists and the woman of the year', *Raritan* (Fall 1983), reprinted in Jardine and Smith 1987: 116-32. Page references are to the latter.

3 A few caveats are in order here. For one, although this difference in opinion in no way really diminishes the power of Showalter's larger argument, my own reading of Eagleton is less negative than hers – I agree there are problems of tone and a lack of acknowledgment of prior feminist criticisms of Richardson, but there is also much in *The Rape of Clarissa* that strikes me as insightful *and* useful for feminists. Second, despite theoretical problems I have with Culler's attempt to talk about 'reading as a woman' in *On Deconstruction*, my intuition is that he is a genuinely sympathetic ally of feminism, and I would not like my repetition of Showalter's criticisms (with which I agree) to come to stand in *my* readers' minds for the person, a man who might be very different from the written traces embedded in a document composed half a decade ago. This goes for all the critics I mention in the course of this essay, from Stephen Heath forwards: I am not judging, when I criticize, the individual person or critic, but rather his or her historical *participation*, at a given moment in time (a panel, a paper, a publication), in the articulation of a critical discourse on men and feminism that may extend beyond that critic's intention or awareness.

4 See, in Jardine and Smith 1987, respectively, Smith's 'Men in feminism: men and feminist theory', pp. 33-40; Heath's 'Men in feminism: men and feminist theory', pp. 41-6; and Ross's 'Demonstrating sexual difference', pp. 47-53. The logistics are slightly more complicated than this listing, however; for Heath's longer essay, 'Male feminism', pp. 1-32, which circulated among all the panelists, male and female, before the convention, is *not* the same as the presentation paper, listed above (in it Heath omits the opening argument about the 'impossibility' of men entering feminism and, in critiquing Smith and Derrida, attempts to refute the whole inclusion/exclusion proposition). But the fact was that everyone's earlier reading of Heath's original essay ensured that its discursive positionings – however unverbalized by Heath during his actual presentation – were palpably *present* throughout the double session, both in rhetorical terms (as others quoted or cited the opinions expressed in it) and on an emotional level.

5 See, in Jardine and Smith 1987, Jardine's 'Men in feminism: odor di uomo or compagnons de route?', pp. 54-61; Mayne's 'Walking the *Tightrope* of feminism and male desire', pp. 62-70: Weed's 'A man's place', pp. 71-7; and Kamuf's 'Femmeninism', pp. 78-84.

6   My feelings in this regard were also verbalized in the papers of several of the women; Jardine comments in her opening statements on 'the very structure of this encounter: two sessions organized by a man, with women once again responding, reacting – as always, in the negative position' (p. 54), while Weed notes that the effect of these men's papers is to produce 'a discursive battlefield which, of course, produces my position of respondent as one already in the fray, a position I would not otherwise choose' (p. 71).

7   The papers were Claridge's 'Shelley's poetics: the female as enabling silence', Christina Zwarg's 'Emerson as "mythologist" in *The Memoirs of Margaret Fuller Ossoli*', Margaret Higgonet's 'Hardy's Tess – an exchange of voice', and Langland's 'E. M. Forster's right rhetoric: the omniscient narrator as female in *Howards End*'. The two panelists that Claridge and Langland selected out of those who responded to the call for papers, Zwarg and Higgonet, wrote extremely subtle and probing essays well worth inclusion on the panel; the irony is not in the quality of any of these presentations *individually* but in the way that *collectively* they delimited the topic announced in the session's title.

8   The following is a very partial list of men working within the field of literary criticism who might make up such an 'ideal' volume. It is based entirely on my own intuitions: about men I've read or heard speak, men I've heard others talk about, acquaintances and friends, and it ranges from graduate students to full professors; thus I can only hope I'm not misrepresenting any of the following names by tentatively including them – and, in parentheses, my fantasies of what they might best write about – under the aegis of 'male feminism': Andrew Ross (whose marxist-feminist perspective deserves a more favorable context than the 'Men in feminism' panel provided him); Michael Moon (on the homosexual 'economies' of Alger, Whitman, and James); Christopher Craft (connecting a Wildean sexual politics to homophobic discourses); Robert Martin (reclaiming Melville's phallicism as non-patriarchal); David Miller (on the policing of sexual desire in Dickens's boy-heroes); Michael Warner (on narcissism in Thoreau); Ed Cohen (whose recent article on Wilde and the construction of homosexual identity appeared in *PMLA*); Michael Cadden (on Broadway and beyond); Lee Edelman (included in the present volume); Joseph Litvak (on Austen and the Brontës); Robert Vorlicky (on the dynamics of all-male cast dramas); Jack Yeager (on women's marginality in French colonial literature); Wayne Koestenbaum (on the implications of male literary collaborations); Tom Richards (on the relation of Victorian concepts of masturbation to capitalism); Peter Stallybrass (on the erotics of the mouth in Renaissance literature); Ross Chambers; Neil Hertz; Robert Caserio . . . the list could go on.

9   Showalter's contribution is a reprint of her *Raritan* review essay; on the contributions of Miller, Schor, and Gallop, see the paragraphs that follow. I suspect that part of the problem I sense here has to do with the fact that some of these essays were either written or conceived before they were solicited for this collection – hence the degree to which they might not directly address the issue at hand. This, of course, points to yet another editorial problem, beyond the forementioned one of economic exigencies, that enters into the solicitation of pieces for an essay collection on a specific topic. The other essays by women added to this volume include Meaghan Morris's 'in any event . . .', pp. 173-81, and Rosi Braidotti's 'Envy: or with my brains and your looks', pp. 233-41.

10   Donoghue's review is reprinted in Jardine and Smith 1987 after Miller's article 'for the reader's convenience' (p. 137); whether or not to include the piece was much deliberated by the editors, who ultimately decided that Miller's analysis couldn't be understood without its referent. The 'compromise' was to print the review in small type, in order to set it off from the other contributions.

11   The irony that seems momentarily to escape Braidotti is that feminists have done as much to decenter the 'subject', precisely in order to give voice to a non-objectified female subjectivity, as anti-feminist men; to imply that this post-structural 'maneuver' is exclusively a recurrence of the 'old metaphysical cannibalism' engineered by men (pp. 237, 238) is thus as unfair to feminists as it is to male critics interested in feminist theory.

12   See Ohmann's 'In, with', in Jardine and Smith 1987, pp. 182-8; Nelson's 'Men, feminism: the materiality of discourse', pp. 153-72; and Owen's 'Outlaws: gay men in feminism', pp. 219-32. I enjoy the way in which Ohmann's and Nelson's titles attempt to subvert what might be called the prepositional impasse of the collection's title; such plays with the pernicious 'in' of 'men in feminism', nonetheless, attest to the shaping influence that the concept has exerted over the entire collection.

13   But as soon as I write this, I am reminded of conversations with male friends (who may be better feminists than myself) who have eloquently argued against the necessity of the appellation, asserting that their interest in exploring masculine constructions of sexuality needn't be labeled one way or the other; their work is on gender, the debt to feminism is obvious but shouldn't either be overworked or allowed to overwhelm their work.

REFERENCES

Auerbach, Nina 1982. *Woman and the Demon*. Cambridge: Harvard University Press.

Castle, Terry 1982. *Clarissa's Ciphers*. Ithaca: Cornell University Press.

Claridge, Laura and Langland, Elizabeth ms., *Escaping Patriarchy: Male Inquiry and Feminist Writing*.

Cohen, Ed 1987. 'Writing gone Wilde: homoerotic desire in the closet of representation'. *PMLA* 102: 5 (October): 801-13.

Culler, Jonathan 1982. *On Deconstruction*. Ithaca: Cornell University Press.

Donoghue, Denis 1986. 'A criticism of one's own', *The New Republic* 194, 10 March: 30-4; repr. in *Men in Feminism*, ed. Alice Jardine and Paul Smith, 1987, London and New York: Methuen.

Dworkin, Susan 1983. *Making Tootsie*. New York: Newmarket Press.

Eagleton, Terry 1982. *The Rape of Clarissa*. Minneapolis: University of Minnesota Press.

Eagleton, Terry 1983. *Literary Theory: An Introduction*. Minneapolis: University of Minnesota Press.

Gilbert, Sandra and Gubar, Susan (eds) 1985. *The Norton Anthology of Literature by Women*. New York: W. W. Norton.

Jardine, Alice and Smith, Paul (eds) 1987. *Men in Feminism*. London and New York: Methuen.

8
Men Against Patriarchy

Toril Moi

Proclaiming himself a 'feminist theorist', Joseph Boone worries about the effects this move may have on his respondent: will she feel unsettled? squeezed out of 'her' field? or perhaps liberated into a new 'field of imaginative play' (p. 172)? Touched as I am by his concern, I am not sure that any of these alternatives apply. I see no reason why a man should not proclaim himself a feminist. On the contrary, I welcome his support. And if Boone wants to be a theorist, I am hardly the right person to object. Feminist theory is not a property to be hoarded among the happy few; I have no desire to see it in short supply. The more feminist theorists there are, the more feminist theory there will be for all of us.

Recognizing Boone's obvious right to call himself a feminist, however, does not oblige me to *agree* with him, any more than I agree with all female feminists. But to disagree is not necessarily to deny that my opponents *are* feminists. On the contrary, the very act of disagreeing signals an implicit recognition of our common, feminist terrain. My major quarrel with Boone's sweet-tempered essay, for instance, is his vision of a 'community *with* phalluses', which strikes me as quite remarkably unlikely to produce a 'cataclysmic change in the structures of our contemporary society' (p. 177). Although he is right to insist that men should not always turn to women for emotional and practical servicing, it does not follow that patriarchy will disintegrate if they start turning to each other instead. The underlying assumption here is that men require a fixed amount of support or 'nurturing' no matter what, and that if women are not to provide it, then men must do so. I would much rather see men give up their excessive demands for support *tout court* and start practising the difficult art of supporting women instead. Such unusual behavior might provoke more change than any number of communities of self-supporting males.

This is not to say, of course, that I suspect Boone of being a patriarchal wolf in feminist clothing: his good faith is obvious. But good faith alone can never stand in for political arguments: the fact remains that Boone does not offer a single reason why patriarchy should fall to the ground if men start to support men. Some would claim that that's what they have been doing all along. But perhaps Boone has in mind men supporting each other in more 'female' ways: the case nevertheless remains to be argued.

There is of course one sense in which Boone's essay obliges me to abandon, if not my identity, at least my own concerns, and enter into his terrain: by focusing on the question of men in/and feminism, he forces me to do so too. Which means that I find myself in the position of having to respond to an essay that presents itself as a response to a book, Alice Jardine and Paul Smith (eds.), *Men in Feminism*,[1] which itself contains a set of essays, responses to those essays and even some responses to the responses. How metacritical can one get? In the hope of escaping at least some of the numbing effects of this somewhat narcissistic series of specularizations, I will try to address myself 'directly' to the question of men in/and feminism. But 'directness' in this case can be no more than an illusion: my essay remains a reply to Boone, Jardine, Smith *et al*.

Feminist / female / feminine

My position - that men can be feminist - is based on the belief that the words 'feminist' and 'female' do not mean the same thing, and moreover, that it is not particularly helpful to confuse 'femininity' with 'femaleness' either. In a general way, I see 'feminism' as a political position, 'femaleness' as a matter of biology, and 'femininity' as a set of culturally defined characteristics.[2]

The words 'feminist' or 'feminism' are political labels indicating support for the aims of the women's movement. 'Feminism' then is a specific kind of political discourse: a theoretical and political practice committed to the struggle against patriarchy and sexism. In the field of literary studies, which is one of Boone's primary concerns, 'feminist criticism' is a criticism committed to this struggle, not simply a concern for gender in literature. There are of course different political views within feminism,[3] and there will always be debatable 'borderline' cases. The question of who is 'inside' or 'outside' feminism will never be settled once and for all: such definitions remain a matter for concrete political debate. Without wanting to unify or totalize the differences between feminists, I nevertheless want to insist that recognizable feminist criticism and theory must in some way be relevant to the study of the social, institutional and/or personal power relations between the sexes, or in other words, what Kate Millett called *sexual politics*.

If feminism is characterized by its *political* commitment to the struggle against patriarchy and sexism, it follows that the very fact of being *female* does not necessarily guarantee a feminist approach. This is not to deny that *women's* experience of oppression forms the starting point for modern feminist theory and practice. Clearly, males and females do not – and cannot – take up the same position in relation to female experience. In this sense they cannot be feminists in the same way. (I shall return to this point.) But it is to deny that feminism can be *reduced* to an expression of female experience. Common female experience (assuming that such a thing exists) does not in itself give rise to a feminist analysis of women's situation. The fact of having the same experience as somebody else in no way guarantees a common political front: the millions of soldiers who suffered in the trenches during the First World War did not all turn pacifist – or socialist, or militarist – afterwards. Unfortunately, the experience of childbirth or period pains is neither common to all women nor particularly apt to inspire a deep desire for political liberation: if that were the case, women would long since have changed the face of the earth. Feminism, then, is something *more* than the effort to express women's experience: it is at once a relatively comprehensive analysis of power relations between the sexes, and the effort to change or undo any power system that authorizes and condones male power over women.

Assuming that men's brains are not structurally incapable of grasping these issues, such an analysis is clearly available to men as well as women. Men can therefore be feminist. But – and this is crucial – they cannot be women. The parallel here is to the struggle against racism: whites can – indeed ought to be – anti-racist, but they cannot be black. Men/whites do not occupy the same *position* in relation to the dominant power structures as women/blacks. This point has a series of important consequences. First of all, it follows that male feminists cannot simply *repeat* the words and gestures of female feminists. Speaking as they do from a different position, in a different context, the 'same' words take on different meanings: this is why the 'same', as many men have experienced, has a disconcerting tendency to become 'different' in their discourse after all. Miming the words of a female feminist, however earnestly, a man signals the fact that he has not considered the differences in power – and therefore in speaking position – between them. He has, in other words, missed one of the most elementary feminist points in the book: the idea that women – not men – are oppressed by patriarchy. (This is not to say that patriarchy is not a contradictory structure, or that all males actively enjoy their dominant position: *noblesse oblige*, as we know.) The main theoretical task for male feminists, then, is to develop an analysis of their own position, and a strategy for how their awareness of their difficult and contradictory position in relation to feminism can be made explicit in discourse and practice.[4] In this context, the idea of 'speaking the male body' is a relevant and interesting, but not sufficient, project.

But if feminism is primarily the struggle against oppressive and exploitative patriarchal power structures, the important thing for men is not to spend their time worrying about definitions and essences ('am I *really* a feminist?'), but to take up a recognizable anti-patriarchal position. It is not enough simply to be interested in masculinity or in male sexuality or in gender differences. Such interests must in some way or other be developed as part of the anti-patriarchal struggle. The question, then, is not so much a matter of territory (whether men should be *in* feminism) as of position (whether they should be *against* patriarchy).

Appropriating feminism: feminism and other struggles

One consequence of wanting to end male dominance over women is pretty obvious: men ought to hold little hope of 'taking over' feminism in the near future. In this sense I understand and support female feminist skepticism about belated male support of feminism, as expressed for instance by Elaine Showalter in 'Critical cross-dressing' (*Men*, pp. 116–32). On the other hand, it does not follow that feminists are right to suspect every case of male praise of feminism as a take-over bid in disguise. Nor is it politically useful. In many situations feminism *needs* male support. Even typical 'women's issues' such as the struggle for women's abortion rights in Norway and Britain could never have been won without male support. Living through the patriarchal backlash of the 1980s, feminists are even less than before in a position to look a gift horse in the mouth. If men on the left express their support and even try to use feminist insights in their work, I see no reason to resent it. Which is not to say that I won't subsequently disagree with them. Feminists can only judge men's words and actions: it is futile to waste feminist time on the imputation of Machiavellian motivations to a would-be male feminist solely on the grounds of his sex. While strongly in favor of taking issue with controversial male and female interventions in feminism, I see little point in engaging in doomed scholastic debates over intentionality, authenticity, and sincerity in order to distinguish men who *pretend* to be trying from those who are *really* trying.

On the evidence of Boone's essay and *Men in Feminism*, few American critics see feminism in the context of other struggles, except from time to time, that of gay rights (another sexual struggle). But both in the USA and in many other countries feminists often work politically with men: female feminists working in socialist and marxist political parties, struggling against racism and imperialism, fighting vicious dictatorships and mobilizing against nuclear war and ecological disaster have always had to work with men.[5] Such experience often produces a more realistic sense of the strengths and limits of feminism than is evident in *Men in Feminism* and 'Of me(n) and feminism'. There is in these texts a disconcerting tendency to see feminism as at once an isolated, self-sufficient enclave located firmly within academia and as the *only* political struggle relevant for women. Every effort to claim that there are sometimes 'larger struggles' than feminism is denounced as either a sell-out or as another male take-over bid. But in the global context today, oppressive sexual power relations are not always the most important (in the sense of the most painful) form of exploitation. While feminists have crucial insights to bring to bear on other struggles (that is, real socialism also presupposes a feminist transformation of society, effective analysis of nuclear armament strategies can only be carried out if they also draw on feminist insights into the nature of power, and so on), it also remains true that these other emancipatory struggles cannot simply be reduced to so many kinds of feminism. For all its virtues, feminism is not a global discourse addressing all possible forms of oppression and exploitation. It is paradoxical, to say the least, to denounce 'male' appropriations of feminism for other struggles in terms which make us sound as if we want to appropriate all other struggles for feminism instead.

Professionalism

There is a sense in which the whole debate about men and/in feminism is, as Rosi Braidotti argues, 'very American' (*Men*, p. 234). First in the positive sense of demonstrating the degree of interest American men take in feminism: I have noticed no such surge of male interest in Scandinavia, for instance. But there is also another, more negative sense in which the debate strikes me as 'American', and that is the degree to which it appears to be a function of institutional struggles within the American literary critical profession.

There is in these texts a deplorable absence of non-academic, or even non-literary critical settings. It is as if the political horizon of these feminists, male and female, stretches no further than to the MLA. But the question of men in feminism is not *identical* with the question of men in feminist literary criticism. While the latter is an interesting and relevant problem in its own right, it is strange, to say the least, not to find a single discussion of the difference between these two questions, not even from the editors of *Men in Feminism*. On the contrary, Jardine and Smith immediately equate the first with the second question, arguing that at first they felt that: 'the question of "men in feminism" was a relatively unpromising one. It seemed in a very real sense elitist and narrow, of interest only within the often somewhat insulated corridors of academia' (p. vii). The parochialism of Boone's essay, consisting as it does almost entirely of anecdotes from various seminars, panels and sessions at Harvard or the MLA is deplorable – and representative. Boone is inconsistent to criticize Stephen Heath for his 'abstract attempts to intellectualize' (p. 165), when his own text, however 'accessible', encloses us far more firmly within the walls of the seminar room. Does Boone really expect outsiders – non-members of the US literary critical community – to take an interest in the seating arrangements of faculty dinners at Harvard, or the time-tabling of various sessions at the MLA? Who exactly did he have in mind as *readers* of his essay?

It is disconcerting for an outsider to notice that so much of the 'political' disagreement in these essays has more to do with petty professional rivalry than with feminist politics. Sometimes I get the impression that in the USA those politics are perceived as nothing but struggles over tenure, publications, reviews and seminar papers. If I choose Boone's essay to exemplify this point, it is not because I consider him the worst offender in this respect, but because I have been asked to respond to his paper and not somebody else's. There is, then, a somewhat unsettling institutional sub-text to Boone's plea for men in feminism. That sub-text is structured over a series of oppositions: old/young, visible/invisible, known/unknown, speaking/silent and so on (see *passim*). But, with one or two awkward exceptions, Boone does not apply these categories to *female* critics. What he is interested in is the agonistic struggle between younger and older, invisible and visible *men*. His whole essay is a plea for the feminist virtues of young, unknown males, his main critique of Elaine Showalter that she has only discussed famous (older) men:

> By not raising the possibility that the most empathetic, least appropriative feminist critical practice might be happening *elsewhere* - away from public view, by precisely those men who lack the academic power, rank or numerous publications of Showalter's 'cross-dressers' - 'Critical cross-dressing' therefore creates the illusion of a discursive field in which 'male feminism' can only be perceived in terms of a struggle for power among superpowers (Showalter versus Eagleton, say), and hence as potentially antagonistic, intrusive, or threatening to those who have fought for years to legitimize feminism within the academy (pp. 161-2).

Boone's essay is littered with remarks antagonistic to older men or to men who are speaking when he is not. Some of them have even committed the unpardonable crime of usurping his presence in the seminar room. *No* other man speaks for *him*, every male voice is a usurper, an inauthentic intruder. (So much for mutual male support.) The invisible, unknown men, on the other hand, that is to say, those who say nothing, are good feminists and *do* represent him, not so much because of their beliefs, as 'by virtue of their age and lack of professional status alone' (p. 165).

There is an astonishing rhetorical manoeuvre going on here: Boone, by seizing the right, 'oppressed' side of the well-known series of patriarchal binary oppositions, and by placing them within his own professional context, is trying to pass every unknown male critic off as 'silent', 'invisible', 'powerless' - in short, as 'feminine', and therefore also as feminist. The implicit equation between femininity and feminism is more than dubious in itself. But even more important is the fact that this manoeuvre is possible because Boone attributes all the characteristics on the left, 'oppressive' side of the oppositions to older, famous males. But how would these young 'silent' men fare if they were cast opposite young *women*? And what would happen to Boone's rhetorical structure if these unknown male intellectuals actually *became* visible, known and so on? Would that make them less feminist? And why does he insert a footnote which does nothing but list *twenty* (!) names of deserving 'invisible' men if their feminist credentials are best preserved by remaining in obscurity?

'Visible' female feminist critics are let off the hook on the grounds that their 'expertise' makes up for their 'visibility'. A 'visible' man, however, can have nothing interesting to say. Boone is actually *surprised* at encountering an exception from this rule: ' "Well known" as he is,' he exclaims, 'Richard Ohmann's prominence doesn't stand in the way of his reflective, frank comments on his involvement in women's studies at Wesleyan' (p. 171). Let us not insist on the obvious Freudian - or Bloomian - connotations of such rhetorical strategies. The invisible, as feminist critics know, is the place where the phallic eye finds 'nothing to see'.[6] Like the 'visible' feminist critics he accuses of sacrificing the topic of men in feminism to their own critical hobby-horses, Boone too, while ostensibly addressing the question of his own relation to feminism, is pushing his own agenda: the palace revolution of the young Turks. In the end, then, Boone's paper is structured as much by his obsession with (predominantly male) professional hierarchies, fame and prestige as by his quite genuine feminist engagement.

NOTES

1 All further references to *Men in Feminism* will be abbreviated to *Men* and given in the text.
2 For a more developed exposition of the consequences of these distinctions for feminist literary criticism, see my 'Feminist literary criticism' (originally entitled 'Feminist, female, feminine') in Jefferson and Robey 1986.
3 For an excellent account of the major political differences in Western feminism, see Eisenstein 1984.
4 Stephen Heath's 'Male feminism' (*Men*, pp. 1-32) is so far the most impressive effort to determine a possible male position in relation to feminism. I am not convinced that *admiration* or *wonder* in Descartes's sense is the only option open to·men, though.
5 I am not in any way trying to say that such feminists never work in women-only groups. Work in women-only groups remains fundamental to feminism.
6 See Luce Irigaray's reading of Freud in Irigaray 1985.

REFERENCES

Eisenstein, Hester 1984. *Contemporary Feminist Thought*. London: Allen & Unwin.
Irigaray, Luce 1985. *Speculum of the Other Woman*. Trans. Gillian C. Gill. Ithaca, N.Y.: Cornell University Press.
Jardine, Alice and Smith, Paul (eds.). *Men in Feminism*. London and New York: Methuen.
Millett, Kate 1969. *Sexual Politics*. Repr. London: Virago, 1977.
Moi, Toril 1986. 'Feminist literary criticism', in eds Ann Jefferson and David Robey. *Modern Literary Theory: A Comparative Introduction*. 2nd edn, London: Batsford, 1986: 204-21.

Part III
Transforming Texts and Subjects

Each essay in this section has a double perspective: it focuses first on how texts are transformed, as in female appropriations of genres like the sublime. Second, each essay analyzes how texts transform readers, contexts, and history. These reconceptualizations are effected by broadening the angle of vision to encompass race as well as gender; by reformulating the relation of the personal to the political; and by theorizing anew about the relations between history and narrative, representation and production. Collectively, the essays profoundly alter our vision of the networks of relations between author, reader, critic, and society.

In 'Toward a female sublime', Patricia Yaeger discusses the historical institutionalization of the sublime as a genre. Feminist writers have appropriated this traditionally masculine genre of domination, turning it into a vehicle for female power and ecstasy. Yaeger identifies three categories of the female sublime: the failed sublime, the sovereign sublime, and the feminine sublime. She draws on the theories of Hélène Cixous and Luce Irigaray to describe the process by which the feminine or pre-oedipal sublime changes the oedipal, phallic agon with the father into a pre-oedipal desire for closeness or nearness with the mother. In the works of Rebecca Harding Davis, Eudora Welty, Carson McCullers and Elizabeth Bishop, Yaeger maps the territory of this recuperated genre, and illustrates its value for feminists searching for potentially transforming modes of intersubjectivity and empowerment.

Concentrating on Cixous and Irigaray in 'At risk in the sublime: the politics of gender and theory', Lee Edelman emphasizes that the feminist rehabilitation of the sublime derives from a lesbian poetics. He stresses the importance of breaking out of binary modes of heterosexist thinking and illustrates the political value of the confrontational sublime by discussing the history-making Lesbian and Gay March on Washington in 1987. Edelman argues that while it may seem theoretically regressive to affirm identity, one must take that risk and make that affirmation in order to attack the politics of gender from a position of power, and to go beyond the present impasse between gender and theory.

In 'The race for theory', Barbara Christian speaks out against philosophy's take-over of literary criticism. She speaks for those who feel intimidated by the theoretical language that now dominates the critical scene. This new language emerged, she argues, at the same time that the literature of peoples of color, of black women, of Latin Americans, of Africans began to move to the 'center'. Nor is it accidental that the theory of the 'death of the author' emerged simultaneously. Monolithic theory has thus effaced the subtle distinctions between races, classes, and ethnic backgrounds. She sees literature as a matter of survival; she is part of a community engaged with literature in order to save their own lives and to ensure the survival of a black literary tradition that would otherwise be lost.

In 'Appropriative gestures: theory and Afro-American literary criticism', Michael Awkward praises Christian's dedication to saving the black woman's literary tradition, but he argues that new readings alone do not ensure the survival of that tradition. The time has come for black and white feminist critics of both sexes to devise theoretical approaches to this tradition. After discussing the ground-breaking work in the field, he shows how critical theory has enhanced our understanding of black textual production. The Afro-American critic is not just appropriating literary theory or being appropriated by it. Instead, by retranslating theory into the black idiom and black traditions, the Afro-American critic radically reconstructs literary theory itself.

9
Toward a Female Sublime

Patricia Yaeger

In recent decades women have begun to write in the sublime mode – a mode which has, conventionally, been the domain of masculine writers and poets. Its most conspicuous practitioners are those writers we have labelled 'French feminists'. In their prose, the desire for feminine power leads to sweeping metaphors equating women's writing with the release of geothermal energies:

> What woman hasn't flown/stolen? Who hasn't felt, dreamt, performed the gesture that jams sociality? Who hasn't crumbled, held up to ridicule, the bar of separation? Who hasn't inscribed with her body the differential, punctured the system of couples and oppositions? Who, by some act of transgression, hasn't overthrown successiveness, connection, the wall of circumfusion?
>
> A feminine text cannot fail to be more than subversive. It is volcanic; as it is written it brings about an upheaval of the old property crust, carrier of masculine investments; there's no other way. There's no room for her if she's not a he. If she's a her-she, it's in order to smash everything, to shatter the framework of institutions, to blow up the law, to break up the 'truth' with laughter. [1]

The burden of French feminist writing is that women must create a new architectonics of empowerment – not through the old-fashioned sublime of domination, the vertical sublime which insists on aggrandizing the masculine self over others, but instead through a horizontal sublime that moves toward sovereignty or expenditure, that refuses an oedipal, phallic fight to the death with the father, but expands toward others, spreads itself out into multiplicity. Luce Irigaray speaks from this zone in 'When our lips speak together':

> Why aspire to the heights of a worthier discourse? Erection doesn't interest us: we're fine in the lowlands. We have so many spaces to share. Because we are always open, the horizon will never be circumscribed. Stretching out, never ceasing to unfold ourselves, we must invent so many different voices to speak all of 'us,' including our cracks and faults, that forever won't be enough time. We will never travel all the way round our periphery: we have so many dimensions. (p. 75)

Although Irigaray does not say so explicitly, her project, and that of Cixous, is to re-invent the sublime as a feminine mode – to invent, for women, a vocabulary of ecstasy and empowerment, a new way of reading feminine experience. The woman writer's strategies for achieving this re-invention will be the subject of my essay. In other words, my project matches the hubris of the French feminists; I want to define a female sublime.

From the beginning I must present this project as a paradoxical one. The Romantic sublime is a genre that is, historically and psychologically, a masculine mode of writing and relationship. It is also a genre that is – in the present age – of questionable use; it is old-fashioned, outmoded, concerned with self-centered imperialism, with a 'pursuit of the infinitude of the private self' that we, in the twentieth century, regard with some embarrassment and keep trying, epistemologically if not politically, to amend. Nevertheless, as a pre-fabricated structure, as a literary genre or moment concerned with empowerment, transport, and the self's strong sense of authority, the sublime is a genre the woman writer needs.

The claim of the sublime is that we can – in words or feelings – transcend the normative, the human. Its structure, as Thomas Weiskel says in *The Romantic Sublime*, is that of joining the great, of enacting a moment when 'the burden of the past is lifted and there is an influx of power' (p. 11). For its Romantic inventors, it offered:

> a remarkably successful way to read . . . a language for urgent and apparently novel experiences of anxiety and excitement which were in need of legitimation. In largest perspective, it was a major analogy, a massive transposition of transcendence into a naturalistic key; in short, a stunning metaphor. (p. 4)

This 'massive transposition of transcendence' was sought and at least fictively achieved in our canon by masculine poets.

In Wordsworth's 'Resolution and Independence', for example, such a moment is held out, at the poem's beginning, as temptation, as promise. Wordsworth's poem begins with a vision of plenitude and reciprocity that threaten to exceed themselves, to carry the poet toward something sublime. The sun is rising, birds are singing, 'and all the air is filled with pleasant noise of waters' (l. 7). The most buoyant of these creatures is the hare who creates her own panoply, an earthy entourage that follows her everywhere as 'with her feet she from the plashy earth / Raises a mist; that, glittering in the sun, / Runs with her all the way, wherever she doth run' (ll. 12-14). Although Wordsworth achieves a human encounter with sublimity later in the poem by staging a scene of spiritual blockage between his speaker and an old leechgatherer, it is the beginning of 'Resolution and Independence' - with its dream of transcending the human, its preoccupation with the animal daemon - that interests me here. I am always struck, in reading Elizabeth Bishop's 'Invitation to Miss Marianne Moore', with the ways Bishop's poem resonates with the beginning of Wordsworth's poem and alters his project. Like Wordsworth's hare, Miss Moore is followed in her imagined trip to New York City by a halo of energy:

> From Brooklyn, over the Brooklyn Bridge, on this fine morning,
>   please come flying.
> In a cloud of fiery pale chemicals,
>   please come flying,
> to the rapid rolling of thousands of small blue drums
> descending out of the mackerel sky
> over the glittering grandstand of harbor-water,
>   please come flying.
>
> (*Complete Poems*, p. 82)

Bishop's poem opens with a comic flourish; it begins as a happy flirtation with the mock sublime. But within its wry, comic structure, its gimcrack world of watery grandstands and small blue drums, a real sublime structure is being prepared. At the end of Bishop's poem Marianne Moore not only trails 'fiery pale chemicals', but substantial, 'unnebulous' words:

> With dynasties of negative constructions
> darkening and dying around you,
> with grammar that suddenly turns and shines

> like flocks of sandpipers flying,
>   please come flying.
>
> Come like a light in the white mackerel sky,
> come like a daytime comet
> with a long unnebulous train of words,
> from Brooklyn, over the Brooklyn Bridge, on this fine morning,
>   please come flying.
>
> (*Complete Poems*, p. 83)

The female poet accompanied by a halo, or fiery trail of language, is a dazzling image, and, with its premonition of *hypsos* – of power and influence, of transport and height – is an image conspicuously absent (with the exception of the poems of Emily Dickinson) from the poetic lexicon of the nineteenth century. Bishop's poem represents a release from a 'tradition' of female disempowerment, for she is not only praising Miss Moore and revising Mr Wordsworth, but creating for herself a female tradition to join. She is initiating a moment of 'joining the great' – one that is not only described in terms of oedipal struggle, but in terms of shared mutuality, of shopping trips to Fifth Avenue as well as unearthly pleasures.

Moreover, this new power struggle is acted out in opposition to a masculine tradition that reserves this breathless sublimity for men; from the beginning of 'Invitation to Miss Marianne Moore' Bishop is playing with and lifting the burden of the tradition that restricts the woman writer's powers of speech. Thus Bishop stages Marianne Moore's flight *over* Brooklyn Bridge instead of under or upon it because this bridge and the water beneath have been used as modes of poetic transport before.

Bishop is not simply playing with Wordsworth; she is also revising Walt Whitman and Hart Crane. In a letter to Waldo Frank written in 1926 Crane writes eloquently about why he was drawn to the idea of making Brooklyn Bridge the center of his monumental *The Bridge*[2]: 'The very idea of a bridge, of course, is a form peculiarly dependent on such spiritual convictions. It is an act of faith besides being a communication' (p. 231). The bridge represents an act of faith about 'bridging' itself, a way of finding access to a past 'that so overwhelms the present with its own worth and vision that I'm at a loss to explain my delusion that there are links between the past and a future destiny worthy of it' (p. 232). For Crane, the bridge is part of a monumental effort to reconnect the grandeur of the past with a dying future, but Bishop will have nothing to do with these prestigious connections. She wants to collide with the past, to fracture the words connecting the female poet to a masculine tradition that threatens to overwhelm her. She wants to re-invent the sublime – not as a genre of empowerment based on the simple domination of others, but as a genre that can include the sociable, the convivial, as well as the grandiose and empowering, and she comes close to inventing a new mode of the sublime: what we might call 'the sublime of nearness'.

How does this revision of the conventional sublime, this 'sublime of nearness' work? In 'The Fish', one of Bishop's most frequently anthologized poems, Bishop once again resists the lure and danger of historical modes of transcendence:

> I caught a tremendous fish
> and held him beside the boat
> half out of water, with my hook
> fast in a corner of his mouth.
> He didn't fight.
> He hadn't fought at all.
> He hung a grunting weight
> battered and venerable
> and homely.
> (*Complete Poems*, p. 42)

'The Fish' is concerned with whether or not to lift this terrible animal (terrible because of what he has lived through, terrible because of the fisherwoman's power over him, her power to expose his gills 'that can cut so badly' to 'the terrible oxygen' of the poet's alien realm) – whether to lift his burden, his weight, his *tremendum* into the poet's drunken boat. The question, in other words, is how one writes poetry about an 'other' who has an extra-human power the self thinks it needs, without destroying that other's alienness. Should the poet kill the fish, eat him, absorb him? If she refuses she may relinquish the possibility of internalizing this venerability, and relinquish as well the enactment of a ritual moment of empowerment, of making herself greater than she was before by absorbing his *tremendum*. However, in 'The Fish' this influx of power happens – the transport, the ecstasy of 'rainbow, rainbow, rainbow!' fills up the poet's little boat – and yet the other is preserved in its otherness; the temptation, through thought, to 'kill the object and assert the subject', is precisely the temptation Bishop's speaker resists.

In letting the fish go – allowing it to remain outside herself, other than herself – Bishop is refusing a moment Shelley cannot resist in his 'Mont Blanc' (pp. 369-73). At first the mountain is beyond him, overwhelming and crushing him, but by the poem's end Shelley's speaker has wrested this power back from the mountain by insisting on his own superior gesture of identity. He identifies with the mountain, with its creative power, in a moment of internalization that obliterates its otherness and moves us back into the safely structured and recognizable world of oedipal identity and the egotistical sublime.

Bishop's speaker also experiences a moment of transport as her homely little boat is filled with transcendent perceptions. But as she lowers the fish back into the water, she also signals her ability to stage a scene of empowerment in which the other is not obliterated or repressed. In place of this incorporation, she begins to invent a new kind of self-other dialectic that allows the object – the fish – to remain something other than the perceiving subject's conception of it, and allows that perceiving subject, in turn, to become something other than a unified ego.

Bishop may revise Shelley's poem in miniature, but how useful is the sublime as habitual mode for the woman writer? In the twentieth century, to be so enthusiastic, so transported by either a fish or a precursor poet (or by the idea of reinventing the sublime as literary genre), is to leave oneself open to the accusation of being old-fashioned, narcissistic, imperialistic, ersatz. As Weiskel comments in *The Romantic Sublime*:

> we have long since been too ironic for the capacious gestures of the Romantic sublime . . . Freud was definitely and remarkably immune to the sublime moment, whose 'oceanic' and daemonic guises he brilliantly exposed. To please us, the sublime must now be abridged, reduced, and parodied as the grotesque, somehow hedged with irony to assure us we are not imaginative adolescents. (p. 6)

A poem like 'An Invitation to Miss Marianne Moore' both risks this outmodedness and pays a heavy price; it has been criticized as a poem too jejune and unsubtle to be worthy of Bishop's best work. It will be useful, then, to expand upon the claim that the sublime is a risky genre for Bishop to re-invent, or for the feminist critic to reaffirm, because it is an outmoded genre that has little relevance for a modernist poetics.

In *The Crying of Lot 49* Thomas Pynchon clinches our sense of the sublime's outmodedness by making the Romantic sublime the stuff of high parody. Driving along the freeway to Los Angeles, his heroine, Oedipa Maas, sees her obscene double staring down at her from a motel marquee:

> A representation in painted sheet metal of a nymph holding a white blossom towered thirty feet into the air; the sign, lit up despite the sun, said 'Echo Courts.' The face of the nymph was much like Oedipa's, which didn't startle her so much as a concealed blower system that kept the nymph's gauze chiton in constant agitation, revealing enormous vermillion-tipped breasts and long pink thighs at each flap. (p. 6)

For all its tawdriness, this sign replicates the conditions of the Romantic sublime in several ways – it is an object of *hypsos*, or height, it is grander than its spectator, and yet invites that spectator's identification and narcissism (evoked in the name 'Echo Courts'), and even establishes itself as an ideal that Oedipa herself could introject, could assimilate – making her potentially more 'powerful' than the introjected figure itself. At the same time, Oedipa experiences a sense of blockage; she feels unable to reach these heights – an inability figured through references to *The Book of Job*:

> Oedipa pulled into the lot, got out and stood for a moment in the hot sun and the dead-still air, watching the artificial windstorm overhead toss gauze in five-foot excursions. Remembering her idea about a slow whirlwind, words she couldn't hear. (p. 6)

Pynchon is evoking this moment of mock-sublimity to reveal the absurdity of Oedipa's yearnings in a world lacking belief in a transcendent dimension. Moreover, he revels in his own bad faith; Pynchon borrows images from an older mode of writing to teach us that the adolescent hopes of an earlier age are still with us, even though those hopes have run amok. In his prose we enter a modern world that will not support any wish for transcendence – that laughs at such a wish, and reveals the longing for the sublime as symptom, as an oceanic longing that has been pre-manipulated by the commercial environment of late capitalism. As Weiskel says, 'it is against this sense of an increasingly constricted and structured world that the ideology of the sublime looms up retrospectively, as a moribund aesthetic' (p. 6).

As 'moribund aesthetic', the Romantic sublime becomes a dangerous genre for the woman writer to revive because its vocabulary is already used up, tawdry, infused with degradation, doubleness, irony. In addition, it is a genre lacking, for the most part, in literary foremothers with whom to identify. That is, the sublime constitutes a tradition that has not only been forbidden to women, but is inimical to their needs. (We glimpse its forbiddenness when Richard King says, in *A Southern Renaissance*, that Southern women writers have been excluded from his book because 'they were not concerned primarily with the *larger* cultural, racial, and political themes that I take as my focus' [p. 9]. Phallocritics will not blink twice at this passage. They do not expect women writers to be concerned with *hypsos*, with transport, with the grand discontinuities.)

But even if women were not forbidden access to the sublime as experience or as literary genre, there are good reasons a feminist writer or reader might want to avoid duplicating the claims of the masculine sublime. The problem with entering the realm of the sublime is that we contract to participate in a power struggle that, even when it is resisted, involves grim forces of possession and domination. These forces can replicate the problems of a Bloomian poetics in which actants are at the mercy of their own oedipal angers and idealizations. A Bloomian poetics is essentially an agon in which the poet, vulnerable to the discursive stratagems of poets of the past, can, by his own aggressive misreadings, make their power, their place of poetic excellence his own - by overgoing and defeating them. As Weiskel points out, 'The poet is uniquely vulnerable to the hypsos of past masters, but his counteroffensive of identification can make the power of hypsos his own' (p. 5). Nevertheless, I do not want to reject this martial vocabulary out of hand because women, as writers and heroines, are clearly in need of feisty, voracious, volatile vocabularies of empowerment. My larger project is to locate and celebrate this volatility.

We can feel the depth of the woman writer's need for this space of sovereignty in Rebecca Harding Davis's *Life in the Iron Mills*, in a scene where Davis gives us the flip side of Pynchon's obscene metal statue:

'At the other side of the works - Kirby, what's that?'
Mitchell started back, half-frightened, as, suddenly turning a corner, the white figure of a woman faced him in the darkness, - a woman, white, of giant proportions, crouching on the ground, her arms flung out in some wild gesture of warning.

'Stop! Make that fire burn there!' cried Kirby, stopping short.
The flame burst out, flashing the gaunt figure into bold relief.
. . . There was not one line of beauty or grace in it: a nude
woman's form, muscular, grown coarse with labor, the powerful
limbs instinct with some one poignant longing. One idea: there it
was, in the tense, rigid muscles, the clutching hands, the wild, eager
face, like that of a starving wolf's. (pp. 31-2)

In the nineteenth century, the sublime offered the writer a way of adding
to his or her text a dimension of 'power and mystery that conventional
empiricisms lacked' (Wolf 1982: pp. 196-7). But the sublime offered this
energy only because it suggested, as well, new forms of aesthetic subterfuge and sublimation. The sublime suggested modes of experience in
which 'an influx of power' could be 'achieved through the liberation and
appropriation of forbidden and illicit forces' (ibid.: p. 205). If Davis's korl
woman offers access to another dimension of aspiration and feeling, if,
touched by the elemental light of the furnace fire this passage flames out
and reminds us not only of the complacency of the capitalist onlookers,
but of our *Sehnsucht* or longing for untried and unfathomed dimensions
of being, it is because the sublime is also the genre of permitted trespass –
a genre in which figures of women can seize the grand roles formerly
allotted to figures of men.

I will argue that this discovery of the sublime as a mode allowing
trespass and appropriation of 'forbidden and illicit forces' speaks to the
woman writer at play – the woman writer who is looking for a genre
permitting the exploration of alternative modes of female experience. The
woman writer who writes in the sublime mode writes differently; in order
to overcome her exclusion from the dialectic of negative power enacted in
the conventional sublime, she produces a prosody of transcendence, but in
a different key. I want to discuss three strategies the woman writer uses to
harness and re-invent a sublimating power that has been too exclusively
associated with male writers. Let us begin with Eudora Welty.

Power, wildness, and sublime exaltation are not the first qualities that
come to mind in thinking of a Welty story, but in 'June Recital', the
second story in *The Golden Apples*, we encounter an example of why this
territory is right. Miss Eckhart's piano students are trapped inside her
house during a tumultuous thunder storm, and she sits down to play for
them:

The thunder rolled and Miss Eckhart frowned and bent forward or she leaned back to play; at moments her solid body swayed from side to side like a tree trunk.

The piece was so hard that she made mistakes and repeated to correct them, so long and stirring that it soon seemed longer than the day itself had been, and in playing it Miss Eckhart assumed an entirely different face. Her skin flattened and drew across her cheeks, her lips changed. The face could have belonged to someone else - not even to a woman, necessarily. It was the face a mountain could have, or what might be seen behind the veil of a waterfall. There in the rainy light it was a sightless face, one for music only - though the fingers kept slipping and making mistakes they had to correct. And if the sonata had an origin in a place on earth, it was the place where Virgie, even, had never been and was not likely to go. (p. 56)

This incredible scene contains all the elements of the conventional sublime. Miss Eckhart's face blends with and disappears into the huge forms of nature - metaphors attesting to her power of transcending the human. This potential for transcendence is underlined by metaphors of transformation - her face changes, her music seems to come from some unearthly realm. Finally, the passage ends with images of Miss Eckhart's oblivion to others, her power over them, her aggression - her arm strikes a child, and another of her pupils, Cassie, stands 'with her whole body averted as if to ward off blows from Miss Eckhart's strong left hand.' In addition to Miss Eckhart's 'height' or *hypsos*, we can define Welty's *hypsos* as well in this passage, for she is expropriating images from Shelley's 'Mont Blanc' to describe Miss Eckhart. The dynamic powers Shelley withholds from himself at the poem's beginning Welty gives to her heroine. ('Thine earthly rainbows stretched across the sweep / Of the aethereal waterfall, whose veil / Robes some unsculptured image. . . . Thy caverns echoing to the Arve's commotion, / A loud, lone sound no other sound can tame; / Thou art the path of that unresting sound - / Dizzy Ravine!' (ll. 25-35). Miss Eckhart becomes the mountain that stares back defiantly at Shelley and will not answer his human call.

However much Miss Eckhart resembles Mont Blanc itself, there is no moment in 'June Recital' comparable to Shelley's identification with the mountain. Instead of 'joining the great', participating in Miss Eckhart's sublimity, her awesome, otherworldly dignity, Cassie protects herself from Miss Eckhart's by-now metaphorical blows by mentally reducing Miss Eckhart to a fallen woman, an untouchable. Cassie remembers an unspeakable incident that reminds us that Miss Eckhart is trespassing – she has entered into this grandiose oedipal plot as actant when her role should be that of victim. It is this victimization Cassie's imagination now forces upon her:

> One time, at nine o'clock at night; a crazy nigger had jumped out of the school hedge and threatened to kill her. . . . She had been walking by herself after dark; nobody had told her any better. When Dr. Loomis made her well, people were surprised that she and her mother did not move away. (p. 57)

Instead of Miss Eckhart's power, her terror, Cassie remembers that 'a terrible thing once happened to her.' And then, saddest of all, Miss Eckhart polices her own excess: 'What were you playing, though,' an onlooker asks. 'I couldn't say,' Miss Eckhart said, rising. 'I have forgotten' (p. 58). To rise and then forget is not a gesture typical of the masculine sublime. In the Stolen Boat episode of *The Prelude* Wordsworth lets shapes of craggy peaks 'black and huge' work in his mind: 'but after I had seen / That spectacle, for many days, my brain / Worked with a dim and undetermined sense / Of unknown modes of being' (I. 390–3). His imagination is populated by 'huge and mighty forms, that do not live / Like living men' (I. 398–9). But while Wordsworth's imagination is extended by these acts of trespass, the little girls' imaginations contract: 'Coming from Miss Eckhart, this music made all the pupils uneasy, almost alarmed. Something had burst out, unwanted, unexpected, from the wrong person's life' (p. 56).

   This mode of incorporating the sublime into women's writing I want to designate as the 'failed sublime'. In texts where it occurs, we witness a woman's dazzling, unexpected empowerment followed by a moment in which this power is snatched away – often by a masculine counter-sublime that has explicit phallic components. What remains in our minds after such scenes is not simply a sense of feminine failure, but a double burden. First, we learn that women, like men, are capable of joining the great. Second, we learn that something in the social order (either something external, or a set of beliefs internalized by the actant herself) intervenes, and the heroine finds herself not only stripped of transcendent powers, but bereft, in a lower social stratum than before.

To cite another example, in Carson McCullers's *The Ballad of the Sad Café*, Cousin Lymon – a hunchback and a dwarf – intrudes in the scene where Miss Amelia – a woman who is strapping, powerful, and six foot two – is about to throttle her estranged husband, Marvin Macie, in a fair fight. Lymon flies through the air and knocks Amelia out; he enters the scene as a flying phallus, an ironic, sadistic incarnation of Emerson's 'the flying perfect'. Once again McCullers's text enacts a woman's sovereignty – her capacious seizure of what she desires – and takes this sovereignty away, revealing, in the process, the social forces that conspire against a female sublime.

The second strategy women writers use to appropriate the sublime as literary mode I will define as the 'sovereign sublime'. In this reinvention of the conventional sublime the woman writer appears to be appropriating a male genre in a straightforward and mimetic way, and thus to be vulnerable to its structure of violence and domination. But in this appropriation something happens to the sublime's tidy structure. Typically, the male poet writing in the sublime mode will stage a moment of blockage which is followed by a moment of imagistic brilliance. That is, the mind fights back against the blocking source by representing its own inability to grasp the sublime object. This representation of inability becomes scriptive proof of the mind's percipience and stability – of the mind's willed relation to a transcendent order, and thus of the mind's powerful univocity – its potential for mental domination of the other.

In the 'sovereign' sublime this economy of domination changes, however, and rather than a vertical flight toward mastery through height or *hypsos*, the woman writer invents either a horizontal sublime, as we saw in Irigaray, or else what we might call a 'sublime of expenditure' in which the writer expends or spills whatever power the sublime moment – in its structure of crisis, confrontation, and renewed domination, has promised to hoard.

In considering this version of a female sublime, Jacques Derrida's and Georges Bataille's description of sovereignty in 'From a general to a restrictive economy' is instructive. According to Derrida, 'once sovereignty has to attempt to make someone or something subordinate to itself, we know that it would be retaken by dialectics, would be subordinate to the slave. . . . It would fail for having wanted to be victorious, for having alleged that it kept the upper hand' (p. 265). The strategy of the sovereign sublime is neither to govern nor 'to be subjugated', and in order to achieve this, 'it must subordinate nothing. . . . it must practice forgetting.' We can locate this sublime of overwrought mimesis and gorgeous expenditure in Nikki Giovanni's 'Ego Tripping'.[3]

> I was born in the congo
> I walked to the fertile crescent and built
> 　the sphinx
> I designed a pyramid so tough that a star
> 　that only glows every one hundred years falls
> 　into the center giving divine perfect light
> I am bad

Giovanni's verse is a parodic recreation of conventional modes of transcendence. She begins by trying to subordinate everything and continues by detailing the intricate pleasures of imperialistic one-up-man-ship:

> I sat on the throne
> 　drinking nectar with allah
> I got hot and sent an ice age to europe
> 　to cool my thirst
> My oldest daughter is nefertiti
> 　the tears from my birth pains
> 　created the nile
> I am a beautiful woman

But 'Ego Tripping' ends by subordinating nothing, by 'practicing forgetting'. Giovanni's speaker spills all that she has saved:

> I am so perfect so divine so ethereal so surreal
> I cannot be comprehended
> 　except by my permission
>
> I mean . . . I . . . can fly
> 　like a bird in the sky . . .
>
> 　　　　　　　(p. 1385)

This is Shelley's skylark revisited, but with this lovely difference. Shelley's speaker purports to be directing his entire being toward the skylark's orphic sound, but his poem is really about the mad aspirations of the 'I', about the desire to dissolve the ecstatic object into the poem so that the poet can dissolve himself into the ethereal and oedipalized 'light of thought'. Shelley employs the bird as a grand metaphor for the ephemeral space his imagination can soar through and make meta-physical. But in Giovanni's alternatively gendered sublime, a resurrected metaphysics is not the poem's goal. Once Giovanni has renamed the world as a feminized, Africanized space, she uses the image of the bird to push away from this possessiveness, to renounce comparative enunciations of grandeur or ephemera and soar into wide open space.

While these first two strategies for inventing a female sublime offer stunning revisions of a 'masculine' sublime, it is the third strategy – the 'feminine' or 'pre-oedipal' sublime – that offers the most striking revision of an 'oedipal' sublime. Here the agon typical of the Romantic sublime is retained as part of a narrative or poetic structure, but this oedipal conflict is rewritten so that the pre-oedipal desire for closeness or nearness with the other that the conventional sublime tries to repress, remains visible and viable; it hums pre-oedipal songs from the ruins of an agonistic and oppositional poetics.

Why do I define the most implicit gesture of sublimity as 'oedipal'? My reading of the conventional sublime as an oedipal structure, and the 'pre-oedipal' sublime as its alternative, relies on observations in Thomas Weiskel's book and Neil Hertz's essay on the sublime[4] – especially their notion that the agon or struggle between self and other that we see in poems like 'Mont Blanc' is really a subterfuge, an oedipal confrontation that masks an oral, primordial desire to merge with (rather than to possess) the mother. Both Weiskel and Hertz suggest that this aspect of sublime desire goes beyond the need for triangulation with the father and asks instead for the earlier and more polymorphously perverse presence of the pre-oedipal mother. In addition, they suggest that these oral and primitive origins of the sublime have been ignored by students of sublimity. In a poem like 'Mont Blanc', the moment of blockage or alienation – of being stalled by the mountain's greater power – is not the poetic motor it seems to be. Instead, this blockage is rhetorically staged by the poet to allow an oedipal screen or scream to mask the initiating desire for the mother's inundation and comfort.

According to Hertz in 'The notion of blockage', the oedipal moment of blockage, as it is staged within the traditional sublime, aims at a moment of 'conflict and structure' in which a 'disarrayed sequence is converted to one-on-one confrontation' which confirms 'the unitary status of self' (p. 76). But while what is being repressed, disguised and re-figured is an initial wish for inundation – a primordial desire to bond or fuse with the other – the poet-ego schooled in defending male ego boundaries reacts to this wish for inundation with ambivalence and fear. And this fear can only be mastered through a reaction formation that takes the form of oedipal aggression. This aggression, in turn, arouses anxiety, for the writer responds to his own aggressive desire to appropriate with a surge of guilt, and a feeling that is quickly followed by a gesture of reparation. This reparation is not directed toward the pre-oedipal other – who has already been disguised and denied – but to the oedipalized self/other dyad who wears the father's imago and cries out to be incorporated and internalized. In 'Mont Blanc' this father-imago, this man-mountain, is absorbed into the ego as an assurance (rather than a disruption) of the incorporative self's ego-boundaries.

I want to add to Hertz's elegant thesis by suggesting that the oedipal poesis that pivots on a reaction formation (on a moment of blindness overtaking a moment of insight) is made visible, is repaired and given a new figurative base in the poetic mode I am calling the 'feminine' sublime. If what is repressed in the 'oedipal' sublime is the desire for pre-oedipal bonding with a mother's body (which, in most Romantic poems, is given an imaginative correlative in the chaos and blissful heterodoxy of the cosmos), in the 'pre-oedipal' sublime these libidinal elements are not repressed; they break into consciousness and are welcomed as a primary, healthful part of the writer's experience, as part of the motive for metaphor.

Thus the 'feminine' sublime is neither old-fashioned, nor outmoded – but addresses our most pressing modern concerns. How do we move away from our Western allegiance to an imperial, Cartesian, Adamic self who is supposed to act as its own triumvirate and tribunal – toward a model of the self that permits both a saving maintenance of ego-boundaries and an exploration of the pleasures of intersubjectivity? As Fred Dallmayr suggests in *The Twilight of Subjectivity*, we have learned that the subject is 'infiltrated with the world' in such a way that 'otherness is carried to the very heart of selfhood'[5], and yet have not found a language to bring home the political and aesthetic consequences of this knowledge, to put this knowledge into praxis. I will suggest that the 'feminine' sublime becomes an arena for discovering this language; it engenders a zone where self-empowerment and intersubjective bliss entertain one another in an atmosphere free of paranoia.

We find the best example of this 'feminine' or pre-oedipal' sublime in Elizabeth Bishop's 'The Moose': a poem in which a huge female animal comes out of the 'impenetrable forest' of masculine discourse and, rather than participating in the battle of super-egos that usually takes place there, comes over to a crowd of people sitting on a bus in order to investigate them. This poem has affinities with certain Wordsworthian moments of a blockage – moments followed in Wordsworth's poems by perceptions of grandeur and sublimity.

Upon seeing the moose, the bus's driver, in a gesture reminiscent of that Wordsworthian moment when 'the light of sense goes out', stops the bus and turns off his lights. The moose – at once homely and other-worldly, saunters over and sniffs this bus's 'hot hood' – she checks out its motor, its imagination, and does not find it blocked, but redolent. The precursor poem to 'The Moose' is Robert Frost's 'The Most of It', a poem which seems to repudiate this, or any other, romance ethos. But while Frost refuses to describe that ordinary, Romantically sublime moment when the world is subsumed by an 'I', while he resists the Romantic sublime as 'moribund aesthetic', his poem depends for its energy upon the binarism, the agonistic moment of blockage characterizing this rejected mode. Like Wordsworth's Romantic men, Frost's jaded hero goes out to the wilderness; he cries out for 'counter-love, original response', but the only sight that greets his cry is:

> the embodiment that crashed
> In the cliff's talus on the other side,
> And then in the far-distant water splashed,
> But after a time allowed for it to swim,
> Instead of proving human when it neared
> And someone else additional to him,
> As a great buck it powerfully appeared,
> Pushing the crumpled water up ahead,
> And landed pouring like a waterfall,
> And stumbled through the rocks with horny tread,
> And forced the underbrush – and that was all.
>
> (*The Poetry of Robert Frost*, p. 338)

Frost's poem depicts two kinds of blockage. The poem begins with what Hertz calls a 'disturbance of cognition' in which 'the mind's confrontation with a seemingly overwhelming natural force' leads to a second form of blockage in which 'a disarrayed sequence is resolved (at whatever sacrifice) into a one-to-one confrontation.' What Frost seems to be refusing in 'The Most of It' is the moment in which blockage is recuperated as 'sublime exultation, a confirmation of the unitary status of the self' (Hertz, p. 76), but his poem exults in this status all the same – the grandiose sublime of the Romantics is simply replaced with the existential sublime of the twentieth century in which an older form of egocentricity is matched with a self-consuming, binary angst.

Bishop's answer to Frost's negations is another form of 'embodiment' – an 'other' appears who enters the poem as a form of abnormal discourse. This discourse, like the abruption of the moose itself, startles the mind into another dimension. There is also a 'disturbance of cognition' in which 'the mind's confrontation with a seemingly overwhelming natural force' gives way to another form of blockage in which 'a disarrayed sequence is resolved into a one-to-one confrontation.' But this confrontation does not demand sacrifice, nor does it lead to confirmation of the 'unitary status of the self'; the moose is greeted by dispersed and heterogeneous responses: ' "Sure are big creatures." / "It's awful plain." / "Look! It's a she!" ' As the passengers are taken out of themselves, as they revel in the mystery of a female creature 'grand' and 'otherworldly', her mystery is punctuated by the driver's single voice:

> 'Curious creatures,'
> says our quiet driver,
> rolling his *r*'s.
> 'Look at that, would you.'
> Then he shifts gears.
> For a moment longer.
> (*Complete Poems*, p. 173)

The moose does not threaten to obliterate the 'I' as both Shelley's mountain and the 'embodiment' in Frost's 'The Most of It' threaten the opponent-poet's imagination. Instead, the moose allows the perceivers to comment and connect while moving from one register of meaning to another. The self, despite its self-centered illusions, is not obliterated, nor is the object swallowed up by the subject that has perceived it, but the moment of self-structuring is revealed in its doubleness. As Adorno says in *Negative Dialectics*, 'the human mind is both true and a mirage. It is true because nothing is exempt from the dominance which it has brought into pure form; it is untrue because, interlocked with dominance, it is anything but the mind it believes and claims to be' (p. 186). To circumvent and heal this concealed ethic of the domination of everything by thought, to rescue ourselves from the myth of our own enlightened rationality we must, according to Adorno, 'love the thing' in a new way:

The reconciled condition would not be the philosophical imperialism
of annexing the alien. Instead, its shapeliness would lie in the fact
that the alien, in the proximity it is granted, remains what is distant
and different, beyond the heterogeneous and beyond that which is
one's own. (p. 191)

In Shelley's 'Mont Blanc' we are left with the subject's predominance,
with the thought that the mountain is nothing without the poet's
imagination. But in Bishop's 'The Moose', when a busload of people
share a Sabbath sight, although their experience consists of what they
make of it, and while the moose is clearly, and only, their concept of
'moose', nevertheless at the end of the poem the bizarre temerity of the
moose's arrival goes beyond both the timidity of 'the beautiful' and the
oppositional clash of the oedipal sublime. In experiencing the beautiful,
'we feel that the mind and the world were designed for each other; they
are one, capable of comprehending each other. The beautiful is a feeling of
vibrant stillness, of animated rest' (Kurrik, p. 49). The beautiful offers a
fusion of subject and object, a world of pleasure, while the sublime offers
more complex feelings – a movement of action and reaction, a negative
pleasure in the checking of vital powers.

Bishop's moose hovers between each of these zones. This homely
creature is more than the site of a collective fantasy that teaches us how
the mind and world are fitted to one another; it is more than its poetic
'idea'. Instead, Bishop's poem insists (as does the sublime mode) that the
imagination's capacity for synthesis is inadequate to experience, even as
it promises (as the sublime does not) that the experience of severance and
difference will not obliterate the self. At the end of the poem the moose's
resonance quite literally remains, external and impenetrable: the odor of
moose drifts through the air, blending with the exhaust from the bus,
even after its audience has disappeared:

> by craning backward
> the moose can be seen
> on the moonlit macadam;
> then there's a dim
> smell of moose, an acrid
> smell of gasoline.
> (*Complete Poems*, p. 173)

Subject and object have entered into an intersubjective dialectic of grandeur in which the poet refuses to annex what is alien, but revels, for a brief poetic moment, in a pre-oedipal longing for otherness and ecstasy.

In domesticating the Romantic sublime as a literary mode – in emphasizing its usefulness as a zone of feminine literary power – I do not want to evacuate the experience of boundlessness and negativity implicit in this form, nor do I want to assert that the 'failed' sublime, the 'sovereign' sublime, and the 'pre-oedipal' sublime are the only sublime structures that women have re-invented. In Elizabeth Bishop's 'Over 2,000 Illustrations and a Complete Concordance', for example, we find an intriguing revision of the mathematical sublime. The poem's strange and beautiful ending suggests a way of incorporating pre-oedipal grief and expenditure into moments of mathematical closure. But there are also numerous women's texts that refuse to take this pre-oedipal route – that employ the sublime as a liberating structure of female violence and aggression. Lois Gould's *A Sea-Change* comes to mind and Isak Dinesen's 'The Monkey'. We need, then, to expand the typology of the female sublime to include categories I have not yet explored in this essay – in particular, to include women writers' celebrations of a violence originating in women. I want to conclude, then, with a brief analysis of Eudora Welty's violent story about her childhood: 'A Memory'.[6] Here a little girl narrator is torn between a Romantic sublime of dynamism and *Sehnsucht* and an ironic mode of narrative closure that would keep the narrator safe from her own inner violence.

'A Memory' explores a little girl's disconcerting day at the beach. Once again a woman is the subject of a sublime vision, only this time the vision is entirely frightening. The little girl of the story sees a woman on the beach who is arrayed with the scary slovenliness of too much flesh. 'Fat hung upon her upper arms like an arrested earthslide on a hill. With the first motion she might make, I was afraid that she would slide down upon herself into a terrifying heap.' Her mouth is also frightening: 'a continuous laugh . . . came through the motionless open pouched mouth of the woman' (p. 153). This is a vision of woman as Ozymandias: her 'legs lay prone one on the other like shadowed bulwarks, uneven and deserted, upon which, from the man's hand, the sand piled higher like the teasing threat of oblivion.' These shifting sands culminate in complete dissolution: 'She bent over and in a condescending way pulled down the front of her bathing suit, turning it outward, so that the lumps of mashed and folded sand came emptying out. I felt a peak of horror, as though her breasts were of no importance at all and she did not care' (p. 156). To a little girl on the beach, there is no way to convert this terrifying vision into increase of power. But this moment represents something other than the disempowerment of the 'failed sublime'. This woman is turning the destructive sands of patriarchy out into the world again; she is revealing her own construction as a frightened and frightening image. The narrator-child finds herself split by this vision into a double image – into an obsessive little girl who looks at the world through a frame made by squaring her fingers, and into a portrait of the artist as young hysteric – the young Welty identifies with the angry daughter of the disintegrating woman. In fact, this woman's daughter, who hurls her body angrily up and down the beach, will not be 'squared' by the narrator's vision. She is curled in her 'green bathing suit like a bottle from which she might, I felt, burst in a rage of churning smoke'. When this young girl explodes, she comes 'running toward the bench as though she would destroy it, and with a fierceness which took my breath away, she dragged herself through the air and jumped over the bench. But no one seemed to notice' (p. 155).

This girl, like her disintegrating mother, becomes the source of a frightening and violent sublimity. In refusing to adapt to the codes of a dominant culture that demands female propriety, she represents woman bursting out of bounds, lifting the burden of the past (however painfully) and experiencing an influx of power. But why is this sublime of violence necessary, and how can it be a source of feminist affirmation? At the end of Shelley's 'Mont Blanc', that which is numinous and external is dramatically interiorized and the poem reminds us of who it is that has been troping all along. Not only is an influx of power achieved, but the self who has seemed so small at the poem's beginning looms large; he claims a grandeur which had initially been defined as external. The weight of empirical being is momentarily lifted and the mind experiences within itself a fund of naturalized supernatural power. For Shelley and Wordsworth the sublime mode permits a normal retrieval of mythic powers that are initially alienated in order to insure their internalization; this energy is finally reappropriated so as to strengthen the ego. But for women, such retrieval is still abnormal or deviant. In 'A Memory' Welty is bent on retrieving lost powers, but this can only be achieved by violating the dominant order, by liberating and appropriating forces nominally forbidden to Wordsworth and Shelley, but actually forbidden to women. Although the girl in the green bathing suit is invisible to everyone else on the beach, although, as she surges over the beach, writes on the sand with her body, 'no one seemed to notice', she becomes an avatar of the woman writer as aggressive heroine; she offers us an angry and empowering version of a female sublime of violence that needs, again and again, to be rewritten.

NOTES

1 Cixous 1980: 258.
2 In Crane 1966: 231.
3 In the *Norton Anthology of Modern Poetry*, ed. Richard Ellmann and Robert O'Clair (New York: Norton, 1973), pp. 1384-5.
4 Weiskel 1976; Hertz 1978.
5 As quoted in Thomas McCarthy, 'Introduction', to Jürgen Habermas, *The Theory of Communicative Action*, vol. 1, *Reason and the Rationalization of Society*, p. viii. See Dallmayr, 'Man and Nature: Prospects of a "Humanistic Naturalism" ', pp. 144-73.
6 In Welty 1936; page references are to this volume.

REFERENCES

Adorno, Theodor W. 1983. *Negative Dialectics*. Trans. E. B. Ashton. New York: Continuum.

Bishop, Elizabeth 1984. *The Complete Poems 1927-1979*. New York: Farrar, Straus, Giroux.

Cixous, Hélène 1980. 'The laugh of the Medusa', in *New French Feminisms*. Amherst: University of Massachusetts Press.

Crane, Hart 1966. *The Complete Poems and Selected Letters and Prose of Hart Crane*. Ed. Brom Weber. New York: Doubleday and Company (Anchor).

Dallmayr, Fred 1981. *The Twilight of Subjectivity*. Amherst: University of Massachusetts Press.

Davis, Rebecca Harding 1972. *Life in the Iron Mills or the Korl Woman*. Ed. Tillie Olsen. New York: The Feminist Press.

Dinesen, Isak 1934. 'The Monkey', in *Seven Gothic Tales*. New York: Simon and Schuster.

Derrida, Jacques 1978. 'From a restricted to a general economy', in *Writing and Difference*, trans. Alan Bass. Chicago: University of Chicago Press.

Frost, Robert 1974. *The Poetry of Robert Frost*. Ed. Edward Connery Lathem. New York: Holt Rinehart and Winston.

Giovanni, Nikki 1973. 'Ego Tripping', in *Norton Anthology of Modern Poetry*, ed. Richard Ellmann and Robert O'Clair. New York: Norton.

Gould, Lois 1976. *A Sea-Change*. New York: Simon and Schuster.

Hertz, Neil 1978. 'The notion of blockage in the literature of the sublime', in *Psychoanalysis and the Question of the Text: Selected Papers from the English Institute 1976-77*, ed. Geoffrey Hartman. Baltimore: Johns Hopkins University Press.

Irigaray, Luce 1980. 'When our lips speak together', in *Signs* 6: 65-79.

King, Richard H. 1980. *A Southern Renaissance: The Cultural Awakening of the American South, 1930-1955*. New York: Oxford University Press.

Kurrik, Maire Jaanus 1979. *Literature and Negation*. New York: Columbia University Press.

McCarthy, Thomas 1981. 'Introduction' to Jürgen Habermas, *The Theory of Communicative Action*, vol. 1, *Reason and the Rationalization of Society*. Boston: Beacon.

Pynchon, Thomas 1986. *The Crying of Lot 49*. New York: Harper and Row.

Shelley, Percy Bysshe 1951. *Selected Poetry and Prose of Shelley*. Ed. Carlos Baker. New York: The Modern Library.

Weiskel, Thomas 1976. *The Romantic Sublime: Studies in the Structure and Psychology of Transcendence*. Baltimore: Johns Hopkins University Press.

Welty, Eudora 1947. *The Golden Apples*. New York: Harcourt, Brace, and World (Harvest).

Welty, Eudora 1936. *A Curtain of Green and Other Stories*. New York: Harcourt, Brace, Jovanovich.

Wolf, Bryan Jay 1982. *Romantic Re-Vision: Culture and Consciousness in Nineteenth-Century American Painting and Literature*. Chicago: University of Chicago Press.

Wordsworth, William 1965. *Selected Poems and Prefaces*. Ed. Jack Stillinger. Boston: Houghton Mifflin.

10
At Risk in the Sublime: The Politics of Gender and Theory

Lee Edelman

I want to begin by considering two compelling moments in Patricia Yaeger's impressive essay, 'Toward a female sublime'. In the first, after persuasively identifying the empowering access to sublimity that Hélène Cixous and Luce Irigaray both invoke and enact in their writings, Yaeger explicitly identifies her critical enterprise with theirs: 'my project matches the hubris of the French feminists; I want to define a female sublime.' Later, after discussing Elizabeth Bishop's revisionary appropriation of the sublime in poems that she reads as socializing or domesticating that mode, Yaeger goes on to insist that 'the sublime is a risky genre for Bishop to re-invent, or for the feminist critic to reaffirm' (p. 196). I should like to consider the way in which Yaeger, in each of these passages, situates her discourse on the sublime within the dynamics of the sublime itself, the way she enacts the gestures of 'hubris', 'risk', and definition through confrontation (definition, here, of the 'female sublime' through confrontation with the 'conventional' or 'oedipal' sublime) characteristic of the very oedipal sublime that her essay explicitly 'refuses'.

This unstable relation between subject and object, between the cognitive mode through which the sublime is conceptualized and the sublime itself as a mode of cognition, seems frequently to assert itself in the analytic of the sublime. David Morris suggests one reason for this when he observes, in his essay on 'Gothic sublimity', that 'the sublime . . . embraces such a variety of historical practices and of theoretical accounts that the quest for a single, unchanging feature or essence is futile. There is no essence of the sublime' (p. 300). This quality of excess, this metamorphic capacity by which the sublime always escapes our efforts to define it, raises to the level of the sublime itself the attempt to wrest comprehensibility from its protean manifestations. Indeed, the sublimity of this intellectual struggle to define or account for or delimit the sublime recalls Kant's positioning of the sublime within a drama of cognition and self-re-cognition on the part of the rational faculties.

Thus Yaeger cannily acknowledges the implication of her critical discourse within the problematic of the sublime, and it behooves me to recognize that my response, like the relationship of responsiveness that governs the structure of our 'dialogue', must find itself inevitably situated within the space of the sublime as well.[1] As an implicitly narrativizing mode – that is, as a relational mode that stages its paradigmatic confront-ations at the bounds of (self-)definition, at the threshold or limen marking the highly charged division of self and other – the sublime can be seen to inform the strategic movements of dialectic (including those movements that seem to dismantle or go beyond dialectic itself), and to constrain us, therefore, to produce distinctive types of narrative structure. This dialogue with Patricia Yaeger, for instance, this attempt to respond to her essay, is destined to enact the coercive logic implicit in the sublime encounter. Indeed, before writing this response I received a letter from Linda Kauffman, expressing her hope that the pairing of essays and responses in this book would generate 'ways to make various discourses critically interrupt each other, throw each other into crisis, reversal, displacement'. What immediately struck me about this, in the context of my response to Yaeger's essay, was the extent to which it expressed a desire for the confrontations that mark the sublime.

What is at stake, though, for gender and for theory, in the staging of these sublime encounters, and what is effected by rehearsing them here as dialogic encounters? This 'dialogue', after all, is necessarily framed by the exigencies of history. Gender and theory are not, at this moment, unproblematically available as subjects for reasoned discussion between the sexes; they are subjects already theorized and gendered in ways that disturbingly identify them with the subjects who are doing the discussing. The old labels have been removed from the identical doors that figure in Lacan's well-known discussion of the symbolic inscriptions of sexual differentiation, and instead of 'Ladies' and 'Gentlemen', we have, within the academy at any rate, 'Gender' and 'Theory' as the contested, but still privileged, signifiers of difference 'between the sexes'.[2] And this leads us to produce by way of response, as the original subtitle of this volume, 'dialogues between the sexes', that could define the territory of difference prepositionally, as the dangerous space 'between' – a space that positions at its threshold those who undertake to frame it, and thus effectively places them within the arena of danger and confrontation that designates the sublime. But the inscription of this uncanny and seemingly inescap-able repetition of an oppositional structure – one that is simultaneously too familiar and too oppressive – appeared only in the volume's original subtitle, which was stand to stand, of course, in supplementary relation to the apparently more harmonious marriage pronounced by the title, *Gender and Theory*. The copular 'and' that links these two heavily gendered and theorized terms interprets them ambiguously as both the subjects under discussion in the 'dialogues between the sexes' and as the specular image of the subjects between whom that dialogue is being conducted. In the process, the 'and' identifies the dialogue itself as a type of union or wedding, thus inscribing within the very framework of the discussion the essential heterosexuality of the project – a project that must always supplement the idealized pairings of 'and' with a reproduction of the confrontational sublime that operates 'between'.

The heterosexual imperative to (re)produce this dialectic finds its emblem in the present volume's pairings of male and female authors in order to produce the effect of 'dialogue' – as if the impasse resulting from the contemporary impulse to theorize gender and to gender theory could be overcome, dialectically resolved, through a dialogue positioned 'between' man and woman. Instead, such a dialogue repositions itself in the mode of the oedipal sublime – the sublime of one-on-one confrontation that aspires to the recuperation of identity through the sudden over-coming of what blocks or constrains. Indeed, the very heterosexuality of this dialogue is what assures that it will reproduce the same hierarchical manifestations of an oppositional sublime.

At least in part this results from the historical moment at which the sexes meet across the hotly disputed boundaries of gender and theory. Even were both parties to bring nothing but good will, even were the explicit political goals of both the same, the relation between the sexes would still unfold in the figuration of a chiasmus that would signal the divergent interests at stake in the male and female efforts to frame the intersection of gender and theory. By and large the attraction of gender studies for (heterosexual) male theoreticians lies in its susceptibility to elaboration within the context of a male-dominated post-structural tradition. The project of deconstructing the subject of discourse finds its 'natural' fulfillment in the reading of 'woman' as a site at which issues of decentering and disarticulation are always already pronounced. Yet as feminist theoreticians like Elizabeth Weed and Rosi Braidotti have argued, it is precisely that condition that leads women to seek a feminist mode of empowerment and articulation. Such a mode – which is the mode of sub-limity at stake in Yaeger's initiating study of the 'female sublime' – would seek to consolidate the identity of a female subject in ways that might seem regressive or conservative to the male theorist intent on dismantling what he sees as an outmoded fiction of identity.[3] But Braidotti brings the matter into focus quite clearly: 'In order to announce the death of the subject one must first have gained the right to speak as one'.[4] Thus the axes of the chiasmus, or schematic crossing, traced by the movements toward and away from the articulation of the subject, cross at – and threaten to cross out – the female occupying the contested space at the intersection of gender and theory. And in this way the heterosexually inscribed 'dialogue between the sexes' assures the repetition of 'condensed, epistemologically loaded confrontations', a phrase that I borrow from Neil Hertz's description in *The End of the Line* of one 'trademark' of the sublime (p. 220).

To put all this another way, *Gender and Theory* risks presupposing the answer to the questions of sexual difference by phrasing its interrogations in terms of what Hélène Cixous, in 'Sorties', describes as 'always the same metaphor; we follow it, it transports us, in all its forms, wherever a discourse is organized' (p. 90). The metaphor that Cixous recognizes as infecting our discourse and effecting the 'transports' characteristic of the sublime is that of the oppositional couple: 'And all the couples of opposition are *couples*. Does this mean something? Is the fact that logocentrism subjects all thought – all of the concepts, the values – to a two-term system, related to "the" couple man/woman?' (p. 91). In fact, by beginning her essay with a discussion of the sublime flights of Cixous and Irigaray, Patricia Yaeger implies the need to recognize how much of the motive force for the contemporary feminist rehabilitation of the sublime is derived from the courage of a lesbian poetics that stands apart from the heterosexually marked dialogues 'between the sexes' and refuses the endlessly repetitive parading of the same differences in response to the same compulsion to pair off and find fulfillment in the alleged complementarity the opposite gender is said to provide. While it is a pleasure, then, to read and respond to Yaeger's wide-ranging and provocative essay, I find the very structure of our responsive relationship problematically captured within the register of 'condensed, epistemologically loaded confrontations'; and I am uncomfortable with the image of our prom-night pairing that requires this dialogue to reproduce the spectacle of heterosexual coupling, especially when it does so across the resonant texts of Cixous and Irigaray – texts that give passionate articulation to women's still brutally silenced desires for the love of other women.

How has the sublime as a genre got us into this situation? And what role, if any, can it play in helping to get us out? Yaeger's encounters with the sublime in her essay can offer some useful direction. As she unfolds the numerous varieties of what she defines as the 'female sublime', Yaeger produces a taxonomy in which the strategies of female empower-ment approach something like the mathematical sublime itself. Indeed, only an act of rational cognition such as Kant locates in the mathematical sublime can bring this ever-expanding typology into the unity effected by so magisterial and comprehensive a rubric as the 'female sublime'. But as Yaeger herself quite properly notes, the sublime is a risky genre 'for the feminist critic to reaffirm' – risky because its effect of empowerment cannot easily be disentangled from the dialectic of its relation to imperialism and domination; Yaeger formulates the issue shrewdly: 'The problem with entering the realm of the sublime is that we contract to participate in a power struggle that, even when it is resisted, involves grim forces of possession and domination.' To her credit, Yaeger refuses simply to disavow those forces of negativity; she recognizes too well how significant they can be in the production of 'voracious, volatile vocabularies of empowerment'.

As her essay insistently demonstrates, however, the sublime exacts a cost: it leaves the critic vulnerable to accusations of imperialism no matter how well-intentioned her or his efforts to disclaim or resist it may be. Yaeger, for instance, exemplifies the female 'sublime of near-ness' by evoking Elizabeth Bishop's poem, 'The Fish'. She directs our attention to the narrator's final gesture of releasing her venerable catch, thereby staging 'a scene of empowerment' in which incorporation is disavowed and 'the other is preserved in its otherness'. As the para-digm for Yaeger's definition of the female sublime, however, this model cannot account for the inescapably incorporative mode of the sublime that operates within the very taxonomy she presents; for as she per-suasively unfolds the vast and endlessly expansive domain of the female sublime, Yaeger's discursive implication within the domain of the sublime itself leads her to constitute 'the female sublime' as a coherent discursive category by invoking the unity of a female Difference (mani-festing the allure of Unity-in-Difference) that can have the effect of sub-suming and effacing the experiential differences played out in women's lives. Thus the specificity of Nikki Giovanni as a black female artist and the distinctiveness of Elizabeth Bishop as a lesbian poet are elided in the service of an economy of Difference that effectively occludes their determining differences in the sublime expansiveness of the female sublime.

This erasure of distinctions in order to produce the unity of a coherent identity constitutes, as we have seen, the distinguishing mark of the oedipal sublime. It is of interest, therefore, that the political realities that lead to Yaeger's own inscription within this problematic can be analyzed most effectively in her discussion of the feminist strategy her essay clearly privileges: that associated with what she defines as the 'feminine' or 'pre-oedipal sublime'. Let me make clear at the outset, however, that it is not my intention to deconstruct or disempower this invocation of the 'pre-oedipal sublime'; rather, I want to attend as responsibly as I can to the desire that is articulated within both the pre-oedipal and its strategic invocations.

'Here,' Yaeger writes of the 'pre-oedipal sublime', 'the agon typical of the Romantic sublime is retained as part of a narrative or poetic structure, but this oedipal conflict is rewritten so that the pre-oedipal desire for closeness or nearness with the other that the conventional sublime tries to repress, remains visible and viable' (p. 204). Now the 'closeness' of the pre-oedipal is bound up with issues of inundation and incorporation, since the determining feature of the pre-oedipal stage is the fluidity of the boundaries between self and (m)other. Incorporation, though, as Yaeger suggests in her reading of 'The Fish', can identify the imperialistic tendency to annul otherness by means of appropriation; and to some extent the pre-oedipal itself can effect a dangerously similar appropriation by focusing on an imaginary reciprocity and interdependence prior to the constitution of gendered subjects in relation to socially constructed difference. It is precisely this focus, however, that accounts for the powerful appeal of the pre-oedipal to contemporary feminist theoreticians: for the pre-oedipal seems to offer the conceptual space to think outside the hierarchical ordering of phallogocentric discourse, and it suggests a ground, or at least a zone, from which to speak a female voice that can otherwise only be figured – and experienced – as the repressed in an oedipalized social formation.

More precisely, though, it is *female* feminists who have been most active in the re- or dis-articulation of psychoanalytic theory through the intervention of a theory and a discourse of the pre-oedipal. For male theoreticians drawn to feminism, the possibility of escaping the economy and logic of phallogocentrism has seemed, in the main, an impossible project, a version of naive or utopian idealism, or even a covert return to a disavowed essentialism. Cixous herself takes account of this response when she repudiates those male theorists – deconstructive and/or psychoanalytic fellow-travelers – who would dismiss works like 'the laugh of the Medusa' as recuperative gestures in an outmoded and discredited philosophical idealism.[5] But the great strength of Cixous's position in 'The laugh of the Medusa' is that while affirming the pre-oedipal as a necessary point of departure for an *écriture féminine*, she self-consciously and strategically mobilizes this call for a reconsideration of the imaginary, this call for a reconsideration of the moment before the institutionaliz-ation of sexual difference, as a canny response to a historical moment in which feminists confront the blockage or impasse that theory (especially male appropriations of feminism in deconstructive and psychoanalytic theory) produces with respect to gender. The recuperation of a female pre-oedipal sublime, then, can be seen as a moment of feminist self-recognition or self-constitution that moves beyond, or before, the paralyzing and endlessly repeated confrontations of male and female across the boundaries of gender and theory;[6] in other words the theor-izing of the pre-oedipal sublime occurs in a diacritical and historically specific relation to the 'epistemological confrontations' of the oedipal sublime itself.

This historical positioning of the pre-oedipal, far from disempowering its desire for the non-appropriative or non-hierarchical, imbues it with the political force of its historical specificity. To disengage it from that context, however, and invoke a universalized pre-oedipal 'sublime of nearness' that is characteristically female, risks emptying that sublime of the experiential conflict – and thus of the element of human suffering – that marks not only the oedipal sublime, but also – and more importantly – the ongoing history of female oppression from which comes the very motiv-ation to produce a sublime of female empowerment. The danger of such an emptying out is largely, but not entirely, evaded in Yaeger's essay. Although she asserts near the end that 'in domesticating the Romantic sublime . . . [she does] not want to evacuate the experience of boundless-ness and negativity implicit in this form' (p. 209), Yaeger does risk scanting that negativity when she frames her project as an attempt to move 'toward a model of the self that permits both a saving maintenance of ego-boundaries and an exploration of the pleasures of intersubjectivity.' (p. 205) Who, after all, are the unspecified subjects gaining access to this pleasurable intersubjectivity here? Can the female sublime, can a pre-oedipal sublime, encompass a pleasurable 'nearness' across the divisions 'between the sexes'? Is there not something crucially significant about the 'homosexual' object choice of the female child in the pre-oedipal stage? Surely it is significant that the instances of the pre-oedipal sublime that Yaeger presents in her essay, insofar as they invoke an intersubjective nearness at all, do so in contexts that specify as female the gender of the subjects experiencing the 'pleasures' of contiguity. They invoke, that is, what might more strategically be called a lesbian rather than a female sublime.[7]

But the empowerment effected by the lesbian sublime, the recognition of the pleasure attainable through a lesbian intersubjectivity, is itself historically situated as a response to the oppressive agencies of a misogynistic and heterosexist society. Its celebration of an Irigarayan pre-oedipal (which Carolyn Burke evokes as a 'lost paradise of mutual affection' [p. 299]) derives significance from its historical inscription in a post-lapsarian cultural text marked by the unleashing of violent forces of domination and subjugation. To situate the act of resistance implicit in this self-constituting lesbian sublime under the universalizing aspect of a 'female' sublime that 'can include the sociable, the convivial, as well as the grandiose and empowering', is, potentially, to ignore the gendered specificity of the society that this sublime would include. And it is to risk, in the process, overlooking the politically contestatory uses to which the oedipal sublime itself can still be put. I would like to conclude this essay, therefore, by inscribing anecdotally within its text my sense of the political value that can attach to the historically specific deployment of the confrontational sublime – a value Yaeger also suggests in her essay's concluding affirmation of 'the female sublime of violence' – and by evoking a moment that can articulate with less protective mediation my own relation to the sublime as it is effected and affected by my sexual positioning.

My nearest approach to an experience of the sublime took place on 11 October 1987, the day of the Lesbian and Gay March on Washington. Like so many of the other gay men and lesbians who traveled from each homophobic corner of America to participate in this passionately outraged response to centuries of oppression, a decade of indifference to our struggle against disease, and the bitter insult of the Supreme Court's decision in *Bowers* v. *Hardwick* to affirm the right of states to criminalize acts of homosexual sodomy, I arrived at the ellipse behind the White House just before the procession was scheduled to begin at noon. In my anticipations of the march I had foreseen a massive and irresistible outpouring of people: I had envisioned a crowd that would overflow the ellipse, that would clog the streets in every direction and render them impassable. But the streets from the direction of my approach were clear and when I saw the open spaces between the groups that had gathered on the ellipse at noon, I suffered a shock of disappointment. We seemed to be so many fewer than I had imagined, so many fewer than I had hoped. Time passed as I talked with friends and students I ran into as we waited for the march to commence, and when we still were not moving by 1 o'clock I began to wonder if the organizers of the march were as ineffectual as I thought so small a crowd must be. But as we made our way forward we discovered that the march had started on time, over an hour ago, and when we finally were out in the streets and marching we discovered that we were part of a crowd that now seemed much larger than it had before.

By the time we reached our destination, the mall in front of the Capitol, we were truly an amazing throng: an enormous crowd stretched out before us and an unbroken procession of people filled the parade route behind as far as we could see – so many people that by 5 o'clock, when the speeches had been going on for almost five hours, contingents of marchers were still first making their way to the mall from the ellipse. Before the march the gay community had hoped for a crowd of 200,000; so when Eleanor Smeal, standing on the stage constructed at the Capitol end of the mall, looked out at this ever enlarging crowd sweeping toward the base of the Washington monument where it rose at the other end and announced that we were half a million lesbians and gay men gathered to assert the force of our numbers, the crowd arose in a spontaneous outburst of dazzled exaltation. We had stunned ourselves with the image our own multitudinous unity and the mathematical sublime produced by our seemingly incomprehensible mass served to reconstitute our identity in the face of all our devastations. That sense of exhilaration, that Wordsworthian access to identification with power after initial blockage or disappointment, was not unmixed with a painful knowledge that the vast territory of the American continent lay behind us with its vaster array of homophobic voices ready to silence, with self-righteous violence, our cries of affirmation. And the empowering sense of our unification into this crowd of half a million strong could only temporarily subordinate the recognition of those ineffaceable differences that necessarily inhabit, and at times divide, the gay community – differences not only between lesbians and gay men, but differences also of color, age, ethnic back-

ground, economic status, and political ideology. The force of the sublime
had configured us into a powerfully enabling facsimile of unity, but the
price of that unity was the momentary occlusion of the real social forces
that so often render the needs and desires of our various constituencies
painfully incompatible.

Now the sublime element evoked by this anecdote, like the sincere but
sentimentalizing pathos that informs its elaboration, operates, I would
argue, in a theoretically regressive way to affirm identity and thereby
constitute a coherent locus of subjectivity under the suspect banner of
unity, idealism, and empowerment. But what is regressive here in theory
can still have, given its historical context – and the context of the march
on Washington was one of institutionally sanctioned homophobia and the
inevitable physical and emotional violence it breeds – powerful and
progressive force within the politics of gender. It is in this sense that I
understand Patricia Yaeger's enterprise in articulating the possibilities of
a contemporary female sublime; and in this sense its gestures of
empowerment – produced, as Gayatri Spivak would put it, even at 'the
risk of essence' (in *Men in Feminism*, p. 58) – should be seen, like
Cixous's risk of 'idealism' in the elaboration of an *écriture féminine*, not
as theoretical backsliding, but as historically and politically imperative
moments in the effort to escape the wearying stalemate of gender and
theory wedded in opposition across the threshold of the sublime.

NOTES

I would like to express my gratitude to Joanne Feit Diehl, with whom I discussed my
thoughts about this essay as I wrote it, and to Joseph Litvak who generously read and
commented on it at every stage of its production.

1   It is appropriate, therefore, that in 'The Most of It', one of the texts Yaeger cites as
    exemplary of the power of the oedipal sublime to produce, in Hertz's words, a
    'confirmation of the unitary status of the self' (1985: 53), Frost depicts a seeker of
    sublimity who cries out for 'counter-love, original response' (p. 338). Response is thus
    already inscribed within the workings of the oedipal sublime, and it necessarily governs
    the articulation of my position here.
2   This is by no means intended to valorize or to naturalize the gender coding of this
    distinction, only to mark the extent to which 'Theory' remains largely conceptualized
    as the purview of a critical and philosophical tradition that is still, for the most part,
    male, and 'Gender' encompasses the domain of women's history, feminist theory,
    lesbian and gay studies, and all the other theoretical explorations of sexuality. These
    distinctions, I should add, are not exclusively imposed by one gender or the other; I can
    recall many occasions at the Seminar on Feminist Literary Theory at Harvard on which
    'Theory' was identified as a hegemonic masculine discourse threatening to appropriate

the question of gender in ways that would trivialize what Alice Jardine identifies as the *'inscription of struggle* - even of *pain'* (Jardine and Smith 1987: 58) in the feminist movement. This association of 'Theory' with a male discourse can also be seen in Cixous's 'The laugh of the Medusa', where she writes: 'Am I dreaming? Am I misrecognizing? You, the defenders of "theory," the sacrosanct yes-men of Concept, enthroners of the phallus (but not of the penis)' (1980: 262).

3   The political valence of the sublime itself has been subjected to critical reconsideration in the work of some contemporary theorists. Jonathan Arac, for instance, takes issue with what he sees as the prevalent reading of the sublime's political force when he asserts that 'the sublime does not always function for liberation' (1987: 219). Donald Pease goes even further and insists that 'despite all the *revolutionary* rhetoric invested in the term, the sublime has, in what we could call the politics of historical formation, always served conservative purposes' (1984: 275).

4   Braidotti 1987: 237. Elizabeth Weed makes a similar observation in her essay, 'A man's place', when she writes: 'Certainly the situation for women is additionally complicated by our need to struggle against the lure of Woman as privileged figure of undecidability, particularly in the texts of male theorists. For the many feminists both inside and outside the academy who work to transform systems of domination, the immediate task entails constructing a female subject in order to obtain for women a better, and in many cases a less oppressive and literally safer place in the social field, while *at the same time* always displacing boundaries, always shifting positions to work against the erection of the same old phallocratic structures in the name of identity and the unifying subject' (p. 75). The problem, as Weed's italics indicate, is in the question of temporality. Like the Derridean double science, feminism must operate simultaneously on the non-coinciding fields of gender and of theory, and what theory, at any given moment, many see as reactionary or naive, may turn out to be, in terms of gender, not only necessary, but radically contestatory as well.

5   'Once more you'll say that all this smacks of "idealism," or what's worse, you'll splutter that I'm a "mystic"' (Cixous 1980: 262).

6   Consider, for example, the sublime moment of breakthrough, transport, and transformation in Irigaray's 'When our lips speak together': 'Our whole body is moved. No surface holds. No figure, line, or point remains. No ground subsists. But no abyss, either. Depth, for us, is not a chasm. Without a solid crust, there is no precipice. Our depth is the thickness of our body, our all touching itself. Where top and bottom, inside and outside, in front and behind, above and below are not separated, remote, out of touch. Our all intermingled. Without breaks or gaps' (1985: 213).

7   This is not to suggest that 'lesbian' and 'female' are necessarily separable from one another; indeed, among the political benefits that accrue from designating a 'lesbian' rather than a 'female' sublime is the possibility of reaffirming the importance of the 'lesbian continuum' that Adrienne Rich sees as providing a context for understanding the entire field of women's relations with other women (1980: 648). By designating this sublime as 'lesbian' we can also try to avoid a repetition of the heterosexual history of denying lesbian lives. Cixous, of course, inscribes this gesture in 'The laugh of the Medusa', when she writes, 'The Americans remind us, "We are all Lesbians"' (1980: 252). See in this context, however, Wenzel 1981, for a discussion of the vexed relationship between Cixous and the concept of lesbianism.

REFERENCES

Arac, Jonathan 1987. 'The media of sublimity: Johnson and Lamb on *King Lear*', *Studies in Romanticism* 26: 209-20.

Braidotti, Rosi 1987. 'Envy: or with my Brains and your Looks', in *Men in Feminism*, ed. Alice Jardine and Paul Smith. London and New York: Methuen.

Burke, Carolyn 1981. 'Irigaray Through the Looking Glass', *Feminist Studies* 7: 288-306.

Cixous, Hélène 1980. 'Sorties', trans. Ann Liddle, in *New French Feminisms*, ed. Elaine Marks and Isabelle de Courtivron. Amherst: University of Massachusetts Press.

Cixous, Hélène 1980. 'The laugh of the Medusa', trans. Keith Cohen and Paula Cohen, in *New French Feminisms*, ed. Elaine Marks and Isabelle de Courtivron. Amherst: University of Massachusetts Press.

Frost, Robert 1974. *The Poetry of Robert Frost*, ed. Edward Connery Lathem. New York: Holt Rinehart and Winston.

Hertz, Neil 1985. *The End of the Line: Essays on Psychoanalysis and the Sublime*. New York: Columbia University Press.

Irigaray, Luce 1985. 'When our lips speak together', in *This Sex Which is Not One*, trans. Catherine Porter with Carolyn Burke. Ithaca, NY: Cornell University Press.

Jardine, Alice 1987. 'Men in feminism: odor di uomo or compagnons de route?', in *Men in Feminism*, ed. Alice Jardine and Paul Smith. London and New York: Methuen.

Morris, David 1985. 'Gothic sublimity', *New Literary History* 16: 299-319.

Pease, Donald 1984. 'Sublime politics', *boundary 2* 12-13: 259-79.

Rich, Adrienne 1980. 'Compulsory heterosexuality and lesbian existence', *Signs* 5: 631-60.

Weed, Elizabeth 1987. 'A man's place', in *Men in Feminism*, ed. Alice Jardine and Paul Smith. London and New York: Methuen.

Wenzel, Hélène Vivienne 1981. 'The text as body/politics: an appreciation of Monique Wittig's writing in context', *Feminist Studies* 7, 2: 264-87.

11
The Race for Theory

Barbara Christian

I have seized this occasion to break the silence among those of us, critics, as we are now called, who have been intimidated, devalued by what I call the race for theory. I have become convinced that there has been a take-over in the literary world by Western philosophers from the old literary elite, the neutral humanists. Philosophers have been able to effect such a take-over because so much of the literature of the West has become pallid, laden with despair, self-indulgent, and disconnected. The New Philosophers, eager to understand a world that is today fast escaping their political control, have redefined literature so that the distinctions implied by that term, that is, the distinctions between everything written and those things written to evoke feeling as well as to express thought, have been blurred. They have changed literary critical language to suit their own purposes as philosophers, and they have re-invented the meaning of theory.

My first response to this realization was to ignore it. Perhaps, in spite of the egocentrism of this trend, some good might come of it. I had, I felt, more pressing and interesting things to do, such as reading and studying the history and literature of black women, a history that had been totally ignored, a contemporary literature bursting with originality, passion, insight, and beauty. But unfortunately it is difficult to ignore this new take-over, theory has become a commodity because that helps determine whether we are hired or promoted in academic institutions - worse, whether we are heard at all. Due to this new orientation, works (a word which evokes labor) have become texts. Critics are no longer concerned with literature, but with other critics' texts, for the critic yearning for attention has displaced the writer and has conceived of himself as the center. Interestingly in the first part of this century, at least in England and America, the critic was usually also a writer of poetry, plays, or novels. But today, as a new generation of professionals develops, he or she is increasingly an academic. Activities such as teaching or writing one's response to specific works of literature have, among this group, become subordinated to one primary thrust, that moment when one creates a theory, thus fixing a constellation of ideas for a time at least, a fixing which no doubt will be replaced in another month or so by somebody else's competing theory as the race accelerates. Perhaps because those who have effected the take-over have the power (although they deny it) first of all to be published, and thereby to determine the ideas which are deemed valuable, some of our most daring and potentially radical critics (and by *our* I mean black, women, Third World) have been influenced, even co-opted, into speaking a language and defining their discussion in terms alien to and opposed to our needs and orientation. At least so far, the creative writers I study have resisted this language.[1]

For people of color have always theorized – but in forms quite different from the Western form of abstract logic. And I am inclined to say that our theorizing (and I intentionally use the verb rather than the noun) is often in narrative forms, in the stories we create, in riddles and proverbs, in the play with language, since dynamic rather than fixed ideas seem more to our liking. How else have we managed to survive with such spiritedness the assault on our bodies, social institutions, countries, our very humanity? And women, at least the women I grew up around, continuously speculated about the nature of life through pithy language that unmasked the power relations of their world. It is this language, and the grace and pleasure with which they played with it, that I find celebrated, refined, critiqued in the works of writers like Toni Morrison and Alice Walker. My folk, in other words, have always been a race of theory – though more in the form of the hieroglyph, a written figure which is both sensual and abstract, both beautiful and communicative. In my own work I try to illuminate and explain these hieroglyphs, which is, I think, an activity quite different from the creating of the hieroglyphs themselves. As the Buddhists would say, the finger pointing at the moon is not the moon.

In this discussion, however, I am more concerned with the issue raised by my first use of the term, *the race for theory*, in relation to its academic hegemony, and possibly of its inappropriateness to the energetic emerging literatures in the world today. The pervasiveness of this academic hegemony is an issue continually spoken about – but usually in hidden groups, lest we, who are disturbed by it, appear ignorant to the reigning academic elite. Among the folk who speak in muted tones are people of color, feminists, radical critics, creative writers, who have struggled for much longer than a decade to make their voices, their various voices, heard, and for whom literature is not an occasion for discourse among critics but is necessary nourishment for their people and one way by which they come to understand their lives better. Clichéd though this may be, it bears, I think, repeating here.

The race for theory, with its linguistic jargon, its emphasis on quoting its prophets, its tendency towards 'Biblical' exegesis, its refusal even to mention specific works of creative writers, far less contemporary ones, its preoccupations with mechanical analyses of language, graphs, algebraic equations, its gross generalizations about culture, has silenced many of us to the extent that some of us feel we can no longer discuss our own literature, while others have developed intense writing blocks and are puzzled by the incomprehensibility of the language set adrift in literary circles. There have been, in the last year, any number of occasions on which I had to convince literary critics who have pioneered entire new areas of critical inquiry that they did have something to say. Some of us are continually harassed to invent wholesale theories regardless of the complexity of the literature we study. I, for one, am tired of being asked to produce a black feminist literary theory as if I were a mechanical man. For I believe such theory is prescriptive – it ought to have some relationship to practice. Since I can count on one hand the number of people attempting to be black feminist literary critics in the world today, I consider it presumptuous of me to invent a theory of how we *ought* to read. Instead, I think we need to read the works of our writers in our various ways and remain open to the intricacies of the intersection of language, class, race, and gender in the literature. And it would help if we share our process, that is, our practice, as much as possible since, finally, our work *is* a collective endeavor.

The insidious quality of this race for theory is symbolized for me by a term like 'Minority Discourse'[2] – a label that is borrowed from the reigning theory of the day but which is untrue to the literatures being produced by our writers, for many of our literatures (certainly Afro-American literature) are central, not minor. I have used the passive voice in my last sentence construction, contrary to the rules of Black English, which like all languages has a particular value system, since I have not placed responsibility on any particular person or group. But that is precisely because this new ideology has become so prevalent among us that it behaves like so many of the other ideologies with which we have had to contend. It appears to have neither head nor center. At the least, though, we can say that the terms 'minority' and 'discourse' are located firmly in a Western dualistic or 'binary' frame which sees the rest of the world as minor, and tries to convince the rest of the world that it *is* major, usually through force and then through language, even as it claims many of the ideas that we, its 'historical' other, have known and spoken about for so long. For many of us have never conceived of ourselves only as somebody's *other*.

Let me not give the impression that by objecting to the race for theory I ally myself with or agree with the neutral humanists who see literature as pure expression and will not admit to the obvious control of its production, value, and distribution by those who have power, who deny, in other words, that literature is, of necessity, political. I am studying an entire body of literature that has been denigrated for centuries by such terms as *political*. For an entire century Afro-American writers, from Charles Chestnutt in the nineteenth century through Richard Wright in the 1930s, Imamu Baraka in the 1960s, Alice Walker in the 1970s, have protested the literary hierarchy of dominance which declares when literature is literature, when literature is great, depending on what it thinks is to its advantage. The Black Arts Movement of the 1960s, out of which Black Studies, the Feminist Literary Movement of the 1970s, and Women's Studies grew, articulated precisely those issues, which came *not* from the declarations of the New Western Philosophers but from these groups' reflections on their own lives. That Western scholars have long believed their ideas to be universal has been strongly opposed by many such groups. Some of my colleagues do not see black critical writers of previous decades as eloquent enough. Clearly they have not read Wright's 'A blueprint for Negro Writing', Ellison's *Shadow and Act*, Chestnutt's resignation from being a writer, or Alice Walker's 'In search of Zora Neale Hurston'.[3] There are two reasons for this general ignorance of what our writer-critics have said. One is that black writing has been generally ignored in the USA. Since we, as Toni Morrison has put it, are seen as a discredited people, it is no surprise, then, that our creations are also discredited. But this is also due to the fact that until recently, dominant critics in the Western world have also been creative writers who have had access to the upper-middle-class institutions of education and, until recently, our writers have decidedly been excluded from these institutions and in fact have often been opposed to them. Because of the academic world's general ignorance about the literature of black people, and of women, whose work too has been discredited, it is not surprising that so many of our critics think that the position arguing that literature is political begins with these New Philosophers. Unfortunately, many of our young critics do not investigate the reasons *why* that statement - literature is political - is now acceptable when before it was not; nor do we look to our own antecedents for the sophisticated arguments upon which we can build in order to change the tendency of any established Western idea to become hegemonic.

For I feel that the new emphasis on literary critical theory is as hegemonic as the world which it attacks. I see the language it creates as one which mystifies rather than clarifies our condition, making it possible for a few people who know that particular language to control the critical scene - that language surfaced, interestingly enough, just when the literature of peoples of color, of black women, of Latin Americans, of Africans, began to move to 'the center'. Such words as *center* and *periphery* are themselves instructive. *Discourse, canon, texts*, words as Latinate as the tradition from which they come, are quite familiar to me. Because I went to a Catholic Mission school in the West Indies I must confess that I cannot hear the word 'canon' without smelling incense, that the word 'text' immediately brings back agonizing memories of Biblical exegesis, that 'discourse' reeks for me of metaphysics forced down my throat in those courses that traced *world* philosophy from Aristotle through Thomas Aquinas to Heidegger. 'Periphery' too is a word I heard throughout my childhood, for if anything was seen as being at the periphery, it was those small Caribbean islands which had neither land mass nor military power. Still I noted how intensely important this periphery was, for US troups were continually invading one island or another if any change in political control even seemed to be occurring. As I lived among folk for whom language was an absolutely necessary way of validating our existence, I was told that the minds of the world lived only in the small continent of Europe. The metaphysical language of the New Philosophy, then, I must admit, is repulsive to me and is one reason why I raced from philosophy to literature, since the latter seemed to me to have the possibilities of rendering the world as large and as complicated as I experienced it, as sensual as I knew it was. In literature I sensed the possibility of the integration of feeling/knowledge, rather than the split between the abstract and the emotional in which Western philosophy inevitably indulged.

Now I am being told that philosophers are the ones who write liter-ature, that authors are dead, irrelevant, mere vessels through which their narratives ooze, that they do not work nor have they the faintest idea what they are doing; rather, they produce texts as disembodied as the angels. I am frankly astonished that scholars who call themselves marxists or post-marxists could seriously use such metaphysical language even as they attempt to deconstruct the philosophical tradition from which their language comes. And as a student of literature, I am appalled by the sheer ugliness of the language, its lack of clarity, its unnecessarily complicated sentence constructions, its lack of pleasurableness, its alienating quality. It is the kind of writing for which composition teachers would give a freshman a resounding F.

Because I am a curious person, however, I postponed readings of black women writers I was working on and read some of the prophets of this new literary orientation. These writers did announce their dissatisfaction with some of the cornerstone ideas of their own tradition, a dissatisfaction with which I was born. But in their attempt to change the orientation of Western scholarship, they, as usual, concentrated on themselves and were not in the slightest interested in the worlds they had ignored or con-trolled. Again I was supposed to know *them*, while they were not at all interested in knowing *me*. Instead they sought to 'deconstruct' the tradition to which they belonged even as they used the same forms, style, language of that tradition, forms that necessarily embody its values. And increasingly as I read them and saw their substitution of their philo-sophical writings for literary ones, I began to have the uneasy feeling that their folk were not producing any literature worth mentioning. For they always harkened back to the masterpieces of the past, again reifying the very texts they said they were deconstructing. Increasingly, as *their* way, *their* terms, *their* approaches remained central and became the means by which one defined literary critics, many of my own peers who had previously been concentrating on dealing with the other side of the equation, the reclamation and discussion of past and *present* Third World literatures, were diverted into continually discussing the new literary theory.

From my point of view as a critic of contemporary Afro-American women's writing, this orientation is extremely problematic. In attempting to find the deep structures in the literary tradition, a major preoccupation of the new New Criticism, many of us have become obsessed with the nature of reading itself to the extent that we have stopped writing about literature being written today. Since I am slightly paranoid, it has begun to occur to me that the literature being produced *is* precisely one of the reasons why this new philosophical-literary-critical theory of relativity is so prominent. In other words, the literature of blacks, women of South America and Africa, etc., as overtly 'political' literature, was being preempted by a new Western concept which proclaimed that reality does not exist, that everything is relative, and that every text is silent about something – which indeed it must necessarily be.

There is, of course, much to be learned from exploring how we know what we know, how we read what we read, an exploration which, of necessity, can have no end. But there also has to be a 'what', and that 'what', when it is even mentioned by the New Philosophers, are texts of the past, primarily Western male texts, whose norms are again being transferred onto Third World, female texts as theories of reading proliferate. Inevitably a hierarchy has now developed between what is called theoretical criticism and practical criticism, as mind is deemed superior to matter. I have no quarrel with those who wish to philosophize about how we know what we know. But I do resent the fact that this particular orientation is so privileged and has diverted so many of us from doing the first readings of the literature being written today as well as of past works about which nothing has been written. I note, for example, that there is little work done on Gloria Naylor, that most of Alice Walker's works have not been commented on – despite the rage around *The Color Purple*[4] – that there has yet to be an in-depth study of Frances Harper, the nineteenth-century abolitionist poet and novelist. If our emphasis on theoretical criticism continues, critics of the future may have to reclaim the writers we are now ignoring, that is, if they are even aware these artists exist.

I am particularly perturbed by the movement to exalt theory, as well, because of my own adult history. I was an active member of the Black Arts Movement of the 1960s and know how dangerous theory can become. Many today may not be aware of this, but the Black Arts Movement tried to create Black Literary Theory and in doing so became prescriptive. My fear is that when Theory is not rooted in practice, it becomes prescriptive, exclusive, elitist.

An example of this prescriptiveness is the approach the Black Arts Movement took towards language. For it, blackness resided in the use of black talk which they defined as hip urban language. So that when Nikki Giovanni reviewed Paule Marshall's *Chosen Place, Timeless People*, she criticized the novel on the grounds that it was not black, for the language was too elegant, too white.[5] Blacks, she said, did not speak that way.

Having come from the West Indies where we do, some of the time, speak that way, I was amazed by the narrowness of her vision. The emphasis on *one way* to be black resulted in the works of Southern writers being seen as non-black since the black talk of Georgia does not sound like the black talk of Philadelphia. Because the ideologues, like Baraka, came from the urban centers, they tended to privilege their way of speaking, thinking, writing, and to condemn other kinds of writing as not being black enough. Whole areas of the canon were assessed according to the dictum of the Black Arts Nationalist point of view, as in Addison Gayle's *The Way of the New World*, while other works were ignored because they did not fit the scheme of cultural nationalism.[6] Older writers like Ralph Ellison and James Baldwin were condemned because they saw that the intersection of Western and African influences resulted in a new Afro-American culture, a position with which many of the Black Nationalist ideologues disagreed. Writers were told that writing love poems was not being black. Further examples abound.

It is true that the Black Arts Movement resulted in a necessary and important critique both of previous Afro-American literature and of the white-established literary world. But in attempting to take over power, it, as Ishmael Reed satirizes so well in *Mumbo Jumbo*, became much like its opponent, monolithic and downright repressive.[7]

It is this tendency towards the monolithic, monotheistic, and so on, that worries me about the race for theory. Constructs like the *center* and the *periphery* reveal that tendency to want to make the world less complex by organizing it according to one principle, to fix it through an idea which is really an ideal. Many of us are particularly sensitive to monolithism because one major element of ideologies of dominance, such as sexism and racism, is to dehumanize people by stereotyping them, by denying them their variousness and complexity. Inevitably, monolithism becomes a metasystem, in which there is a controlling ideal, especially in relation to pleasure. Language as one form of pleasure is immediately restricted, and becomes heavy, abstract, prescriptive, monotonous.

Variety, multiplicity, eroticism are difficult to control. And it may very well be that these are the reasons why writers are often seen as *persona non grata* by political states, whatever form they take, since writers/artists have a tendency to refuse to give up their way of seeing the world and of playing with possibilities; in fact, their very expression relies on that insistence. Perhaps that is why creative literature, even when written by politically reactionary people, can be so freeing, for in having to embody ideas and recreate the world, writers cannot merely produce 'one way'.

The characteristics of the Black Arts Movement are, I am afraid, being repeated again today, certainly in the other area to which I am especially tuned. In the race for theory, feminists, eager to enter the halls of power, have attempted their own prescriptions. So often I have read books on feminist literary theory that restrict the definition of what *feminist* means and overgeneralize about so much of the world that most women as well as men are excluded. Seldom do feminist theorists take into account the complexity of life – that women are of many races and ethnic backgrounds with different histories and cultures and that as a rule women belong to different classes that have different concerns. Seldom do they note these distinctions, because if they did they could not articulate a theory. Often as a way of clearing themselves they do acknowledge that women of color, for example, do exist, then go on to do what they were going to do anyway, which is to invent a theory that has little relevance for us.

That tendency towards monolithism is precisely how I see the French feminist theorists. They concentrate on the female body as the means to creating a female language, since language, they say, is male and necessarily conceives of woman as other.[8] Clearly many of them have been irritated by the theories of Lacan for whom language is phallic. But suppose there are peoples in the world whose language was invented primarily in relation to women, who after all are the ones who relate to children and teach language. Some Native American languages, for example, use female pronouns when speaking about non-gender-specific activity. Who knows who, according to gender, created languages. Further, by positing the body as the source of everything French feminists return to the old myth that biology determines everything and ignore the fact that gender is a social rather than a biological construct.

I could go on critiquing the positions of French feminists who are themselves more various in their points of view than the label which is used to describe them, but that is not my point. What I am concerned about is the authority this school now has in feminist scholarship – the way it has become *authoritative discourse*, monologic, which occurs precisely because it does have access to the means of promulgating its ideas. The Black Arts Movement was able to do this for a time because of the political movements of the 1960s – so too with the French feminists who could not be inventing 'theory' if a space had not been created by the women's movement. In both cases, both groups posited a theory that excluded many of the people who made that space possible. Hence one of the reasons for the surge of Afro-American women's writing during the 1970s and its emphasis on sexism in the black community is precisely that when the ideologues of the 1960s said *black*, they meant *black male*.[9]

I and many of my sisters do not see the world as being so simple. And perhaps that is why we have not rushed to create abstract theories. For we know there are countless women of color, both in America and in the rest of the world, to whom our singular ideas would be applied. There is, therefore, a caution we feel about pronouncing black feminist theory that might be seen as a decisive statement about Third World women. This is not to say we are not theorizing. Certainly our literature is an indication of the ways in which our theorizing, of necessity, is based on our multiplicity of experiences.

There is at least one other lesson I learned from the Black Arts Movement. One reason for its monolithic approach had to do with its desire to destroy the power which controlled black people, but it was a power which many of its ideologues wished to achieve. The nature of our context today is such that an approach which desires power singlemind-edly must of necessity become like that which it wishes to destroy. Rather than wanting to change the whole model, many of us want to be at the center. It is this point of view that writers like June Jordan and Audre Lorde continually critique even as they call for empowerment, as they emphasize the fear of difference among us and our need for leaders rather than a reliance on ourselves.

For one must distinguish the desire for power from the need to become empowered – that is, seeing oneself as capable of and having the right to determine one's life. Such empowerment is partially derived from a knowledge of history. The Black Arts Movement did result in the creation of Afro-American Studies as a concept, thus giving it a place in the university where one might engage in the reclamation of Afro-American history and culture and pass it on to others. I am particularly concerned that institutions such as black studies and women's studies, fought for with such vigor and at some sacrifice, are not often seen as important by many of our black or women scholars precisely because the old hierarchy of traditional departments is seen as superior to these 'marginal' groups. Yet, it is in this context that many others of us are discovering the extent of our complexity, the interrelationships of different areas of knowledge in relation to a distinctly Afro-American or female experience. Rather than having to view our world as subordinate to others, or rather than having to work as if we were hybrids, we can pursue ourselves as subjects.

My major objection to the race for theory, as some readers have probably guessed by now, really hinges on the question, 'For whom are we doing what we are doing when we do literary criticism?' It is, I think, the central question today, especially for the few of us who have infiltrated academia enough to be wooed by it. The answer to that question determines what orientation we take in our work, the language we use, the purposes for which it is intended.

I can only speak for myself. But what I write and how I write is done in order to save my own life.[10] And I mean that literally. For me literature is a way of knowing that I am not hallucinating, that whatever I feel/know *is*. It is an affirmation that sensuality is intelligence, that sensual language is language that makes sense. My response, then, is directed to those who write what I read and to those who read what I read - put concretely - to Toni Morrison and to people who read Toni Morrison (among whom I would count few academics). That number is increasing, as is the readership of Walker and Marshall. But in no way is the literature Morrison, Marshall, or Walker create supported by the academic world. Nor given the political context of our society, do I expect that to change soon. For there is no reason, given who controls these institutions, for them to be anything other than threatened by these writers.

My readings do presuppose a need, a desire among folk who like me also want to save their own lives. My concern, then, is a passionate one, for the literature of people who are not in power has always been in danger of extinction or of cooptation, not because we do not theorize, but because what we can even imagine, far less who we can reach, is constantly limited by societal structures. For me, literary criticism is promotion as well as understanding, a response to the writer to whom there is often no response, to folk who need the writing as much as they need anything. I know, from literary history, that writing disappears unless there is a response to it. Because I write about writers who are now writing, I hope to help ensure that their tradition has continuity and survives.

So my 'method', to use a new 'lit. crit.' word, is not fixed but relates to what I read and to the historical context of the writers I read *and* to the many critical activities in which I am engaged, which may or may not involve writing. It is a learning from the language of creative writers, which is one of surprise, so that I might discover what language I might use. For my language is very much based on what I read and how it affects me, that is, on the surprise that comes from reading something that compels you to read differently, as I believe literature does. I, therefore, have no set method, another prerequisite of the new theory, since for me every work suggests a new approach. As risky as that might seem, it is, I believe, what intelligence means – a tuned sensitivity to that which is alive and therefore cannot be known until it is known. Audre Lorde puts it in a far more succinct and sensual way in her essay 'Poetry is not a luxury':

> As they become known to and accepted by us, our feelings and the honest exploration of them become sanctuaries and spawning grounds for the most radical and daring of ideas. They become a safe-house for that difference so necessary to change and the conceptualization of any meaningful action. Right now, I could name at least ten ideas I would have found intolerable or incomprehensible and frightening, except as they came after dreams and poems. This is not idle fantasy, but a disciplined attention to the true meaning of 'it feels right to me.' We can train ourselves to respect our feelings and to transpose them into a language so they can be shared. And where that language does not yet exist, it is our poetry which helps to fashion it. Poetry is not only dream and vision; it is the skeleton architecture of our lives. It lays the foundations for a future of change, a bridge across our fears of what has never been before.[11]

NOTES

This essay is reprinted (with changes) with permission from Barbara Christian and first appeared in *Cultural Critique* 6 (Spring 1987): 51-63.

1 For another view of the debate this 'privileged' approach to Afro-American texts has engendered, see Joyce A. Joyce, ' "Who the Cap Fit:" unconsciousness and unconscionableness in the criticism of Houston A. Baker, Jr, and Henry Louis Gates, Jr', *New Literary History* 18 (1987): 371-84. I had not read Joyce's essay before I wrote my own. Clearly there are differences between Joyce's view and my own.

2 This paper was originally written for a conference at the University of California at Berkeley entitled 'Minority Discourse', and held on 29-31 May 1986.

3 See Ellison 1964; Farnsworth 1969; Gayle 1971; Jones, L. 1966; Neal 1971: pp. 357-74; Walker 1975; Wright 1937.

4 Walker 1982. The controversy surrounding the novel and the subsequent film are discussed in Hernton 1987, chs 1 and 2.

5 Giovanni 1970.

6 Gayle 1975.

7 Reed 1972.
8 See Jones A. R. 1981.
9 See Jordan 1981; Audre Lorde, 'The master's tools will never dismantle the master's house', in Lorde 1984: pp. 110-14.
10 This phrase is taken from the title of one of Alice Walker's essays, 'Saving the life that is your own: the importance of models in the artist's life', in Walker 1983.
11 Audre Lorde, 'Poetry is not a luxury', in Lorde 1984.

REFERENCES

Ellison, Ralph 1964. *Shadow and Act*. New York: Random House.
Farnsworth, Robert M. 1969. 'Introduction to *The Marrow of Tradition* by Charles Chesnutt'. Ann Arbor, Michigan: Michigan Paperbacks.
Gayle, Addison, Jr (ed.) 1971. *The Black Aesthetic*. Garden City, New York: Doubleday Anchor Press.
Gayle, Addison, Jr 1975. *The Way of the New World: The Black Novel in America* Garden City, New York: Doubleday Anchor Press.
Giovanni, Nikki 1970. Review of Paul Marshall, *Chosen Place, Timeless People, Negro Digest* 19.3 (January): 51-2, 84.
Hernton, Calvin 1987. *The Sexual Mountain and Black Women Writers*. New York: Doubleday.
Jones, Ann Rosalind 1981. 'Writing the body: toward an understanding of *l'écriture féminine'*, *Feminist Studies*, 7.2 (Summer): 247-63.
Jones, LeRoi 1966. *Home: Social Essays*. New York: William Morrow.
Jordan, June 1981. *Civil Wars*. New York: Beacon Press.
Lorde, Audre 1984. *Sister Outsider*. Trumansburg, New York: Crossing Press.
Neal, Larry 1971. 'The Black Arts Movement', *The Black Aesthetic*, ed. Addison Gayle Jr. Garden City, New York: Doubleday Anchor Press: 272-90.
Reed, Ishmael 1972. *Mumbo Jumbo*. Garden City, New York: Doubleday Anchor Press.
Walker, Alice 1975. 'In Search of Zora Neale Hurston', *MS* 3.9 (March).
Walker, Alice 1982. *The Color Purple*. New York: Harcourt Brace Jovanovich.
Walker, Alice 1983. *In Search of Our Mothers' Gardens: Womanist Prose*. New York: Harcourt Brace Jovanovich.
Wright, Richard 1937. 'A blueprint for negro writing', *New Challenge* 11: 53-65.

12
Appropriative Gestures: Theory and Afro-American Literary Criticism

Michael Awkward

Barbara Christian's 'The race for theory' leaves no doubt in the mind of its readers that the esteemed black feminist critic is - in the words of the controversial Steven Knapp and Walter Benn Michaels essay - against theory. Christian's reaction to theory, however, differs from that of Knapp and Michaels, who seek to discredit theory by discussing what they argue are its fallacious oppositions - meaning/intent, knowledge/belief. She also differs from Afro-American critic Joyce Joyce, who discusses what she views as the ideologically deficient theoretical practice of several black critics in order to demonstrate an incompatibility between practical Afrocentric criticism and contemporary literary theory.[1] For Christian neither systematically attacks what she believes are the inadequacies of its most basic tenets nor attempts to address in specific ways what she holds are the flawed critical practices of Afro-Americanist uses of theory. Instead, Christian asserts that theory is a putatively radical enterprise which has done little to change the *status quo* or advance our comprehension of the processes of literary production, and that its ideologically radical practitioners have been 'co-opted into speaking a language and defining their discussion in terms alien to and opposed to our needs and orientation' (p. 226).

The particulars of Christian's attacks on theory certainly are not original, nor are they, I believe, particularly persuasive. By condemning the discourse of literary theory, calling those who employ theoretical paradigms 'critic[s] yearning for attention', and implying that literary theory has gained a significant hold on our attention primarily because 'so much of the literature of the West has become pallid, laden with despair, self-indulgent and disconnected', Christian rehearses old arguments which, frankly, I am not interested in addressing. I am aware of no evidence which convincingly suggests that today's literary critics are, as a group, any more egotistical than their predecessors, or that figurations of despair historically have proven any less *analytically* provocative than those of any other psychological/emotional state. What I am interested in exploring – and arguing against – are Christian's specific reasons for viewing as counterproductive the theoretical practice of black feminist criticism and other non-hegemonic – non-white male – schools of literary analysis. For I believe that the strategies of reading which she deplores offer the Afrocentric critic a means of more fully and adequately decoding the black literary text and canon than what the critic Daniel O'Hara might call the 'fly-by-the-seat-of-one's-pants'[2] approach Christian advances at the end of her essay as a corrective to 'the race for theory'.

Christian characterizes her own critical practice as an effort to save the emerging, under-appreciated Afro-American woman's text from the types of critical marginality and canonical oblivion that had previously been the fate of early- and mid-twentieth century products of black female imaginations. Clearly, Christian's preservatory impulses are commendable and historically well founded. Despite the inroads some Afro-American women's texts have made in small areas in the canon, black women's literature still does not assume the prominent place in courses and criticism that those who devote a great deal of scholarly attention to it feel it merits. I do not, then, object to the tenets which inform Christian's critical practice, nor do I feel that it is correct to dismiss out of hand the works of those scholars in the field which are not obviously informed by post-structuralist theories. The types of re-readings of neglected black women's texts and 'first readings' of new works to which Christian has devoted herself can be, when performed in the energetic manner with which she approaches her work, quite helpful to our understanding of what she has called 'the development of the tradition' of black women's literature. What I do object to where Christian's discussion of Afro-American critical engagement of literary theory is concerned is her consistent refusal to acknowledge that its employment by several clearly Afrocentric critics has indeed deepened our received knowledge of the textual production of black writers.

Christian sees literary theory as a coercive hegemonic force which has begun to poison the discourse of 'some of our most daring and potentially radical critics (and by *our* I mean black, women, Third World)' (p. 226) whose adoption of post-structuralist modes of reading suggests that they 'have been influenced, even co-opted' by a hegemonic critical discourse.

While here, as at most points in her essay, she is unwilling to name
victims or villains, Christian suggests that, as an enterprise, literary
theory has corrupted a previously methodologically sound black feminist
criticism, forcing its practitioners either into silence or into the defensive
postures of black female natives invaded by an alien, white, phallocentric
critical discourse that they employ against their will and better judgment.
While the imagery she uses resonates with historically significant indig-
nation – the black female critic as pure Afrocentric maiden corrupted by
an institutionally all-powerful white male post-structuralist theory –
Christian's representation of theoretically informed black female (and
other non-caucasian and/or male) critics as 'co-opted' can only be read as
an attack on their personal integrity and recent work. She apparently
cannot even conceive of the possibility that these critics *choose* to employ
theory because they believe it offers provocative means of discussing the
texts of non-hegemonic groups, that theory indeed is viewed by them as
useful in the critical analysis of the literary products of 'the other'.

Further, Christian's 'resistance to theory' leads her to overstate her
claims about a purely descriptive, non-theoretical stage of black feminist
criticism. One of its earlier and most eloquent statements, Barbara
Smith's groundbreaking essay 'Toward a black feminist criticism', is
essentially a theoretical – if not post-structuralist – discussion of critical
practice and textual production. In this much-anthologized essay, Smith –
like all theorists – prescriptively asserts what she believes ought to be the
informing principles of the critics she wants to persuade. She defines the
limits of the black feminist interpretive project, telling aspiring black
feminist critics how Afro-American women's texts ought to be read and
suggesting what sorts of findings such readings ought to uncover. Smith
says: 'Beginning with a primary commitment to exploring how both
sexual and racial politics and Black and female identity are inextricable
elements in Black women's writings, she would also work from the
assumption that Black women writers constitute an identifiable literary
tradition. . . . [S]he would think and write out of her own identity and not
try to graft the ideas or methodology of white/male literary thought upon
the precise materials of Black women's art' (pp. 174-5).

While post-structuralist theorists might intervene here and censure
Smith's overdetermined collision of biology and ideology – Smith assumes
that the black feminist critic will necessarily be a black woman, that
whites and black men are incapable of offering the types of analyses she
advocates because they 'are of course ill-equipped to deal [simultaneously]

with the subtleties of racial [and sexual] politics' (p. 170)[3] - it is in her move from theory to practice that contemporary critical theory could be most helpful to her project. For Smith problematically believes that her (now generally accepted) theoretical suggestions - that one analyze in black women's texts figurations of the relationships between race, gender and class, as well as demonstrate the contours of the black woman's literary tradition - will lead necessarily to critical acts such as her still-controversial reading of Toni Morrison's *Sula* as a lesbian novel. Unlike Deborah McDowell, who in 'New directions for black feminist criticism' argues that the problems with Smith's analysis result from a lack of a precise definition of the term 'lesbian' and from the fact that Smith's ' "innovative" analysis is pressed to the service of an individual political persuasion' (p. 190), I feel that the problems with Smith's critical manuevers lie in her lack of awareness of the contemporary literary theories that Christian devalues. Combined with her own convincingly articulated black feminist approach, an engagement of reader-response theory and theories about the textual construction of gendered/ideological readers might have led Smith to be even more innovative. Rather than arguing that Morrison's is a black lesbian text (a reading to which Morrison herself forcefully objected in a recent interview[4]), she might instead have offered a theory of a *black lesbian reader*. Rather than involving herself needlessly and unprofitably in discussions of authorial intent,[5] Smith might have focused on the *effects on the reader* of *Sula*'s clear and consistent critique of heterosexual institutions, on the text's progressive 'lesbianization' of the reader. Whether Morrison *intends* this is, to a certain extent, beside the point; the point of Smith's theorizing is that such a process does - or at least *can* - indeed occur as a necessary function of careful, ideologically informed reading of Morrison's novel. The problem with the move from practical theory to theoretical practice in 'Toward a black feminist criticism' is not, as Christian's perspectives suggest, Smith's attempt to 'overgeneralize', to *theorize*, about the process of reading, but her insufficient awareness of advances in reader-response theory that would have allowed her to discuss in a more convincing manner her perceptions of the effects of reading Morrison's novel.

My own intent here is not to discredit Smith's essay, which I believe remains the most influential work in the area of black feminist criticism. Rather, it is to suggest the misconceptions that mar Christian's three most forcefully articulated arguments against a black feminist engagement of literary theory: 1) that black feminist criticism and literary theory are essentially incompatible enterprises; 2) that post-structuralism is the cause of (premature) attempts at black feminist literary theory; and 3) that black feminist literary theory has not – and should not have – emerged before the practice of reading black women's texts is more firmly established. Clearly, Smith's essay – and its careful analysis – serves to challenge the general applicability to black feminist criticism of Christian's suppositions. For Smith's 1977 essay (however problematically) *theorizes* despite its lack of a clearly informed awareness of deconstruction, reader-response theory, semiotics, or any of what Smith terms 'the ideas or methodology of white/male literary thought', and does so *while* bemoaning the paucity of black feminist critical acts. Despite an obviously antagonistic relationship to white/male hegemony, Smith believes, like the villainous post-structuralist theorists of Christian's essay, that she can offer a prescription, a theory, of how most profitably to read literary texts.

Unlike Smith, Christian is concerned primarily not with theorizing about profitable means by which to approach Afro-American women's literature, but with 'help[ing to] ensure that [the black woman's literary] tradition has continuity and survives' by offering 'first readings' of new works by Afro-American women. As a consequence, she perceives as quite problematic the insistence that black feminist critics devise theoretical ways of approaching the Afro-American woman's literary tradition. She says:

> Some of us are continually harassed to invent wholesale theories regardless of the complexity of the literature we study. I, for one, am tired of being asked to produce a black feminist literary theory as if I were a mechanical man. For I believe such theory is prescriptive – it ought to have some relationship to practice. Since I can count on one hand the number of people attempting to be black feminist literary critics in the world today, I consider it presumptuous of me to invent a theory of how we *ought* to read. (p. 227)

Certainly Christian's anger is justified if, as she suggests, the requests she has received to offer theoretical models adequate to a discussion of black women's literature have indeed taken the form of intellectual harassment. But she can argue that critical practice in the last fifteen years has not adequately prepared the way for new theories of black women's textual production only by being as restrictive in her definition of 'black feminist literary critics' as she accuses feminist literary theorists of being when they define the term 'feminist'. (Are black feminist critics only black women? If so, they number much more than a handful. Can a gendered and/or racial other learn the ideology, speak the discourse, of 'black feminist literary critics'? If not, how should we label such essential works on black women writers as Robert Hemenway's biography of Zora Neale Hurston, Barbara Johnson's essays on Hurston, Calvin Hernton's *The Sexual Mountain* and *Black Women Writers?*) A multitude of readings – by black and white women and men – have appeared in journals, collections of essays, and books that analyze black women's texts in terms of 'the intricacies of the intersection of language, class, race, and gender', enough at least to suggest to Christian, as it has to other black female critics, that black feminist criticism has reached an appropriate time in its history to begin theorizing about its practice and the literary production of Afro-American woman writers.

In *The Resistance to Theory*, Paul de Man suggests:

> Literary theory can be said to come into being when the approach to literary texts is no longer based on non-linguistic, that is to say historical and aesthetic, considerations or, to put it somewhat less crudely, when the object of discussion is no longer the meaning or the value but the modalities of production and of reception of meaning and of value prior to their establishment. (p. 7)

I believe that the time has indeed arrived for the black feminist critical move beyond simply 'non-linguistic' analyses of the texts of black women writers. As illuminating as a Barbara Christian 'first reading' of Toni Morrison's *Beloved* or of new works by Gloria Naylor, Paule Marshall, Alice Walker, Ntozake Shange and Toni Cade Bambara would undoubtedly prove, such readings will do little to insure the survival of the black women's literary tradition. I firmly believe that the tradition's critical establishment has in the past required, and still requires, such self-consciously preservatory acts. But if the literature of black women is to continue to make inroads in the canon, if it is to gain the respect it doubtlessly deserves as an ideologically and aesthetically complex, analytically rich literary tradition within an increasingly theoretical academy, it will require that its critics continue to move beyond description and master the discourse of contemporary literary theory.

I do not mean that Christian must herself undergo a miraculous change in perspective and become a Derridean, Foucauldian or Barthesian post-structuralist critic. I do believe, however, that literary theory provides Afro-Americans and other non-hegemonic groups with a means by which to begin to offer other, currently even more essential, types of responses: text-specific theories of the modalities of black textual production. Whatever the strictly personal or specifically 'tribal' uses to which members of oppressed groups put their writers' texts, I believe it is the literary critic's responsibility – whenever he or she acts in the role of critic – to discuss such works in as full, complex, and sophisticated ways as possible. Henry Louis Gates states his view of this responsibility in the following way:

> This is the challenge of the critic of black literature in the 1980s: not to shy away from literary theory; rather, to translate it into the black idiom, *renaming* principles of criticism where appropriate, but especially *naming* indigenous black principles of criticism and applying these to explicate our own texts. It is incumbent upon us to protect the integrity of our tradition by bringing to bear upon its criticism any tool of sensitivity to language that is appropriate . . . *any* tool that enables the critic to explain the complex workings of the language of a text.[6] (p. xxi)

Zora Neale Hurston has argued that the Afro-American is an 'appropriative' creature, that 'while he lives and moves in the midst of a white civilization, everything he touches is re-interpreted for his own use' (p. 28). Certainly one of the means by which Afro-Americans have, in Christian's words, 'managed to survive with such spiritedness the assault on our bodies, social institutions, countries, our very humanity' has been by successfully appropriating putatively superior Western cultural and expressive systems – Christianity, the English language, Western literary genres – and transferring them into forms through which we expressed our culturally distinct black souls. It is this history that suggests that we need not stand before even the most apparently obscure literary theories as silenced, confused, and discursively 'blocked' victims of recent developments in the study of literary texts. Literary theory is, despite its origins and white androcentric uses to which it has generally been put, a tool that Afro-American critics can – and have begun to – successfully employ in explications of our own traditions' texts and intertexts. To continue to assert, despite its wonderfully provocative and *useful* employment by figures such as Gates, Hortense Spillers, Houston Baker, and Mary Helen Washington, that literary theory cannot serve the best, *blackest* interests of our literary tradition is to devalue in significant ways these critics' recent contributions to our understanding of black textual production. Such critics have demonstrated irrefutably that theory can be appropriated in ways that will allow us to continue to further our comprehension of Afro-American texts, and to insure both their survival and their impact.

NOTES

1 See Knapp and Michaels 1985, and Joyce 1987.
2 In Mitchell 1985: 37.
3 For a fuller discussion of this collision of biology and ideology in black feminist criticism, see my 1988 essay 'Race, gender, and the politics of reading', *Black American Literature Forum*, 22.1 (1988): 5-27.
4 In her interview collected in Tate 1983, Morrison asserts – obviously with Smith's comments in mind: 'Nobody ever talked about friendship between women unless it was homosexual, and there is no homosexuality in *Sula*' (p. 118).
5 The problems with Smith's discussion of *Sula* are most glaringly manifested in her attempts to distinguish between textual meaning and authorial intent. She argues that despite the novel's 'consistently critical stance toward the heterosexual institutions of male-female relationships, marriage, and the family' (p. 175), Morrison's failure to 'approach . . . her subject with the consciousness that a lesbian relationship was at least a possibility for her characters' results from the novelist's overdetermined 'heterosexual assumptions [that] can veil what may logically be expected to occur in a work' (p. 181).
6 Gates 1987.

REFERENCES

Awkward, Michael 1988. 'Race, gender, and the politics of reading', *Black American Literature Forum* 22:1: 5-27.
Baker, Houston A., Jr 1980. *The Journey Back*. Chicago: University of Chicago Press.
Baker, Houston A., Jr 1984. *Blues, Ideology, and Afro-American Literature*. Chicago: University of Chicago Press.
Christian, Barbara. 'The race for theory', ch. 11 in this volume.
Gates, Henry Louis, Jr (ed.) 1984. *Black Literature and Literary Theory*. New York: Methuen.
Gates, Henry Louis, Jr 1987. *Figures in Black*. New York: Oxford University Press.
Gates, Henry Louis, Jr 1987. ' "What's love got to do with it?" Critical theory, integrity; and the black idiom', *New Literary History* 18:2 (Winter): 345-62.

Hemenway, Robert 1977. *Zora Neale Hurston: A Literary Biography*. Urbana: University of Illinois Press.

Hernton, Calvin 1987. *The Sexual Mountain and Black Women Writers*. New York: Doubleday.

Hurston, Zora Neale 1934. 'Characteristics of negro expression', in *Negro: An Anthology*, ed. Nancy Cunard. Repr. London: Negro University Press, 1969: 24-31.

Johnson, Barbara 1984. 'Metaphor, metonymy and voice in *Their Eyes Were Watching God*', in Gates 1987: 205-19.

Johnson, Barbara 1986. 'Thresholds of difference: structures of address in Zora Neale Hurston', *'Race,' Writing, and Difference*, ed. Henry Louis Gates. Chicago: University of Chicago Press.

Joyce, Joyce A. 1987. 'The black canon: reconstructing black American literary criticism', *New Literary History* 18.2: 335-44.

Knapp, Steven and Michaels, Walter Benn 1985. 'Against theory', in Mitchell 1985: 11-30.

McDowell, Deborah 1987. ' "The Changing Same": generational connections and black women novelists', *New Literary History* 18.2: 281-302.

McDowell, Deborah 1985. 'New directions for black feminist criticism', in *The New Feminist Criticism*, ed. Elaine Showalter. New York: Pantheon: 186-99.

Man, Paul de 1986. *The Resistance to Theory*. Minneapolis: Minnesota University Press.

Mitchell, W. J. T. (ed.) 1985. *Against Theory: Literary Studies and the New Pragmatism*. Chicago: University of Chicago Press.

Morrison, Toni 1974. *Sula*. New York: Knopf.

Morrison, Toni 1987. *Beloved*. New York: Knopf.

O'Hara, Daniel 1985. 'Revisionary madness: the prospects of American literary theory at the present time', in Mitchell 1985: 31-47.

Smith, Barbara 1985. 'Toward a black feminist criticism', in *The New Feminist Criticism*, ed. Elaine Showalter. New York: Pantheon: 168-85.

Spillers, Hortense 1985. 'Cross-currents, discontinuities: black women's fiction', in *Conjuring: Black Women, Fiction, and Literary Tradition*, ed. Marjorie Pryse and Spillers. Bloomington: Indiana University Press: 249-61.

Tate, Claudia (ed.) 1983. *Black Women Writers at Work*. New York: Continuum.

Washington, Mary Helen 1984. ' "Taming all that anger down": rage and silence in Gwendolyn Brooks's *Maud Martha*', in Gates 1984: 249-62.

Index